Lightweight Camping
for
Motorcycle Travel
Revised Edition

Frazier Douglass

iUniverse, Inc.
New York   Bloomington

Lightweight Camping for Motorcycle Travel

iUniverse books may be ordered through booksellers or by contacting:

iUniverse
1663 Liberty Drive
Bloomington, IN 47403
www.iuniverse.com
1-800-Authors (1-800-288-4677)

ISBN: 978-1-4401-7645-6 (pbk)
ISBN: 978-1-4401-7647-0 (cloth)
ISBN: 978-1-4401-7646-3 (ebk)

Printed in the United States of America

iUniverse rev. date: 9/23/2009

Dedication

In memory of
my mother, Jean Duval Douglass, and
my grandmother, Francis Bagby Duval

Together they showed me the high road of life.

Contents

List of Summary Charts

Information for Non-Campers
Information for Veteran Campers
Differences between Backpacking and Motorcycle Camping
Camping Gear Vendors
Motorcycle-Only Campgrounds
Pre-Trip Checklist
Two-Person Tents
Three- and Four-Person Tents
Down Bags
Synthetic Bags
Bags for Big Guys
Essential Gear Checklist
Clothing Checklist
Kitchen Gear, Grocery Items, and Supplies Checklist
Optional Gear Checklist
Motorcycle Packing List
Defensive Riding Practices

Preface to the First Edition

In the fall of 1998, I got the itch to pack some camping gear and a few clothes on my motorcycle and spend a night at a campground about 140 miles away from my home. I had been camping for most of my adult life and riding motorcycles for over ten years, but I had never tried to do both activities together. Initially I thought the trip would be easy, but it proved to be more difficult than I had imagined.

After returning home from that trip, I began searching for information that could teach me how to have drier, warmer, and more comfortable trips. I found several sites on the Web (such as the BMW Motorcycle Owners and the International Brotherhood of Motorcycle Campers) that provided some information and advice. I also discovered the book *Motorcycle Camping Made Easy*, by Bob Woofter. But none of these resources provided all the information I wanted. After a while, I expanded my search and bought several general books on camping, but they also failed to provide the information I wanted. A few years later, I discovered *Backpacker* magazine. Although I had no plan to go backpacking, this magazine provided useful information that could be applied to motorcycle camping—but still not everything I needed.

I had dozens of questions, first about tents. For example, when buying a tent for a motorcycle camping trip, what specifications should I look for? What specific tent models are best suited for motorcycle camping trips and why? Where could I purchase one of the better models? How much do they typically cost? How could I find the best prices? How should I pack my tent on a motorcycle? What factors should I consider when deciding where to set up my tent in a campsite? How should I take down and pack my tent when the time comes to move on?

I had many more questions about sleeping bags, sleeping pads, kitchen supplies, cooking, and many other camping-related items. I wanted to know what items I could easily pack on a motorcycle—without a trailer or a chase vehicle—and how to pack them safely when riding two-up. I also wanted to know how to stay dry in wet weather and how to stay warm in cold weather. I wanted to find the solutions to dozens of practical problems I might encounter on a motorcycle camping trip. After three years of searching, I finally realized that the answers to many questions could not be found in any single reference source. Much of it is out there, but it is scattered among various books, magazines, Web sites, retail store catalogs, and other sources. Some of it is only available by word of mouth.

Eventually I decided to write this book to combine as much information and advice as possible and to provide a comprehensive and organized analysis of one specific approach to camping—lightweight camping—because this approach is best suited for motorcycle touring and travel. In this book I have purposely ignored issues exclusively pertaining to backpacking and issues pertaining to car camping.

My book begins by summarizing the homework you should do before taking your first motorcycle camping trip. Then it proceeds through each step of a camping trip by describing personal experiences that taught me valuable lessons; addressing important issues; summarizing available factual information; and presenting recommendations based upon expert opinion and my own experiences. I hope you will find this book to be both encouraging and useful in planning your future motorcycle trips.

Preface to the Revised Edition

After submitting the manuscript for the first edition of this book, I began thinking about topics that deserved further explanation and new topics that should be added. As a result, I began revising the book long before it was published in September 2008. The book you are now reading is the product of my efforts. It was written both for people who have never camped before and for veteran campers. Regardless of your past camping experience, you will find lots of useful information. The two charts on the following pages summarize important points that both non-campers and veteran campers will find throughout the book.

This revised edition provides much more information about topics discussed in the first edition, adds several new topics, and includes many new photographs. Overall it provides more information and practical suggestions than could be found in any other camping book. For example, this edition discusses sleeping bags for big guys and provides specific information that will help larger men find models that best suit their needs and pocketbook. Other information that could not be found in other camping books include a summary of overall injury risks associated with state and national park use and a historical overview of the American conservation movement. Many chapter titles and section headings have been modified to provide a better description of their content. Readers can now find information and suggestions related to many camping-related topics without having to read through unrelated content.

You will notice that several themes are repeated throughout this book. For example, you will find information and suggestions regarding environmental and ecological issues in several chapters. If everyone will do their part to help preserve our great natural resources, we can preserve them for our neighbors, our children, and our grandchildren. Accordingly several chapters in this book describe common attitudes and habits that conflict with long-term environmental needs and offer suggestions for more eco-friendly actions. You will also notice other themes that run through this book: using alcohol and other drugs responsibly, understanding important differences between backpacking and motorcycle camping, being safety conscious while riding and camping, exploring great camping destinations in the eastern United States, and riding Harley-Davidson motorcycles on camping trips.

I hope the information in this book will motivate you to take more motorcycle camping trips and help you discover ways to have dryer, warmer, and more comfortable camping experiences. Furthermore, I hope this book will inspire you to become an advocate for the environment and show kindness toward all people.

Acknowledgments

First of all, I would like to thank my employer, Athens State University. For the past twenty years Athens State has supported me during life's good times and bad times. Some of the people who have provided special support include Ron Fritze, James Gadberry, Randy McIntosh, Tim Jones, Bruce Thomas, Celeste Bedingfield, Debbie Kelley, Mary Simpson, Betty Marks, Steve Clarke, and Tracy Hicks. I am especially grateful to Celeste Bedingfield for reading the entire manuscript and to Tracy Hicks for preparing my photographs for print.

I would also like to express deep appreciation to my entire family. For many years they have listened to my babbling and acted like they were interested in what I had to say. Furthermore, they have joined me on many camping trips. Robin, my longtime companion (and former wife), has joined me on dozens of camping adventures and has read my manuscript several times. My two sons, Shel and Lyle Douglass, camped with me when they were less than one year old and have joined me on several camping trips over the past thirty years. My sisters, Jean Douglass Baswell and Cecelia Douglass Herndon, have raised their families and have recently joined me on a few camping trips. My daughter-in-law, Amy Douglass, retouched the photograph used on the cover of this edition.

I want to thank the guys in the service department at Foster Harley-Davidson in Tuscumbia, Alabama. Harold and his mechanics have done a great job keeping my old motorcycles running in "like new" condition for several years.

Finally, I would like to express appreciation to all the people who purchased copies of the first edition of this book. I hope that you were not disappointed and that you will appreciate the additional material that has been included in this revised edition.

Information for Non-Campers

You will learn that camping is economical.
- Campsites cost about $20 per night, while motel rooms cost about $75.
- Good-quality essential gear costs about $550 (tent = $200; sleeping bag = $100; air mattress = $80; headlight = $35; tarp = $10; towel = $30).
- After 10 nights, you pay for your gear and save at least $55 per night.

You will learn that camping is safe.
- State parks have established campgrounds with gates, campground hosts, and park rangers who provide nighttime security.
- Many families bring their children camping
- Established campgrounds have telephones and/or cell service for help, if needed.
- Dangerous critters (bears, snakes, etc.) usually do not live near established campgrounds.

You will learn that camping can be comfortable.
- Most parks have drive-in sites with water and electricity nearby.
- Most parks have flush toilets, hot showers, and laundry facilities.
- Good tents have waterproof floors and rain flies that will keep you dry if it rains.
- Good air mattresses and sleeping bags will keep you warm and comfortable so you won't feel like you are sleeping on the ground.
- You can cook great-tasting meals in your campsite or ride to nearby restaurants.
- You can read books, listen to music, watch movies, or do whatever you want to do in your campsite.

You will learn that camping can be educational.
- Many parks have nature centers and educational programs.

- You can learn more about American history, plants, wildlife, geology, ecology, environmental issues, and other interesting topics.
- You will learn how to be more independent and self-sufficient.

You will learn that camping can be relaxing.
- You will enjoy the sunlight, wind, and other elements of the great outdoors.
- You will enjoy smelling the fresh air, flowers, trees, campfires, and food being cooked in the campground.
- You can enjoy walking and hiking scenic trails.
- You will enjoy relaxing in a hammock and sitting by the campfire.

You will learn that camping is easy if you do your homework.
- Basic gear can be purchased for a reasonable price.
- State and national parks are located near your home.

Information for Veteran Campers

You will learn how to stay dry in rainy weather.
- Learn recent improvements to consider when buying a tent.
- Learn how to use light-weight rain gear, boots, and gaiters to stay dry.
- Learn how to set up rain flies over your camp table.

You will learn how to stay warm in cool weather.
- Learn how to combine sleeping bags, sleeping pads, hats, thermal layers, and insulated garments to stay warm even when the temperature drops below 35 degrees Fahrenheit.
- Learn why moisture-wicking underwear and thermal layers are best for camping.
- Learn how to layer base and mid-layer garments with insulated jackets and outer shells to stay warm on cool days.

You will learn how to pack camping gear and clothing for two on a motorcycle.
- Learn to distinguish between essential items needed for camping and optional items.
- Buy compressible garments and travel-sized personal items.
- Be able to estimate your Gross Vehicle Weight Rating (GVWR).
- Learn the Motorcycle Safety Foundation (MSF) principles for carrying loads.
- Learn other practical packing tips.

You will learn how to set up comfortable campsites.
- Learn how to select the best campsites.
- Learn how to set up tents, kitchen areas, clotheslines, and hammocks.
- Learn how to tie and use several useful knots.
- Learn how to find good firewood and build campfires.

You will learn how to cook great-tasting meals.
- Learn how to cook meat and vegetables in aluminum foil over the campfire.

- Learn about backpacker stoves, cookware, dinnerware, and utensils.
- Learn what food staples you will need and how to acquire them.

You will learn information about common camping problems.
- Learn how to avoid falls and burns and poisonous plants, insects, snakes, and other animals.
- Learn basic steps to take when injuries occur.

You will learn how to prolong the life of your camping gear.
- Learn how to prevent rips, tears, mold, mildew, and animal damage.
- Learn how to repair and recycle your camping gear.

You will learn more about environmental and conservation issues.
- Learn the history of the American conservation movement.
- Learn the seven Leave No Trace principles.
- Learn about carbon footprint and the environmental effects of toxic chemicals.

Introduction

This book offers a detailed description of *lightweight camping,* which in terms of required gear and comfort level falls between car (or family) camping and ultra-light camping. To clarify the distinctions between these three different approaches, let me first describe car camping and then describe ultra-light camping.

Car camping emphasizes comfort. To achieve that end, car campers typically purchase large family tents with multiple rooms, pop-up campers, or travel trailers. In addition, they typically purchase large dining tents and many other items such as comfortable chairs, large coolers, stoves, kitchen utensils, lights, heaters, TVs, and other electrical appliances. They like to camp in established campgrounds where water, electricity, and sometimes sewer facilities are immediately accessible and where bathrooms and showers are only a few yards away from their site. When electricity is unavailable, they sometimes purchase generators to run their electrical appliances. They frequently purchase cots and comfortable bedding. Many car campers pack large boxes of food and typically bring much more than they could possibly eat. Car campers also pack lots of bulky clothes, jackets, and shoes from their closets. To haul all their gear, family campers usually purchase large SUVs, pickup trucks, vans, and trailers.

At the opposite end of the continuum is ultra-light camping. The ultra-light approach to camping is usually adopted by serious backpackers, canoe campers, and mountain climbers. In this approach, emphasis is placed upon being able to survive and conquer remote wilderness areas with the absolute least amount of gear. These campers weigh everything and constantly strive to reduce their packed weight. They typically purchase large backpacks, small tents or shelters, highly compressible sleeping bags, bear-proof containers, and snakebite kits. They carry a minimum amount of water and plan to catch the water they need from streams and lakes along the way. Consequently, they must pack water-purification equipment. They also must pack all the food they will need for the trip and thus must rely on dehydrated foods that can be packed in pre-portioned sizes in small plastic bags and be combined with water when it is time to eat. They typically pack only one change of clothes and thus must wash underwear and socks every day or two. Since bathrooms are unavailable in remote areas, they must pack a shovel and toilet paper. And they frequently go several days without bathing. Finally, since they will be traveling and camping several hours away from roads and other people, ultra-light campers must be prepared to survive many different types of weather and injury emergencies. To do so, they should complete several hours of survival training before attempting their trips.

Lightweight motorcycle camping falls between these two extremes. It combines much of the comfort associated with the car-camping approach with much of the weight/space consciousness associated with ultra-light camping. Motorcycle campers typically camp in established campgrounds with access to potable water, toilets, and showers. They frequently have electricity available in their campsites for charging their cell phones and for operating a few electrical appliances. Motorcycle campers are able to eat great-tasting meals without having to pack much food or cooking gear because most campgrounds are located near restaurants and grocery stores. Because they do not need much of the gear required for ultra-light camping, motorcycle campers typically have space to pack larger, more comfortable tents, several changes of clothes, small soft-sided coolers, and other personal items.

I will make three important assumptions throughout this book. First, I assume that camping can in itself be an enjoyable recreational activity and not just a means of sleeping while taking long-distance trips or attending motorcycle rallies. Second, I assume that motorcycle riders are able to pack everything they will need for a comfortable trip on their motorcycles and thus do not need trailers or chase vehicles to carry their gear. Finally, I assume that many motorcycle riders have backseat companions and that riding two-up does not preclude them from enjoying lightweight camping trips. Although camping is more difficult when riding two-up than when riding solo, we know from years of personal experience that couples will be able to pack all their camping gear and clothing on their bike if they do their homework and buy the right gear and clothing.

As we travel about the country and camp in different parks, we are happy to see that other motorcycle riders are also camping. Most of them ride solo. One couple we met several years ago at a private campground near the Smokies had each ridden their own bike all day down from Michigan. Since they had two bikes, they were able to split their gear and clothing by packing half of it on each bike. After setting up their camp, they got onto one bike and rode together to a restaurant for dinner. Other couples ride together on one bike and use a trailer to haul their camping gear. Sometimes the trailer is a cargo trailer and other times it is a small pop-up tent.

Few couples attempt to ride together on one bike and pack all their gear on the same bike. In fact, many couples seem to think it is impossible to get two people, their clothes, and all the camping gear they will need packed on one bike. But we know from experience that it can be done. A few years ago we met another such couple at Potowatomie State Park near Sturgeon Bay, Wisconsin. They were touring the state of Wisconsin and had packed their tent, some camping gear, and all their clothes on an Electra Glide Standard (with no tour pack). After arriving at their site, the woman set up camp while the man rode to a nearby store for supplies and firewood.

If you enjoy riding a motorcycle with a companion and you enjoy camping, you should try camping on future motorcycle trips. Or if you just like riding but have never camped, you should give camping a try. At first it may seem impossible to pack enough gear and clothing for two people on your motorcycle without a trailer or a chase vehicle. Indeed it is difficult, but it can be done! The secret is to do your homework, purchase the right gear, develop a system for packing your gear on your bike, and learn how to use your gear in the field to assure maximum comfort. If you do your homework and master a few basic skills, you will be able to have many enjoyable camping trips.

Camping on your trips (rather than staying in motels) will yield considerable financial savings but will also provide many more intangible pleasures. At the end of this book, I will describe many of the things we enjoy about our motorcycle camping trips. If you begin camping on your motorcycle trips and learn the basic camping routine, you will probably experience many things that I have failed to mention. Moreover, if you take several camping trips to different destinations, you will probably add more things to your list after every trip. The pleasures you get from motorcycle camping are sometimes difficult to explain to others who have not yet undertaken motorcycle camping trips.

Background

Motorcycle riders have been touring and camping out under the stars since motorcycles were first introduced to the public in the late eighteen hundreds. Perhaps the first reported motorcycle camping trip across the country occurred in 1915—twelve years after William Harley and Arthur Davidson made their first motorcycle. Effie Hotchkiss (twenty-one years old) and her mother rode her Harley-Davidson twin equipped with a sidecar from New York City to San Francisco. According to *Heroes of Harley-Davidson*, the two women packed a tent, blankets, pots, pans, two rubber ponchos, a pistol, a medicine kit, an ax, and a toolbox. A year later, W. H. Wallace published an article in *Recreation* magazine entitled "Camping trips with a motorcycle." In this article, Wallace describes his "camping outfit," how he packed it on his Indian motorcycle, how he prepared his meals, and how he used many items to enhance his comfort. A copy of this article can be found in the 2009 Rider Wearhouse catalogue and Web site.

Over the next forty years, camping became an enjoyable recreational activity as well as a necessary part of motorcycle travel. In the 1960s, Roger Hull founded a new magazine called *Road Rider* that broke away from traditional motorcycle magazines. Rather than focusing upon engine modifications, troubleshooting, racing, and hill climbing (like other motorcycle magazines), this new magazine focused on long-distance touring trips and frequently offered camping tips. The magazine featured frequent articles on camping written by Cliff

Boswell. These articles describe camping trips to the Sierra Nevada Mountains of California, Mexico, Canada, and Alaska.

By 1969 motorcycle touring and travel had became very popular. The movie *Easy Rider*, for example, told the story of two men who rode across the country and camped out several nights along the way. Many other long-distance riders probably slept out in the woods on their trips—some because they wanted to and others because they had no other option.

A few years later, Peter Tobey collected several articles related to motorcycle touring and published these articles in 1972 as a book entitled *Two Wheel Travel: Motorcycle Camping and Touring*. This book, now out of print, included detailed articles on several topics such as tents, sleeping bags, food, clothing, and loading a motorcycle. Over the years, these topics continue to define the basic core of information that must be mastered to camp comfortably. Tobey's book also included chapters on other topics related to motorcycle touring but not necessarily to camping. Some of these later topics include insurance, credit cards, fairings, buying used motorcycles, sidecars, and troubleshooting on the road.

In 1972, a group of BMW owners formed the BMW Motorcycle Owners Association (BMWMOA). The purpose of this organization was to establish camaraderie and friendship among BMW motorcycle owners. Rallies were organized, and group camping became a major part of these rallies. Today the BMWMOA Web site (www.bmwmoa. org) has over a dozen short essays dealing with various aspects of motorcycle camping. These essays give tips about tents, cooking gear, and other topics related to camping.

In 1973, Cliff Boswell and other riders formed the International Brotherhood of Motorcycle Campers. One of the distinguishing characteristics of this organization was that it welcomed riders of all motorcycle makes. Today this organization hosts several campouts all over the country. Their Web site (www.ibmc.org) lists all the upcoming campouts and has lots of pictures of past campouts.

Since the 1970s, motorcycle camping has continued to grow in popularity, and many sites on the Web attest to this fact. If you search the Web for the topic "motorcycle camping," you will get several hundred sites. These sites offer a wide range of information and advice regarding motorcycle camping. Some provide lists and descriptions of good camping gear. Others describe how to accomplish various camping chores. Others describe interesting camping destinations.

And others provide pictures and videos of past motorcycle camping trips.

Despite this growing interest in motorcycle camping, only one other book has been published on this topic in the past thirty years. This book, entitled *Motorcycle Camping Made Easy,* was written by Bob Woofter and published in 2002. It gives an introduction to motorcycle camping and presents a brief overview of camping products, such as tents and sleeping bags, that could be used on a camping trip. It also includes interesting information about other topics, such as GPS receivers and how to pick up a fallen bike.

In 2007, the movie *Wild Hogs* was released. Its story line revolves around four older professional men who decide to ride their Harleys from Cincinnati out to the West Coast. They start their trip by trying to camp out, but they obviously were not properly prepared to camp, and their camping adventure quickly turned into a disaster.

For most of my life, I have enjoyed traveling both by car and by motorcycle. My family had only modest means and barely helped me go to college. I had to work at part-time jobs to help pay the rest of my bills. As a result, I had little money for entertainment and travel. To be able to travel, I had to find a way to do it on a shoestring budget.

My first motorcycle camping experience occurred in 1965. I was a twenty-year-old student at Auburn University. One night, a friend and I decided to take a trip to Panama City Beach, Florida, on my Yamaha Big Bear (305 cc). We left after work with almost no money in our pockets. We thought we could find someone who would allow us to sleep on a motel room floor. But alas, we had no such luck and had to spend two nights sleeping on the beach. At the time, we viewed the experience as bad luck, but perhaps it was preparation for later motorcycle camping trips.

I soon discovered that camping was the way to travel without having to pay expensive motel bills. In 1967 I bought a used army surplus tent with two doors and no floor and a used army mess kit and began to camp out on my trips.

When I was twenty-three, my wife and I took a three-week car camping trip out west (Grand Canyon, Utah, Colorado, Kansas) and camped almost every night. After our children were born, we continued to camp as much as possible. During the summer of 1974, we spent forty-five days in a small pop-up trailer with a two-year old son and a nine-month old son. That summer we camped in Canada, Colorado, Iowa, Wisconsin, and Florida.

After a divorce, I met my current riding companion (Robin). She had been raised in a camping family and seemed to enjoy camping as much as I did. During the last twenty years of our relationship, we have camped extensively throughout the eastern United States. We worked two summers as campground hosts at Brigham County Park near Madison, Wisconsin.

For most of my life I viewed motorcycle riding and camping as two mutually exclusive activities. Some weekends we chose to ride the motorcycle, and other weekends we chose to go camping. But in the mid 1990s, I sold my pop-up camper and bought a trailer to haul my motorcycle plus a family-sized tent. Now we were able to go camping and take my motorcycle on the trailer. After setting up camp, we used the motorcycle to sightsee and ride to restaurants or local attractions.

In the fall of 1998, I decided to try something new. I packed some camping gear on my motorcycle and rode to a campground for an overnight trip. Thus began my motorcycle camping adventures. Since that first trip, Robin and I have taken several motorcycle camping trips over the past eleven years. During this time, we have enjoyed many pleasurable camping experiences and suffered through several learning experiences. Through these experiences we have discovered ways to make our trips easier and more comfortable. The key to having comfortable motorcycle camping trips is to do your homework. You must learn as much as you can about what gear to purchase, how to pack it on your motorcycle, how to use it in the field, and how to care for it after each trip. If you do your homework and are willing to exert a little effort, you will able to enjoy many dry, warm, and happy motorcycle camping trips.

1. Homework

Preparation and planning are basic principles in almost all activities. If you want to do something well, you have to prepare. Children are taught this principle when they are admonished to do their homework before coming to school. They must do their homework so that they will be prepared for the day's lessons and so that their teacher can see how well they understand past lessons. The Boy Scout motto, "Be Prepared," emphasizes the importance of this principle, not just in Scouting activities but also in all other areas of life. Athletics, band, dance, gymnastics, and many other activities require hours of practice before a game or concert. The military certainly recognizes the importance of training before placing soldiers in the field. And successful businessmen understand the importance of "doing their homework" before entering into any business venture.

Motorcycle camping is no different. If you want to have a dry, warm, and happy camping experience, you must do your homework. You must learn how to plan a trip, how to purchase the best gear, how to pack that gear on your bike, and how to use that gear effectively in the field.

My first motorcycle camping trip:
I tied a tent, two cotton sleeping bags, and a small soft-sided cooler
on the backseat and packed the rest of my gear in a sissy bar bag.

When I first decided to try camping on a motorcycle in 1998, I did not understand the importance of doing my homework. My first trip came about as a result of an impulsive last-minute decision. I was a veteran car camper and thought I knew all there was to know about camping. I got the itch to go a week before Thanksgiving. Even though it was late November, the weather had been very mild for several days. It was Saturday morning, and I had no plans for the weekend. I had a tent and a couple of old cotton-filled sleeping bags in my closet, so I tied them on my bike and headed to the Cherokee National Forest near the Ocoee River, Tennessee, for a solo overnight camping trip. My destination was 140 miles from my home. I had camped there in the past and knew the location of a nice campground. Unfortunately I did not think to look at the weather forecast.

The ride to the campground was very pleasant. I arrived at my destination an hour before dusk. So far, so good! I quickly set up my tent and began to look for firewood. To my surprise, I could find no firewood on the ground or for sale. It seemed as though every piece of wood had been scavenged before I arrived. And, although there was a travel trailer parked in the camp host site, no other people were in the campground. *Oh, well,* I thought, *I really do not need a fire. I will just ride to a restaurant, have a nice meal, come back, and read a book.*

My first motorcycle camping campsite:
Parksville Lake in the Cherokee National Forest

When I finished my meal it had turned dark—very dark. Thick clouds obscured any light from the moon and stars. As I rode back to the campground, I noticed that the temperature was falling. When I got back to the campsite, I was unable to do much. I wanted to read my book, but I had only a flashlight and found it difficult to read the book while holding the flashlight. So I gave up on the book, took a shower, and went to bed. I used one sleeping bag as a mat and the other as my sleeping bag, but both were summer bags. The temperature continued to drop all night. I had packed only a few clothes because my trip was going to be just "an overnighter." As the temperature dropped, I put on every article I had and got into the bag. What a miserable night! I never was able to get warm, and I shivered all night long, having no fire, not enough clothing, and insufficient bedding.

The next morning a heavy fog kept me from getting on the road early. I decided to take a hot shower to get my body temperature up, but I did not have the clothes to keep me warm as I waited for the fog to lift. Finally, at about 10:00 AM, I hit the road. The weather was still somewhat foggy, damp, and cold (around forty degrees). My trip home was miserable! I started shivering and could not stop. I stopped at gas stations and fast food restaurants along the road to try to warm up. I should have stopped in a motel to take a hot shower, but all I could think of was *I want to get home as fast as possible.* I probably had a mild case of hypothermia.

I survived that trip by the grace of God. Had that trip been my only camping trip, I probably would have never tried it again. But I had been a lifelong camper and had many previous enjoyable camping experiences. Thus I was determined to learn more about motorcycle camping and try again.

An important moral of the story is this: Before setting out on your first camping trip, do your homework and get the right gear. You are going to be outside for long periods; you should expect the temperature to feel colder than it really is; you may not have a convenient place to get out of the cold; you should be prepared for rain; and you must have the right gear and clothing to stay dry and warm. To acquire the gear that will best suit your needs, you must gather a lot of information and make decisions based upon that information. Proper planning takes a lot of time but will help assure that you are prepared for most any situation, and thus that you will have an enjoyable trip.

You must learn about the best destinations, the best camping gear to buy, the best ways to pack your gear safely on a motorcycle, and the best ways to stay dry, warm, and comfortable during your camping trips. This book gives a lot of information about these topics, but after finishing it, you should look through other sources. Search the Web and you will find a variety of books, magazines, and individual sites that provide information and advice about a wide range of topics related to motorcycle camping. In your search, use key phrases such as "motorcycle camping," "lightweight camping," and "tent camping." You will find one other book on motorcycle camping, several books on car (or family) camping, several books on backpacking, and several dozen Web sites on motorcycle camping. All of these sources present some useful tips.

A good time to start planning your camping trips is during the winter months after the holidays have passed. You probably will not be able to get out very much and you will likely have some free time. A cold winter night is the perfect time to sit by the fireplace or heater and plan some camping trips for the next summer. If you begin planning during the early winter months, you will have plenty of time to determine the gear you will need, acquire this gear, and increase your chances of having that perfect camping experience you have envisioned.

Learn Camping Skills

When you start looking for information about camping, you will find lots of sources. These books, magazines, and Web sites are typically written for backpackers, backwater canoeists, mountain climbers, and other wilderness campers whose activities take them several hours away from modern conveniences. Much of the information is designed to teach these campers how to survive in the wilderness with a minimum amount of gear. However, some of the information in these references could also be applied to motorcycle camping as well. A major principle discussed in all of these references is to buy gear that packs small but has many uses in your camp. This principle is also important for motorcycle camping.

Several books present useful information about camping and outdoor activities in general. Two of my favorites are *The Backpacker's Handbook* by Chris Townsend and *Camping Made Easy* by Michael Rutter. Other good books include *The Backpacker's Field Manual* by Rick Curtis, *Lightweight Backpacking and Camping* by Ryan Jordan, *Backpacker Tent and Car Camper's Handbook,* by Buck Tilton with Kristin Hostetter, and *Camping's Top Secrets*, by Cliff Jacobson. Some potentially valuable topics include preparing meals outdoors, dealing with insects and animals, first-aid, keeping warm and dry, and the use of ropes and knots.

One book, *Motorcycle Camping Made Easy* by Bob Woofter, specifically focuses upon motorcycle camping. This book presents an overview of camping gear that could be used by motorcycle campers and has lots of pictures showing tents and motorcycles together. But it seems to assume that motorcycle campers may have either a trailer or a chase vehicle to haul some of their gear and seems to focus on primitive camping during motorcycle rallies and camping in motorcycle-only resorts. It gives a considerable amount of information about pull-behind trailers for your motorcycle, luggage accessories, servicing your bike, GPS navigation, and how to pick up a fallen bike. The book also provides some technical details about how tents and sleeping bags are manufactured.

Magazines such as *Backpacker* and *Outside* also present lots of information that can be applied to motorcycle camping. Some of the topics discussed in these sources include selecting good campsites, staying warm, preventing and treating injuries, building campfires, choosing gear that best meets your needs, cooking, campsite recipes, and first aid. In addition to tips and suggestions, these sources describe many great destinations and present many product reviews and advertisements that can help you find the best gear.

The next place to learn more about motorcycle camping is the Web. To begin your search, visit my site (www.motorcyclecampingtips. com). Next search the Web using the phrase "motorcycle camping" or "motorcycle camping trips" and you will find dozens of sites. One of the best sites is the BMW Motorcycle Owners of America (BMWMOA) Web site. This site has several articles written by different BMW owners that provide useful information and tips related to motorcycle camping. The site presents opinions about the best gear, lists designed to remind you of everything you need to take on your trip, and tips as to how to pack a bike, how to cook good-tasting meals, and how to deal with different types of camping-related problems.

Another popular site is Bill Johns' Excellent Motorcycle Camping Guide. This site gives tips and opinions on a variety of motorcycle camping equipment such as luggage, tents, sleeping bags, mattresses, stuff sacks, stoves, and utensils. It also shares several thoughts on cooking, packing the bike, and several other topics and presents a list of camping gear to pack for your trip, divided into six categories: camping equipment, cooking/eating equipment, clothing, personal effects, bike paraphernalia, and tools.

The Easy Reader Tourguide by Gary Sosnick is another helpful site. This site's description of a typical day on the road is an excellent guide for planning your days. And like Bill Johns' site, it presents a list of gear to pack, but it is divided into four categories: clothes, gear, cookware, and tools.

After viewing the above-described sites, you will find many other good sites with lots of suggestions and insights regarding motorcycle camping. Some of the sites give tips and advice regarding the best gear, how to plan your day, and how to approach various camping tasks. Other sites describe motorcycle-only (or motorcycle-friendly) campgrounds, such as 29 Dreams Motorcycle Resort near Birmingham, Alabama, and Two Wheels Only in Suches, Georgia. Yet other sites describe various camping-related products, such as trailers and pop-up tent trailers that can be pulled behind your bike.

Finally, visit sites related to backpacking and tent camping. For example, you may wish to visit www.outsideonline.com. This site provides lots of general camping information and tips that can make your camping trips more comfortable and enjoyable.

While the gear and skills needed for motorcycle camping and backpacking are similar, there are important differences between these two camping strategies, and these differences must be understood before you can consistently plan dry, warm, and comfortable motorcycle camping trips. For example, backpackers must pack water-purification equipment and all the food they will need, while motorcycle campers do not need these items and can use the space to pack more clothing or other items that will make their trip more comfortable. Backpackers would never pack tablecloths because tablecloths add unnecessary weight to the pack, require valuable packing space, and may not be used since there are few tables in back-country campsites. Similarly, backpackers would not pack tarps to be used as dining flies or tarp support poles because these items would add considerable weight to the pack, would take valuable packing space, and are not essential.

Motorcycle campers, on the other hand, could easily pack all these items. They will likely have the space to pack these items on their motorcycles and need not be too concerned about the extra weight. Plus, having a covered table area and tablecloth in your campsite would greatly enhance your camping comfort. Motorcycle campers have the ability to pack many items (that backpackers must forgo) that could make camp life much more comfortable.

One of the goals of this book is to describe important differences between the backpacking and motorcycle camping approaches and explain how these differences should guide your decisions regarding the best gear to purchase, the best way to pack it on your motorcycle, and the best way to use it in your campsite. At the end of this chapter, you will find a chart that summarizes some of the important differences between these two camping approaches. Throughout the book, you will find many more differences between backpacking and motorcycle camping that have important practical implications.

Another important point to understand is that overnight camps require less gear and less work than base camps. Sometimes you just need a place to camp overnight. Perhaps you are traveling to a distant destination but need to spend the night along the way. Sometimes you just want to spend your vacation time riding rather than hanging around a campsite. When morning arrives, you want to get on the road as quickly as possible. For these overnight camps, you want a campground that offers basic conveniences, is close to your travel route, and is safe. You only need a parking area, a small spot to pitch your tent, a table, and a bathhouse with showers. You really do not need privacy, trees, hiking trails, or scenic beauty. When you set up camp, you probably will not set up your tarp over the table or your hammock, and you may not cook supper or breakfast in your campsite. Your main priority is to set up simple sleeping quarters that will allow you to pack up quickly the next morning and get an early start on the road. If your entire trip consists of one or more overnight camps, you would not have to pack kitchen gear and other optional gear. Some of the best places to make overnight camps are state parks—they are close to major highways and easily located on most state road maps—and private campgrounds that are usually located next to major highways.

On the other hand, sometimes you want to camp in one place for several nights, using your campsite as a base camp for relaxing and for venturing out each day. When we stay in a base camp for several days, we typically set up a dining fly and kitchen. We cook breakfast in our site each day, go out for the day's activities, and then cook supper. If you plan to set up a base camp, you may wish to pack your cooking gear, a tarp (to be used as a dining fly), hammocks, and perhaps some other optional gear. Once you set up your camp, you can ride to a grocery store or discount department store and buy groceries, ice, firewood, food, and perhaps a couple of cheap folding chairs.

Assemble the Right Gear

The next step in preparing for your motorcycle camping trip is to determine the items (e.g., a tent, sleeping bags, etc.) that you will need and to collect detailed information (such as weight, features, and price) about available models. If you need a sleeping bag, for example, determine the different models that would suit your needs and your budget. After acquiring this specific information, you will be in a better position to narrow your search down to the one model that best suits your needs.

In addition to the information presented in this book, two good places to find detailed information and advice about camping gear are the REI and Campmor Web sites. These sites provide detailed information about specific models and good advice for selecting gear that will meet your needs and fall within your price range. Furthermore, both sites offer a broad range of gear at reasonable prices. Both companies have free catalogs, and if you need to talk with a person, they have toll-free phone numbers and knowledgeable staff who can answer most, if not all, of your questions. In addition to REI and Campmor, several other Web sites offer useful information and items for sale. Some of these sites, with their contact information, are listed in a summary chart at the end of this chapter.

Another place to go for information is the Web site of popular companies that sell outdoor gear. Some of the best-known companies are Big Agnes, Coleman, Eureka, Kelty, MSR, The North Face, Mountain Hardware, and Sierra Designs. Type the name of the company into your Internet search engine and you will quickly find their Web site, where you will be able to get more detailed information about each item and model. The final place to go is to the Trail Space Web page. This site has product reviews of almost any specific model of outdoor gear you can imagine. Reading these reviews will quickly alert you to the strengths and limitations of any specific product you are considering.

Once you have gathered sufficient information, you should be able to decide upon the particular model that best suits your needs and wallet. Then you may wish to shop around to find the best price. You may want to start your search by visiting retailers in your hometown. Sales personnel will usually be willing to help. Also check reputable mail order companies such as REI and Campmor. REI requires you to become a member of their co-op to get their best prices. Several other possible vendors are listed in a table at the end of this chapter. Another place to look, if you feel comfortable shopping there, is eBay.

Identify Possible Destinations

A good way to start planning a motorcycle camping trip is to think about possible destinations. Perhaps you have read a magazine article describing a scenic trip. Perhaps you have always wanted to visit a certain place but never had the chance to go. Perhaps you'd like to attend a motorcycle rally. Or maybe you have visited a place in the past and would like to visit there again. At first, think of as many different destinations as possible. You can narrow the list and prioritize it later. Think of several destinations within a day's ride. Also think of one or two longer trips that would require more travel time.

Once you get some ideas, go to the Web to get more information about each destination. Visit chamber of commerce Web sites and other community Web sites. Purchase or borrow travel brochures or books that provide details about attractions, events, etc. Libraries typically have lots of travel information. If you are a member of AAA, call for information. Determine if any festivals or special events are scheduled for the locations you are investigating. Look for possible attractions that would interest you, such as motorcycle museums, racetracks, plays, and concerts.

I plan several trips every year. Most of them are short weekend trips to destinations within a day's ride. Some of the trips are to places I have visited in the past. For example, I try to revisit the Smoky Mountains National Park every summer. I especially enjoy camping in Cades Cove (Tennessee) and at Deep Creek (North Carolina). Other favorite destinations are Fall Creek Falls State Park (Tennessee), Cloudland Canyon State Park (Georgia), Unicoi State Park, (Georgia), and Fort Pickens National Seashore (Pensacola, Florida). I also plan trips to new destinations such as Big South Fork National River and Recreation Area (Tennessee/Kentucky) and Cumberland Falls State Park (Kentucky).

Deep Creek Campground in the Smokies is one of my favorite destinations.

Take Short Trips before Attempting Longer Ones

If you have never been on a motorcycle camping trip, it is be a good idea to take a few weekend practice camping trips. Select campsite destinations that are within a hundred miles of your home, pack your gear, and ride over to the site. Unpack your bike and set up your camp. Make a fire, cook your meals, enjoy park programs, and relax. After a day or two, pack up and ride back home. Taking such short trips will help you determine whether you are ready for longer trips. When taking these short trips, you can determine if you are able to pack the all the camping gear you need and if your body (in particular, your butt) is able to sit in the saddle for more than two hours. If you have problems on a trip, you can get back home fairly easily and decide what corrective actions need to be taken. Once things go smoothly, you are ready for that longer trip.

Regardless of the type of campground you select, parks with established campsites will probably have the following conveniences in each campsite:

- Parking Area: Typically there will be a paved or gravel parking area at (or near) your site where you can park your motorcycle. In fact, there will be room to park two or three motorcycles, if you are riding with friends.

- Picnic Table: Since you will probably not have folding chairs, the picnic table will be the primary place where you can sit, eat, and relax. If you are lucky, your table is not permanently affixed to the ground and can be moved around the site. Having a table that can be moved is ideal because you can first determine the best location for setting up your tarp and then move the table under it, as you would like. Unfortunately, because of vandalism and theft, many parks have switched to permanently positioned (stationary) tables—frequently made from concrete. In this situation, you may have to be creative to set up your tarp so that it covers the table.

- Tent Pad: Most campgrounds provide an elevated gravel pad for your tent. This pad usually has good drainage and thus eliminates the need to dig trenches to drain rainwater away from your tent. In fact, trenching, which used to be considered necessary, is now considered environmentally undesirable because repeated trenching promotes soil erosion and creates a negative impact upon the land. Some parks require you to place your tent on the pad so as to minimize damage to fragile plants near your site. Use the pad if it is provided.

- Fire Ring or Grill: Most campsites will have a fire ring or grill. You should use the fire ring wherever it is placed and confine your fires to these locations.

A typical campsite at Tims Ford State Park, Tennessee

In addition, many sites will have fresh drinking water and electricity (for charging your cell phone) located at (or near) the site. Most established campgrounds also have flush toilets, a shower, and laundry facilities. All of these campsite features will help you stay dry, warm, and comfortable during your stay.

State parks usually are great places to learn basic motorcycle camping skills. In most regions of the country, one can be found within a hundred miles or so of any starting point. They usually have good nighttime security to assure a safe camping experience and have designated campsites with tent pads, tables, and parking areas. Drinking water, bathhouses, and hot showers are usually located near campsites. They have sturdy brick or stone buildings that can provide emergency shelter if severe weather conditions develop. In general, state parks provide basic conveniences to assure comfortable camping experiences and enough ruggedness to help you learn basic camping skills. After my first disastrous trip to Parksville Lake campground, I took several short trips to Monte Sano State Park, which is about thirty miles from my home. Through trial and error, I acquired the right gear, learned how to pack it on my motorcycle, learned how to set it up in a campsite, and learned how to use it to stay dry, warm, and comfortable in a variety of weather conditions.

National parks and recreation areas are also great places to learn basic camping skills. They usually have most of the conveniences found in state parks plus they offer a wide range of recreational and educational activities. For example, Mammoth Cave National Park offers several cave tours, hiking trails, and nature programs. Land Between The Lakes National Recreation Area offers a living history interactive farm, a planetarium, a bison range, an excellent nature center, and lots of water recreational activities.

Another type of campground you may wish to consider is a motorcycle-only campground or motor camp. Most of these campgrounds are located in the southeast near the Appalachian Mountains. They are fun to visit, just for the experience. Frequently they have a cafe where you can buy food and beer, and on weekends they usually have entertainment and lots of motorcycle riders who also enjoy camping. It is always interesting to gab with other riders, hear their stories, and learn new tips. My limited experience with motorcycle-only campgrounds is that they have excellent bath facilities and security. Some have cabins or lodges for riders who do not have camping gear. The only possible limitation of these camps is that they may charge by the head. If you are riding solo, it is a bargain; but if you are riding two-up, the cost of the campsite may be a little higher than the price of a state park site. A partial list of motorcycle-only campgrounds, with contact information, can be found at the end of this chapter.

Other options are county and city parks. In our experience, the quality of these campgrounds varies considerably. Some, such as Point Mallard Campground in Decatur, Alabama, and Brigham County Park near Madison, Wisconsin, are very nice campgrounds, but many other city and county parks are not as nice. The problem we have most often experienced in city and county parks has been drunkenness and rowdiness due to inadequate nighttime security. After several unpleasant experiences, we are now reluctant to camp in these campgrounds unless several families are camping there and good security will be present during the night.

Campgrounds differ in terms of several desirable qualities. For example, campgrounds vary in terms of the quality of bathroom facilities, nighttime security, privacy, noise levels, recreational activities, natural beauty, and price. If we are planning to stay several nights in a base camp, we prefer to camp in national parks or national recreation areas, if possible. These campgrounds usually offer good nighttime security, a lot of privacy, educational programs and activities, and natural beauty at a low price. Their disadvantages are that they may be located several miles away from major highways and their bath facilities are sometimes limited. National recreation areas are usually good choices, but some of the more isolated parks may not have adequate nighttime security. If there is limited nighttime security, you may be disturbed by people who want to drink and party all night. We know—we have had difficulty sleeping because of noise on several occasions. Now when we are considering whether to stay at a particular campground, we determine the degree of security before making our decision.

Campgrounds also differ in terms of two other qualities that may be important for motorcycle riders: terrain and road surface. Many campgrounds (e.g., Smokemont Campground in the Great Smoky Mountains National Park) are basically flat with only a few small hills, while other campgrounds are developed on the sides of mountains (e.g., Edgar Evins State Park, Tennessee). I do not know about other riders, but I personally find it more difficult to ride at a slow speed on steep hilly campground roads (especially if they have speed bumps and sharp turns) than on relatively flat surfaces. This problem of instability is compounded if you are riding two-up. The second feature to consider is the surface of roads in the campground.

Most campgrounds have paved roads, but a few have gravel roads. If you decide to stay at a campground that has steep gravel roads (e.g., Hillman Ferry Campground in the Land Between The Lakes NRA or a KOA campground near Chattanooga, Tennessee), you may have considerable difficulty keeping your bike under control. My Electra Glide is extremely unstable on those steep gravel roads and could easily dump me in a heartbeat. In conclusion, when doing your homework on campgrounds, also pay attention to descriptions of the terrain and road surface.

The bathhouse at Fall Creek Falls State Park, Tennessee, is very comfortable.

Occasionally you may hear that some campgrounds are not "motorcycle friendly." A few books and magazine articles state or suggest that some campgrounds refuse camping privileges to motorcycle riders solely because they are riding motorcycles. We have never personally encountered such a problem. We have camped throughout the South and Midwest and never been refused camping privileges because we were riding a motorcycle. Granted, most of our camping has been in state and national parks rather than in private campgrounds. It is possible that these reports refer to RV parks. We have learned from past experience that some RV parks such as State Fair Park in Milwaukee, Wisconsin, do not allow tent campers, regardless of the vehicle they are driving. But we have never been refused because we were riding a motorcycle. Perhaps a few campground owners have been reluctant to admit motorcycle riders because of past problems or because of the number of the riders in a group or because of their behavior (drunkenness or loud exhaust pipes). If you have any concerns, call the campground before your departure to determine whether or not you will likely encounter problems.

Plan Long Trips

Many motorcycle riders dream of taking a long cross-country trip to Sturgis, Daytona, Laughlin, or some other distant destination. The movie *Wild Hogs* tells the story of four Harley riders who live this dream. They ride from Cincinnati to the West Coast. Although they apparently planned to camp out each night, they were ill prepared and encountered major problems on the first night of their trip. Perhaps others can learn from this example and do a little more homework before departing on that long trip.

The first step in planning long camping trips is to look at state highway maps or go to the MapQuest Web site. Determine the best routes to and from your destination. What is the total length of your trip in miles? How many miles would you ride each day? Four hundred to 450 miles per day is the most to expect, especially when camping. If your destination is 750 miles away, for example, you should plan at least two days to get there and two more days for the return trip (assuming no problems). As you review the map, also look for possible side trips to other points of interest along the way.

To plan your itinerary, first use MapQuest to determine the mileage between points along your route. This information will help you determine the approximate destination for each day. Then look for campgrounds near each day's approximate destination.

On any given trip, you will likely have several different campgrounds from which to choose. Our first choice is a state park. Every state has dozens of them. To find them, look at the state highway map. In all probability, the map will show several located along your travel route. The map will also give useful details, such as phone numbers, driving directions, services available, the number of sites, and the types of recreational activities available. These parks are conveniently located near major highways, have good facilities and security, and are reasonably priced. Sometimes they offer both developed and primitive (or walk-in) sites. Primitive sites are frequently less expensive than developed sites and are located away from the RVs, but they usually are also located further away from bath facilities. When traveling, we usually prefer to pay the extra money and stay in developed sites with water and electricity.

The next place to look for campgrounds is the Web. Search for accommodations near your approximate overnight stops and final destination. For example, if you want to go to Helen, Georgia, for Oktoberfest, search for "Helen Georgia campgrounds" and you will find the Unicoi State Park plus a dozen or more private campgrounds. Read the information about each campground and its facilities and make your first and second choices.

Another good site is Woodall's Web site. This site provides valuable information (such as directions, phone numbers, overall campground quality, quality of bath facilities, and security) about any national, state, or private campground near your destination. Woodall's also publishes this information as a book entitled *Woodall's North American Campground Directory.* A similar book is *Trailer Life's RV Parks, Campgrounds, and Services Directory.*

Another source of information about good campgrounds for motorcycle riders is a series of books written by Johnny Molloy and others entitled *The Best in Tent Camping.* Each book describes the best campgrounds suitable for tent camping in a particular state or popular tourist region such as the Appalachian Mountains. In addition to state parks, these books describe many excellent campgrounds that may not be identified on state highway maps. For example, one of these books that I frequently consult is *The Best in Tent Camping—Tennessee.* In addition to some of the best Tennessee state parks, it describes dozens of great campgrounds operated by the Tennessee Valley Authority, the U.S. Forest Service, the National Parks Service, the Army Corps of Engineers, and other federal agencies. Many of these campgrounds are not identified on Tennessee state highway maps.

When state parks are not available, we will consider camping in private campgrounds or RV parks. Sometimes, when we are anxious to get to a distant destination and just have to spend the night en route, a private campground may be the best choice. Private campgrounds are conveniently located near major highways, especially near large cities. Perhaps the best-known private campgrounds are KOA and Yogi Bear's Jellystone Park. These parks usually have nice sites for tents, good bath facilities, laundry facilities, and a covered clubhouse or recreation room where you could get in out of the rain. Sometimes they have swimming pools, which can be very relaxing and refreshing after a long, hot day of riding. When planning your trip, you may want to visit the KOA and Yogi Bear's Web sites to see if one of these parks is on your route.

When considering private campgrounds, be aware that they typically have limited privacy and little natural beauty. In addition, their prices tend to be higher than the prices for state and national parks. Their bath facilities vary considerably. Some private campgrounds have nice bath facilities, but others have small (and sometimes unsanitary) bath and toilet facilities. Furthermore, some private campgrounds serve as permanent residences for homeless people. Investigate before you decide to stay. If you are considering staying at a private campground, you may want to check Woodall's or Trailer Life's directory before leaving your home. These directories provide ratings that help you assess the quality of bath facilities and the campground as a whole.

Many campgrounds fill to capacity on nice summer and fall weekends—especially on holiday weekends. If you are planning to travel and camp on weekends, you should consider calling the campground office to determine your best strategy for securing a campsite. If the campground will likely fill, you might be able to make a reservation. Some campgrounds accept reservations, while others do not. If the campground does not accept reservations, you should make every effort to arrive as early as possible. Try to get there by early Friday afternoon. Or you could look for other campgrounds in the area as second and third choices if your first choice campground is full when you arrive.

In finalizing the details of a long trip, consider a few other factors. For example, determine the temperature extremes you will likely encounter, especially the predicted low temperature, because this information will tell you what clothes you will need to pack. Understand that riding two-up requires a lot of packing space for clothing and thus reduces the amount of room for packing kitchen gear and other optional gear. Finally, realize that details such as the total number of days of the trip, the approximate number of miles to travel each day, and campgrounds in the vicinity of each night's rest will determine how much and what type of clothing, gear, and personal items you will be able to pack and use. If you want to get your trip off to a happy start, you would be wise to coordinate these details with your companion.

Once you have all of the details, prepare a sheet of paper listing each day of your trip and summarizing the route you plan to take and your destination for the day. Be sure to list names and phone numbers of campgrounds, bike service centers, and any other businesses you may need to contact. When preparing this itinerary, consider the following suggestions:

- Summarize the route and highway numbers you plan to ride each day.

- List names and phone numbers of each campground destination.
- Plan to get an early start (7:00 AM).
- Plan to take a break every one to one and a half hours.
- Plan to ride no more than eight hours per day.
- Plan to travel no more than 400 to 450 miles a day.
- Plan to stay in established campgrounds.
- Plan to arrive at your campground destinations before 5:00 PM.
- Plan to limit Sunday travel (because emergency service is unavailable or expensive).
- Plan to call a friend or relative at the end of each day to verify your location and to discuss plans for the next day.
- Make a copy for a friend or relative.

The overall rationale for these suggestions is to help you have a safe, trouble-free, and enjoyable trip. Getting on the road early in the morning, especially during summer months, allows you to ride during the coolest time of the day. Taking frequent breaks to stand and walk around allows you to overcome fatigue and replenish oxygen rich blood to your brain. This oxygen-rich blood will, in turn, refresh your mind and help you become more alert. Ending your day by 5:00 PM keeps you off the road during peak traffic times. Ending your day by 5:00 PM and limiting your Sunday travel also helps you avoid all the problems associated with breaking down after normal business hours (e.g., waiting long hours until a wrecker can get to you, having to pay extra money for after-hours service, and having to wait overnight before repairs can be made to your bike). Furthermore, arriving at your campground by 5:00 PM gives you plenty of time to register, set up camp, go for food and supplies, cook, clean up, bathe, pack, and relax before going to bed.

The long trip I hope to take someday is a touring trip around the state of Wisconsin. I lived in southeastern Wisconsin and later in Milwaukee several years ago, and I have returned to this area for vacations many times. But I have very little knowledge of the western and northern parts of the state. On the first day of my touring trip, I plan to ride from Alabama up to central Illinois and, depending upon the miles I can cover, camp at either Walnut Point, Kickapoo, or Moraine View State Park. On the second day, I plan to ride up to Freeport, Illinois, and then ride up through Monroe, through the Swiss village of New Glarus, through the Norwegian town of Mount

Horeb, and then over to Dodgeville to spend the night at Governor Dodge State Park. The third day, I want to ride up to Spring Green and then along the Wisconsin River over to Prairie du Chien, then turn north up the Great River Road along the banks of the Mississippi River to the River Falls area. I understand that this river road is a good place to see eagles, so I will be on the watch. I will probably camp at Willow River or Interstate State Park.

Then I want to proceed on up to Superior, where I will ride along the shore of Lake Superior over to Bayfield, where I will spend some time exploring the Apostle Islands National Lakeshore. From there, I will ride down to Minocqua-Woodruff area and eat a good walleye fish dinner; next I will ride over to Green Bay and then up to Door County, where I will camp at Peninsula State Park and enjoy a fish boil and an outdoor play or concert. On the way home I will ride down through Milwaukee, where I will take a tour of a Harley-Davidson assembly plant and enjoy some good German food at Karl Rasch's. To finish the trip, I will ride back over to Madison to visit a friend and then head home through Janesville. Returning home through Chicago would shorten my trip, but I want to avoid the heavy traffic. The total distance from my home, around the state of Wisconsin, and back is about 2,700 miles. I'll allow about ten days for the trip.

Prepare for Rain and Cold

Unless you are exceptionally lucky, you will likely experience rain and perhaps cold weather on many of your trips. Over the past five years we have taken several trips to the Smoky Mountains and have encountered rain almost every time. On many other trips, we have gotten chilled because we were unprepared for the weather. Now we know to expect rain and colder temperatures than forecasted. Some of the things you can do to prepare for rain are:

- Coat boots with a waterproof product.
- Pack a good rain suit. See chapter 4 for details.
- Pack your sleeping bags inside a large waterproof compression sack.
- Pack a tarp to cover your table. See chapter 9 for details.
- Wear and pack the right clothing. See chapter 5 for details.
- Take a book or radio to pass the time.
- Be ready to put on gaiters at the first sign of rain; if you do not, your socks will act like wicks and quickly soak the insides of your boots.

- Be prepared to pack wet and dry clothes separately.
- Know how to select sites with good drainage. See chapter 9 for details.
- Be prepared to cover your bike at night.
- If the rain gets too heavy or is predicted to last for several hours, be prepared to find a motel room for the night.

Some of the things you can do to prepare for cold are:

- Pack an insulated air mattress. See chapter 3 for details.
- Pack a good sleeping bag. See chapter 3 for details.
- Pack the right clothing. See chapter 5 for details.
- Layer clothes for warmth. See chapter 5 for details.

Prepare Checklists

As the date of a trip nears, you must make sure your motorcycle is ready for the trip, assemble all the gear you will need, and gather a variety of personal items. You must attend to many details to assure a problem-free trip. To help you remember everything, prepare checklists and use them to pack for every trip. The first checklist to prepare is a list of specific things to do in the weeks and days before departing on a trip. Specific activities on this first checklist are briefly introduced below and are summarized at the end of this chapter. Additional checklists will be introduced in subsequent chapters of this book.

One or two months before departure

Prepare your trip map. Obtain a good map of the route you plan to travel and seal it in a plastic cover. You can purchase clear plastic map pockets from motorcycle supply vendors or you can use a one-gallon plastic food-storage bag. Mark your route and your planned camping areas on the map and then seal it in a plastic cover so it won't get wet.

Be sure your bike is ready for a trip. A month or two before your trip, check your records to determine whether your bike should be serviced before the trip. Be sure that fluids have been changed according to your bike's manufacturer's recommendations, that cables and controls have been properly inspected and serviced, and that your brakes are working well. Also determine the number of miles on your tires and visually inspect the tires themselves for any signs of damage. If necessary, have repair work performed and tires replaced before departing. These actions should reduce the chances that you will break down on the road or have to spend large amounts of time waiting for your bike to be repaired. If your bike is in good shape, you should not have to pack many tools or spare parts and thus you will have more room for your camping gear.

Assemble your gear. A month or two before your trip you should also assemble the gear you will need. Be sure you have everything you will need and that everything is in good repair. This is a good time to determine whether you need to replace old items or to purchase additional items. Perhaps you might put a box or two in a closet and start packing your gear, including your tent, sleeping bags, mattresses, essential gear, and optional gear. By assembling your gear ahead of time, you will have a general idea about the amount of space required when you pack your bike. If you have too much gear, you will have time to make adjustments.

Plan for emergency service. Most trips go without a hitch. But problems occasionally do occur. Thus you need to plan for the possibility of a breakdown. Many riders purchase roadside assistance insurance. There are several possible carriers. The Harley Owners Group has a good plan, as does the American Motorcycle Association (AMA) and AAA. AAA requires you to be a member for a year before they will provide motorcycle coverage, but if you are a member of AAA, the company will provide travel maps, brochures, and route suggestions to help you plan your trip. And, if you are a member, they will provide contact information for wrecker service even if you do not have motorcycle coverage.

Another precaution you may wish to take is to pack a few basic tools for your bike. If you keep your bike properly serviced, the odds are you will never have to open the kit or lift a wrench to make emergency repairs, but pack a few basic tools anyway, including a roll of duct tape in case you need to make an emergency repair. Several recent books and articles about motorcycle camping agree that carrying an excessive amount of tools and parts is unnecessary. If you have an emergency, your best tools will be your cell phone and your credit card.

One week before departure

Pack your prescription medicines. If you take prescription medicine, be sure you have enough for the entire trip plus a few extra days. This item can be easily overlooked until the day before your departure. If you do not have enough medicine, your trip could be delayed. It can be a hassle trying to get medicine at the last minute or in another state. If you take a controlled substance (i.e., schedule medicines with a potential for abuse), you must leave it in its original container with your name and prescription details printed on the container.

Inspect your bike. Be sure that your brakes, lights, throttle, and other controls work properly. Also look for signs of oil leaks and check air pressure in tires (and shocks). Adjust the preload on your shocks according to the weight you will be carrying. If you see a problem, fix it before you depart. The last thing you want is to break down with a problem that could have been remedied before starting the trip.

Be sure your documents are current. It is easy to forget your motorcycle operator's license, proof of insurance, and vehicle registration, but if you get stopped, you may lose valuable time waiting to get copies of important documents.

Become familiar with motorcycle laws. You may know the laws in your own state, but make sure you are familiar with those in all states along your route. You will especially want to be familiar with helmet laws, high-bar laws, passenger laws, and laws pertaining to noise. Be sure you are able to comply with the laws in every state in which you plan to ride.

Apply waterproof treatment to your boots. I usually use Kiwi Mink Oil or Camp Dry. Several other products such as NikWax have been reported as providing excellent waterproofing.

Sharpen your knife and ax. Camping will frequently require the use of a knife or ax. If these tools are sharp, your tasks will be relatively easy. But if you have dull tools, you may have to exert more effort, thereby increasing the risk of accidentally injuring yourself. Moreover, I have discovered that using sharp tools is one of life's special pleasures. Once you become accustomed to using sharp tools, you will never be satisfied using a dull knife or ax again.

We sharpen our knives with this Smith's tool.

Pack most of your gear, clothes, and personal items. You might be surprised when you first attempt to pack. Clothing and personal items for two people can take a considerable amount of room, even when you try to pack sparingly. Because of limited space, you and your companion will have to make hard decisions regarding the clothing and gear that you will be able to pack. Be sure to purchase travel-sized personal items and containers. Only take what you must have and only what you know you will wear. Your clothing should be able to keep you warm but yet should pack as small as possible. Garments made from cotton are poor choices. Garments made from polyester and nylon are much better choices. They provide considerable warmth, they allow body moisture to evaporate quickly, and they require a small amount of packing space. Depending upon the amount of space consumed, you may have to forgo your kitchen supplies and most optional gear. Large garments such as denim jackets, sweaters, and blue jeans cannot be compressed and should be avoided. Try to leave hair dryers at home, because many restrooms have hot-air hand dryers. In warm weather, natural air-drying will do the job. If you have to take one, buy a small travel-sized dryer.

Give a copy of your itinerary to a relative or friend. If you have made any changes, be sure to note them. Once your itinerary is accurate, make a copy for a family member so he or she will know how to contact you in case of an emergency.

One day before departure

Get cash, debit card, and credit cards. Make sure you have enough money to enjoy your trip and get back home. Bring enough money to cover unexpected expenses.

Charge your cell phone. Be sure your cell phone is fully charged so that you can check in with relatives to let them know that your trip is going as planned. In addition, you may need to call for road service or contact local businesses or campgrounds. While on your trip, make sure to charge your phone often.

Fill your gas tank. The most efficient way to travel long distances is to get an early start and cover as many miles as possible before the temperature gets too warm and before the traffic gets too heavy. After starting out, you should be able to ride for at least an hour before making your first rest stop. Having a full tank will give you the confidence that you will be able to ride as long as necessary before making that first stop.

If you do your homework, you can have a great camping trip.
This was my campsite at the Deep Creek Campground, Great Smoky Mountains
National Park.

Check your tire pressure. Always check your tires before riding. Tires should be inflated when cold. Since you may be riding two-up on a packed bike, your tires should be inflated to their recommended maximum pressure.

Tie tent, sleeping pads, and sleeping bags on your bike. The night before you depart, tie your tent, sleeping bags, and sleeping pads on your bike's luggage rack or backpack. I prefer to use small nylon cord, which is strong enough to hold your gear on your motorcycle but small enough to pack into a small space when you do not need it. When you get to your campsite, you can use the cord for a variety of purposes, such as making a clothesline or securing your tarp over the picnic table.

Check the weather forecast. Be sure you are not riding into strong storms and/or exceptionally cold weather. If the forecast is good, you can be relatively assured you will not have a weather-related problem that could ruin your trip. If the forecast is bad, you may want to delay your trip or consider an alternate route or destination.

Additional checklists are presented in the following chapters. They can be used to remember all the gear you need to pack and how to pack it on your motorcycle. You can copy these checklists or use them to make your own personal lists.

Conclusion

How can you prepare for motorcycle camping trips in a variety of weather conditions? Whether you are a first-time camper or an experienced camper, you should do your homework. You must learn a few basic camping skills, acquire the right gear, plan your trip, prepare for rain and cold weather, and use checklists to remember important pre-trip details. If you do your homework, you should have a dry, warm, and enjoyable camping experience.

After reading this chapter, you can find many more resources to help with your homework. For more information about camping gear, visit your local camping supply store or visit any of the Web sites listed at the end of this chapter. For more information about trip planning, look for guidebooks describing the area you plan to visit. For example, I read *Upper Mississippi Valley by Motorcycle* by Kay Fellows and *The Best in Tent Camping—Wisconsin* by Johnny Molloy to plan my long trip around the state of Wisconsin. For more information about your route and attractions you may want to contact AAA and visit MapQuest (www.mapquest.com) and Woodall's (www.woodalls.com) Web sites.

Differences between Backpacking and Motorcycle Camping

Backpacks
: Backpackers must purchase medium to large backpacks that typically cost $150–$500 to haul all their gear.

  Motorcycle campers do not need backpacks. If they want to take short hikes, they could pack small daypacks that typically cost $25–$100.

Shelters
: Many backpackers sleep under tarps or in hammocks. If they buy tents, they will buy the lightest possible ones (usually one- or two-person tents) that provide minimal space and comfort.

  Most motorcycle campers are able to pack three- and four-person tents that provide more space and comfort.

Sleeping bags
: Backpackers prefer down-filled bags because they provide the greatest amount of warmth for the least amount of weight.

  Motorcycle campers should consider synthetic-filled bags because they keep you warm even when wet.

Food
: Backpackers must pack all their food in their backpack. Consequently, they must eat energy bars and rehydrated foods the entire trip.

  Motorcycle campers do not have to pack food because they can easily ride to stores or restaurants every day. They typically eat freshly prepared foods.

Kitchen gear
: Backpackers must pack a stove, fuel, pots, utensils, dishes, and cups in their backpacks.

  Motorcycle campers have more options. They can pack some kitchen gear if they want to cook or they can leave it at home.

Water
: Backpackers must pack water-purification equipment and draw their water from creeks or ponds.

  Motorcycle campers do not need water-purification equipment because they usually camp in established campgrounds that have clean potable water close to each campsite.

Clothes	Backpackers have very little space to pack clothes. Typically they pack one change (T-shirt, underwear, and socks) and wear their clothes two or more days before washing.
	Motorcycle campers can easily pack up to three changes of clothes. They can wash clothes in laundry mats or sinks in most campgrounds.
Bathing	Backpackers may not bathe during their trip. If they do, they typically use washcloths and a little water to wipe away dirt and sweat.
	Motorcycle campers can take hot showers every night because they typically camp in established campgrounds that have bathhouses.
Optional items	Backpackers typically have little space to pack optional items.
	Motorcycle campers have much more space and can pack hammocks, radios, cameras, extra tarps, hair dryers, and other items.
Survival skills	Backpackers should learn basic survival skills because they may camp in remote places where emergency medical assistance is difficult to obtain.
	Motorcycle campers typically camp in established campgrounds that have phone coverage, paved roads, and trained park rangers.

Camping Gear Vendors

Company	Phone	Home page
Back Country	800-409-4502	www.backcountry.com
Back Country Gear	800-953-5499	www.backcountrygear.com
BentGear	800-470-2368	www.bentgear.com
Cabela's	800-237-4444	www.cabelas.com
Campmor	800-226-7667	www.campmor.com
Camp Saver	877-883-6276	www.campsaver.com
Coleman	800-835-3278	www.coleman.com
Gear Zone	801-796-6096	www.gearzone.com
L. L. Bean	800-441-5713	www.llbean.com
Moontrail	800-569-8411	www.moontrail.com
Mountain Gear	800-829-2009	www.mountaingear.com
Mountain Gear Now	none given	www.mountaingearnow.com
Outdoor Gear Exchange	888-547-4327	www.gearx.com
ProLite Gear	406-582-0508	www.prolitegear.com
REI	800-426-4840	www.rei.com
Sierra Trading Post	800-713-4534	www.sierratradingpost.com
Sun Dog Outfitter	866-515-3441	www.sundogoutfitter.com
Travel Country	800-643-3629	www.travelcountry.com

Motorcycle-Only Campgrounds

East of the Mississippi River

Southern Eagle Motorcycle Resort, Haleyville, Ala.   205-486-2408
  (75 miles NW of Birmingham)

29 Dreams, Vandiver, Ala.   205-672-0309
  (15 miles SE of Birmingham)

Two Wheels Only, Suches, Ga.   706-747-5151
  (82 miles NE of Atlanta)

Shiloh Motor Hotel & Campground, Seymour, Tenn.   865-428-5710
  (14 miles E of Knoxville)

Punkin Center Campground, Maryville, Tenn.   865-856-4879
  (16 miles S of Knoxville)

Cherohala Motorcycle Resort, Tellico Plains, Tenn.   423-253-6544
  (71 miles S of Knoxville)

Motorcycle Vacation Resort, Sequatchie, Tenn.   423-942-8688
  (30 miles W of Chattanooga)

Deal's Gap Resort, Tapoco, N.C.   800-889-5550
  (Southern boundary of Smoky Mountains National
  Park)

Blue Ridge Motorcycle Campground, Canton, N.C.   828-235-8350
  (31 miles W of Ashville)

Rider's Roost, Ferguson, N.C.   336-973-8405
  (36 miles N of Hickory)

High Country Cycle Camp, Ferguson, N.C.   336-973-3911
  (36 miles N of Hickory)

Kickstand Lodge, Stecoah, N.C.   828-479-6069
  (81 miles W of Ashville)

Iron Horse Motorcycle Lodge, Stecoah, N.C.   828-479-3864
  (81 miles W of Ashville)

Willville Motorcycle Camp, Meadows of Dan, Va.   276-952-2267
  (62 miles S of Roanoke)

Rustling Leaves Resort, Buena Vista, Va.   540-264-0042
   (56 miles S of Roanoke)

West of the Mississippi River
Valhalla Motorcycle Campground, Homer, La.   318-927-1008
   (52 miles NE of Shreveport)
Iron Horse Stables, Eureka Springs, Ark.   479-253-0440
   (113 miles N of Fort Smith)
Sawmill Town, Newton, Texas   409-379-3851
   (149 miles NE of Houston)

Pre-Trip Checklist

One or Two Months before Departure
- Prepare trip map.
- Prepare itinerary.
- Service bike.
- Assemble gear.
- Plan for emergency service.

One Week before Departure
- Pack prescription medicines.
- Sharpen knife and ax.
- Pack gear, clothes, and personal items.
- Inspect bike.
- Check license, proof of insurance, and registration.
- Review state motorcycle laws.
- Give copy of itinerary to a family member.
- Waterproof boots.

One Day before Departure
- Get cash, debit card, and credit cards.
- Charge cell phone.
- Fill gas tank.
- Check tire pressure.
- Tie tent, sleeping bags, and sleeping pads to bike.
- Check weather forecast.

2. Shelter

When you decide to try motorcycle camping, the first thing to buy is a good tent. Your tent will be the center of your camping experience and will play an important role in determining how much enjoyment you will have from the experience. It may be your most expensive piece of gear, so do your homework before purchasing one. Choose carefully, because your decision could make the difference between having dry and fun trips and wet and miserable ones.

Tents are available in an almost overwhelming number of styles, sizes, features, and prices. There are cabin tents, family tents, three-season backpacking tents, four-season tents, convertible tents, hoop tents, dome tents, and pyramid tents. Within some of these groups, there are one-, two-, three-, and four-person tents. In addition to all these tents, some backpackers prefer to sleep in hammocks, in bivy sacks, and under tarps or ultra-light shelters to lighten their load. How can a motorcycle camper make sense of this chaos?

The Kelty Gunnison 4 is long and spacious.

For me, finding the right tent has been an expensive lesson of trial and error. Over my lifetime I have owned and camped in approximately twenty different tents. My first tent was an old canvas army surplus tent with wooden poles and no floor. After using this tent for a while, I decided to move up to a tent with a floor. I went to a local discount department store and found an economy family tent that looked fairly nice in the picture. I bought it, but after a few uses I became dissatisfied with it, primarily because it leaked in the rain. So I bought another, and then another, and so on for a while. I was displeased with each of these discount department store tents because they all leaked. After going through a variety of tents, I eventually decided to step up and buy a more expensive weatherproof tent. The first of these good tents was the REI Camp Dome 4 (a four-person family tent).

When I decided to try a motorcycle camping trip in 1998, I only owned one tent—the REI Camp Dome 4. I had used it on several car camping trips and was pleased with its spaciousness and weather resistance. At the time, it seemed small enough to pack on my bike. I later realized it was a little too big for two-up motorcycle camping trips. The tent, along with its footprint, weighed eleven pounds, ten ounces. It was not a problem on my first trip because the trip was a solo one.

But when we tried to pack the Camp Dome 4 for a two-up trip, we ran into problems. It required so much space that we did not have room to pack many other items we wanted to take. In particular, we had no room to pack sleeping bags and sleeping pads. We thought we could compensate by packing lightweight flannel blankets rather than sleeping bags, but this turned out to be a mistake. It was obvious that in order to pack two sleeping bags and two sleeping pads with our tent, all of these items had to be as small and lightweight as possible. We decided that we needed a smaller tent.

In looking for the best motorcycle camping tent, I was confronted by an almost overwhelming amount of information. There were many tents, specifications, and terms. I went to the BMWMOA Web site for guidance and found an article that listed several models and their specifications, but I could not tell what features were important and which were not important. I read books that described and pictured several different tents, but they also failed to provide the direction I needed. I knew I needed a tent that packed into a smaller space and weighed less. But there were so many different choices that I could not identify the specific tent or tents that were best suited for motorcycle travel.

I decided to try another approach. One day I drove up to the REI store in Franklin, Tennessee, just south of Nashville. I looked at tents on the floor and talked with a salesperson. He was very knowledgeable and allowed me to set up a couple of tents on the floor—including a two-person tent. By comparison with my large tent, the two-person tent seemed extremely small. I concluded that I could never be happy with such a small tent, even though it had two doors and two vestibules.

Eventually I decided upon a Kelty Gunnison 4—a four-person, three-season tent. (In 2008 Kelty redesigned this tent and now offers three versions—the Gunnison 4.1, 3.1, and 2.1.) My Gunnison 4 had a very comfortable floor plan and interior height. Furthermore, it packed a lot smaller than my Camp Dome 4. Later I determined that with a ground cloth and poles (but not stakes) it weighed eight pounds, eleven ounces. We have used it on several trips and are satisfied that it was a good choice for two-up camping. It is extremely weather tight. We know this fact personally, because we have spent several stormy nights in it. It also has good interior space and a lower weight (i.e., a good space-to-weight ratio). But after a few trips, I began to notice that it was a little bigger and heavier than most other three- and four-person, three-season tents. Packing it with our sleeping bags and pads seemed to take a little more space than I would like. Although we were generally pleased with it, I thought I could find the same degree of comfort in a smaller tent, so I began looking for another one.

I began my search by reading several articles and reviews written by backpackers. They all seemed to praise the two-person tents, so I thought I should reconsider my first impression of these small tents. Perhaps with the vestibule, they are not as small as they appear on the showroom floor. In particular, I found several positive reviews of the REI Half Dome 2, so I purchased one. It packed very small and seemed to be perfect for my bike. Along with its footprint (or ground cloth), it weighed only six pounds. It packed into a very small bag and required very little packing space. Robin and I took it on a two-day trip to the Smokies. Without a doubt, the tent offered excellent wind and rain protection—it stormed both nights. Furthermore, the two vestibules provided a little extra space to aid with gear storage.

But I quickly realized that at six feet, two inches tall and 260 pounds, I am a lot bigger than the backpackers who wrote those reviews. The doors were both located at one end of the tent, and the interior space was too small for two normal people to turn around. We had to decide whether to enter the tent head first or feet first. It was easy to enter the tent headfirst and sleep with our heads toward the back of the tent. But sleeping with our heads near the back end made it difficult to exit and was very hot on warm summer nights. We had to turn around inside the small tent to go out the door. On the other hand, if we wanted to sleep with our heads near the door where it was cooler and where we could easily exit the tent, we had to enter the tent feet first. I concluded that this tent may be okay for short weekend trips and may be necessary when riding a bike with limited packing space but would make us feel very confined on longer trips, especially in the rain. So I sold the tent and once again resumed my search for the ideal motorcycle camping tent.

After more research, I bought a 2006 Sierra Designs Sirius 3 on closeout sale. It seemed like the perfect motorcycle camping tent. It had forty-one square feet of floor space, was over four feet high, and weighed (with its footprint) only five pounds, fourteen ounces. Thus it required relatively little packing space on my bike. Its weight is reduced by a unique design. It is partly a single-wall tent and partly a double-wall tent. In other words, it only has half a rain fly. The primary fault I found with this tent is that its floor length was a little short for my six-foot two-inch frame. When I stretched out, both my head and my feet touched the walls. Furthermore, I understand that this tent could leak if it is set up in a manner that allows the wind to blow water into the vestibule. I would have to take into consideration the direction of the wind (usually from the southwest) and the probability of rain when setting it up. After a few trips in the Sirius 3, I decided to begin looking again for the perfect motorcycle camping tent.

The next tent I purchased was a Mountain Hardwear Light Wedge 3. It is eight feet long, has forty-four square feet of floor space, is very weather tight, and only weighs six pounds, five ounces. Furthermore, the door zipper slides as smoothly as any tent zipper I have used. I have taken it on several trips and believe it will be my choice for motorcycle camping for several years to come.

Tent Specifications

With several years of trial-and-error experience behind me, I think I am in a position to save you considerable time and expense as you look for your tent. I have come to the conclusion that when shopping for a tent you should consider five important features in addition to price. These five features are: length, area, weight (which is directly related to packed size), weather resistibility, and interior height. Assuming that you may occasionally share your tent with a companion, you should look for tents that are large enough for two people and their gear. Hopefully these observations will help you find the tent that best suits your needs.

Length. First of all, you need a tent that is long enough to stretch out in without touching the walls. Ideally your tent should be at least seven feet long—and longer if you are over six feet tall. I am six feet, two inches tall and prefer tents that are eight feet long. The reason you need a longer tent is that most tents, especially dome tents, have walls that slope toward the top center of the tent. As a result of the slope, you lose several inches of floor space around the edge where the floor and the wall meet. Consequently, when your tent is only a few inches longer than your height, your head and feet will touch the walls. The longest tents for tall guys are Cabela's XPG Ridgelight 3 and the Eureka Timberline 4. Other long tents include the Kelty Gunnison 4.1, the Mountain Hardwear Lightwedge 3, and the ALPS Mountaineering Extreme 3. Some manufacturers have devised ways to reduce the slope of their walls and thus to allow tall guys to stretch out with shorter floors. These tents usually advertise that they have near vertical walls. Examples of such tents include the MSR Mutha Hubba and several "frog" design tents such as The North Face Tadpole.

Area. Ideally the floor of your tent should be about five feet wide to accommodate two twenty-five-inch-wide sleeping pads. A quick guide to a tent's floor space is its square footage. A tent that is eight feet long by five feet wide would have forty square feet of floor space. This size tent seems ideal for two motorcycle campers. Tents with forty or more square feet of floor space are usually called three- or four-person tents, but they are only suitable for two normal-sized adults with some clothing and gear to store.

You might be able to get by with a smaller tent (i.e., a two-person tent) if you and your companion are relatively small and the tent has two doors and two vestibules. In fact, you may need a smaller tent if you ride a cruiser or sport bike with limited packing space. If you choose a smaller tent, you could put some of your gear (particularly your boots and helmets) inside a large waterproof bag and leave them in a vestibule. A tent with two doors allows each person to enter and exit the tent without having to crawl over his or her companion. This convenience is especially important if either of you have to get up in the middle of the night.

When you begin to look for tents, you'll find that manufacturers frequently give floor dimensions in inches. These figures do not include the vestibule, which is counted separately. To determine whether the tent is large enough for your needs, convert each dimension into feet. For example, a length of 90 inches divided by 12 is 7.5 feet; a width of 63 inches rounds to 5.3 feet. Then multiply length by width to determine the square footage. The floor for the tent described above would be 7.5 x 5.3 = 39.75 square feet. After you calculate the square footage, check to see if your value matches the manufacturer's reported square footage. Most of the time, it should match, but occasionally your value may be different from the area reported by the manufacturer. The discrepancy usually indicates an irregular floor shape. The Mountain Hardwear Light Wedge 3, for example, is six feet, two inches wide at the door but only four feet, ten inches wide at the rear.

Weight. Backpackers are acutely aware of a tent's weight. They consider it to be one of the most important, if not *the* most important, considerations when purchasing a tent. For them, every ounce of weight carried on their back is important in determining their long-range endurance. Because of this fact, the *minimum weight* of a tent will usually be included in the tent's description or specifications. This weight usually includes the tent, rain fly, and poles but does not include the ground cloth, stakes, and doormat. Sometimes, manufacturers give other weights for their tents. Look carefully. The *fast weight* or *trail weight* may be a partial weight that is lower than the actual weight you would carry on your bike; the *packed weight* may include the packing box and instruction manual and thus be a few ounces more than the tent's actual weight.

Motorcycle campers should also be concerned about a tent's minimum weight, because it is directly related to packed size. Selecting the smallest tent possible gives you more space to pack other items, such as sleeping bags and sleeping pads. Selecting a small tent is also important because tents are typically packed high on luggage racks where they, along with a backseat companion, can make your bike more top-heavy and difficult to control, especially in low-speed sharp turns. Furthermore, many manufacturers specify a weight limit for their luggage racks of approximately ten to fifteen pounds.

Backpackers frequently weigh each item of gear to determine the total weight they are packing. This practice also may be helpful for motorcycle campers. So I weighed all of my tents, with their ground cloths and doormats. I found that my older Kelty Gunnison 4, with its poles, ground cloth, and doormat, weighed nine pounds, eleven ounces, which was one pound heavier than the manufacturer's specifications (eight pounds, eleven ounces). My older Sierra Designs Sirius 3 with its poles and footprint weighed five pounds, fifteen ounces, which was eleven ounces more than the manufacturer's specifications (five pounds, four ounces). In general, the actual weight of a tent, with its ground cloth and doormat, is about a pound more than the manufacturer's listed packed weight.

If you ride solo or two-up on a touring bike with a luggage rack, you could easily pack a tent that weighs up to nine pounds. If you ride two-up on a cruiser or sport bike with limited packing space, you probably should drop this weight limit to seven pounds. In general, two-person tents typically weigh about four to five pounds. One of the lightest two-person tents is the MontBell Thunder Dome. Most three- or four-person backpacking tents weigh between five and nine pounds. Two very light three-person tents are the Sierra Designs Sirius 3 and the REI Quarter Dome UL. Two or three pounds difference may not sound like much, but for both backpackers and motorcycle campers, each additional pound will seem enormous.

The REI Half Dome 2 is lightweight and packs into a small space.

Weather resistibility. Buy a tent that is able to withstand moderately high wind and rain. Although you may not plan to camp in a storm, it will happen. We have experienced rain on more than half of our camping trips. When we go to the Great Smoky Mountains National Park (one of our favorite destinations), we expect a rain shower or two with strong winds every day.

Therefore it is important to select a tent that is able to withstand moderate wind and rain without leaking or collapsing. Yes, some tents will collapse. If you find this hard to believe, walk around a campground after a storm. You will likely see one or more tents that have collapsed due to the wind and weight of the water. They are typically some of the more economically priced tents.

The best guide to a tent's wind and rain resistibility is its price. Higher-priced tents are generally constructed to provide superior weather protection. They usually are constructed of lightweight, breathable, waterproof fabrics and have bathtub floors, waterproof sealed seams, aluminum (or strong composite material) poles, and full-coverage waterproof storm flies that serve as large umbrellas. Lower-priced tents may serve you well in fair weather, but they will likely be made from heavier materials with seams that may leak, small fiberglass poles that may bend or break with high wind, and small storm flies. If you decide to purchase a low-priced tent, seal its seams with a silicone sealer and erect a tarp over it to help deflect the rain and wind. These steps will usually make an economy tent more weatherproof. Before purchasing your tent, read reviews on Trail Space and other Web sites of several tents within your price range. You will easily determine the weather and waterproof properties of each tent.

Interior height. Buy a tent that has as much interior height as possible. Ideally it should be approximately four feet high, but many lightweight tents are not that tall. Two average-sized adults will need about four feet of interior height to move around comfortably. Smaller people may be able to get by with a little less height. In general, the more interior height you have, the larger the door and the easier it will be to enter and exit your tent. Taller tents also make it easier to enter and exit your sleeping bag. You will especially appreciate this feature if you or your companion has to get out of the sleeping bag in the middle of the night. Taller tents also make it easier to dress and to engage in various housekeeping or recreational activities.

Tent Features

As you begin looking at different tent models, you will quickly notice that tent makers use a lot of terms to describe and promote their particular models. You probably have heard most of these terms before and generally understand their meaning, but I want to define several frequently used terms and explain their practical significance in regard to motorcycle camping.

Three-season (versus four-season) tents. All of the tents discussed in this chapter are three-season tents. Three-season tents are those that are intended for spring, summer, and fall use—the seasons that motorcycle riders would likely camp. They are not intended for cold weather and especially not for snowy or icy conditions.

Four-season tents are intended for harsh winter weather. They typically have more poles and are heavier than the three-person tents. Most are priced well over four hundred dollars. Since four-season tents are heavier and more expensive and since few motorcycle riders are likely to need a tent designed to camp in such cold, wintry conditions, these tents do not seem to be good choices for motorcycle camping. If you want to learn more about four-season tents, you will want to visit the Hilleberg tentmaker Web site.

Condensation. The term "condensation" refers to moisture droplets that frequently accumulate inside waterproof tent materials or rain flies. Small amounts of condensation develop almost every night. Warm, humid air in the tent rises to the top and sides and is trapped by the waterproof material. When the temperature drops, the humid air is cooled by the cool tent wall and forms water droplets that cling to the sides of the tent. Condensation is especially heavy when a cool front with a rain shower or thunderstorm passes in the night after a warm, humid day. This condensation can be aggravating, because movement in the tent or a gust of wind can shake the tent material and release these droplets to shower you while you are sleeping. Or your sleeping bag or clothing may accidentally contact the wet wall when you are sleeping and become soaked. Or you may accidentally brush against the wet wall when exiting or entering the tent and soak your clothing.

Tent makers have devised several methods to reduce condensation. For example, most dome tents are constructed with two parts—an inner tent made with a considerable amount of mesh that allows moisture to pass and an outer rain fly that has a vent or two near the top and sides that do not reach all the way to the ground. Theoretically, cool outside air can come under the rain fly sides and help push the warm humid air out through the vents. Other tents typically have larger vents or windows that can be left open to facilitate the evaporation of moisture-filled air. Regardless of the way your tent is constructed, you must open vents and windows as much as possible at night to facilitate the evaporation of moisture-filled air.

Ventilation. Tent manufacturers and testers frequently use the term "well-ventilated" to refer to the apparent ease with which air can circulate through the tent and reduce condensation. Some people use the term *breathability* instead. Well-ventilated tents allow cool air to enter and circulate easily during warm nights. More importantly, well-ventilated tents allow moisture-filled air (from a temperature drop on humid nights or from your breathing) to exit the tent easily. If you purchase an economy or a mid-range tent, you probably will have to leave windows partially open on rainy and cool nights to move the moisture out of the tent. If you purchase a more expensive tent, you usually do not have to take extra measures, because the tent will likely be designed to provide excellent ventilation when properly set up without having to open any windows.

Single-wall versus double-wall construction. Single-wall tents basically have a single wall that is made from a waterproof fabric. They have mesh windows that can be left open or closed with a solid piece of fabric that zips around the window. Sometimes they may have a small rain fly that only covers the top of the tent. Their design is very simple, and thus they are usually lighter than double-wall tents. Their major limitation is the tendency to develop condensation. Examples of some single-wall tents suitable for motorcycle camping include Cabela's XPG Ridgelight 3, Black Diamond's Firstlight, Eureka's Zeus, and The North Face's Vario.

Double-wall tents are like two tents in one—a small inner tent covered by a larger tent. The inner tent is typically constructed with large mesh panels that do not have closable windows. To provide protection from the rain, the outer tent is a large waterproof rain fly that completely covers the tent and extends almost to the ground. The outer tent is usually larger than the smaller tent and thus provides a covered vestibule in front of each door and allows air to come under the wall into the tent. Double-wall tents are usually well ventilated but weigh more due to the additional materials needed to make the two separate tents. Most backpacker dome tents would be classified as double-walled tents.

Doors. Most lightweight backpacking tents have one or two relatively small doors that require campers to get down on their hands and knees and crawl into the tent. One popular dome tent design has two doors—one on each side of the tent. Since the doors are on the sides, each camper could arrange his or her sleeping area with the head toward either end of the tent and could easily enter and exit the tent by the door that is directly beside his or her sleeping area—without having to crawl over his or her companion. If the doors are positioned near the center of the side, the camper can enter the tent and immediately lie in his or her sleeping area without having to turn around inside the tent. Examples of tents with two doors on the sides suitable for motorcycle camping include the Black Diamond Vista, the L.L. Bean Mountain Light, the Marmot Aeolos, and The North Face Rock.

Another popular tent design has one door on one end of the tent. This design can be found on all hoop tents and some dome tents. Having only one door helps to reduce the weight (and packing space) of the tent but requires each camper to turn around inside the tent after entering it. The best sleeping arrangement is to position your heads near the door end. After entering the tent and turning your body around, you can easily unzip the door and exit without bothering your companion. Personally, I prefer this design partly because the doors are a little taller than doors on side entry tents. Examples of tents with one door on the end include the Eureka Autumn Wind, the

Mountain Hardwear Lightwedge, The North Face Tadpole, and the REI Hoodoo.

Occasionally you may find dome tents with one door on the side or two doors on the ends, but these designs are relatively rare because they are either impractical or add unnecessary weight.

The Mountain Hardwear LightWedge 3 packs small but is very spacious.

Vestibules. This term refers to an additional area of the tent that is covered by the rain fly but is not counted in the calculations of floor space. Virtually all higher-priced tents and some mid-range tents offer vestibules. Some tents have two vestibules, while others only have one. The number of vestibules usually correlates with the number of doors. In other words, most tents with two vestibules have two doors and most tents with one vestibule have only one door. Vestibules provide an additional storage area for helmets, boots, shoes, packs, or other items that you may not need in the tent. They provide good protection from dewfall and from light rain. However, if the rain is moderately hard, some dirt will splatter on items in the vestibule. Thus it is advisable to place these items in waterproof bags.

Backpackers seem to prefer tents with vestibules because they want the lightest possible tents that may not have enough room inside for their backpacks filled with clothing and gear. They typically place their backpacks in the vestibule overnight where it can be protected from heavy rain and where it can be easily accessed. Backpackers sometimes hike with their dogs and allow them to sleep in the tent vestibules.

Motorcycle campers, on the other hand, do not need vestibules, because they are able to carry larger tents on their motorcycle that can hold most of their gear and because they have saddlebags and other luggage on their motorcycle that can hold the rest of their gear. In the event of rain, they can cover their bike and gear with rain covers. In fact rain flies are sometimes inconvenient because when they are properly staked-out to make vestibules, they can make entrance and exit from tents more cumbersome. However, most high-end tents are made with vestibules, and we must learn to live with them.

Freestanding. The term "freestanding" has been applied to a range of tent styles. Technically it means that the tent does not require stakes driven into the ground to stand up. Usually you assemble the poles, slide them through their respective sleeves, if any, insert them into their designated seats, and attach clips onto the poles. The tent is quickly set up and ready to enter. After setting up the tent, you can easily pick it up and move it to a new location, if you so desire. You do not have to disassemble the tent or remove stakes to move it. Or if necessary, you could set it up on a rock ledge or concrete floor without stakes. Examples of freestanding tents include the Ozark Trail Sport Dome, the Coleman Exponent Sun Dome, the Eureka Timberline, and other tents that do not have vestibules.

Non-freestanding tents, on the other hand, cannot stand without stakes driven into the ground. To set these tents up, you must first stake the corners before inserting the supporting poles. To move this type tent to another location, you must first remove all stakes and then re-stake it in the new location. Although non-freestanding tents are a little less convenient, some backpackers prefer them because they have shorter and/or fewer poles and thus have less weight. Many of these non-freestanding tents are called hoop tents—their poles make a hoop or two that extend from one side to the other. Examples of non-freestanding tents include the Exped Aries Mesh, Mountain Hardwear Lightpath, and the Kelty Crestone.

Most backpacking dome tents fall between these two extremes. They are called freestanding tents but in reality should be considered semi-freestanding. They typically have an inner mesh tent that is freestanding, but their outer rain fly must be staked to the ground to provide complete weather protection and to form the vestibules. Many tents that are called freestanding actually require as many as five or more stakes to be correctly set up. Examples of these semi-freestanding tents include the Kelty Gunnison 4.1, the REI Half Dome, and the Mountain Hardwear Lightwedge 3.

Whether the tent is freestanding or semi-freestanding, it needs to be staked to the ground after setting it up to prevent it from being blown and damaged by gusty winds. Thus the presumed advantage (e.g. mobility) of a freestanding tent is not as great as one might assume.

Bathtub floor. This term refers to a method of tent construction that minimizes or eliminates water leaks around the edges of the floor. Economy tents may not have this feature. They may allow rain that hit the tent roof and walls to run down the side and accumulate at the bottom of the side where the floor and the sides are sewn together. When the water remains on the seam, it will eventually begin to seep into the tent and will soak your sleeping bag and clothing. On the other hand, tents with bathtub floors use a single piece of waterproof material to make the floor and the lower side of the tent. Approximately twelve inches above the ground, the bathtub floor is sewn to the tent walls. Water rolls past the seam to the ground and thus does not have the opportunity to enter the tent.

Clips versus sleeves. Many tents are constructed with small plastic clips or hooks that can be attached to the poles easily to hold the tent in place. These clips make it very easy to set up and take down your tent. But they add weight and packed space to the tent. Cheaper tents with weaker fiberglass poles frequently use sleeves for the poles to add stability and reduce weight. Four-season tents frequently use sleeves to enhance the tent's stability in high wind. To set up tents with sleeves, you must slide the assembled tent pole through the sleeves before inserting them into their seats. When taking down the tent, you must pull the poles back through the sleeves. You must be careful when pulling the poles back through the sleeves to prevent them from snagging on the fabric. If you get in a rush and snag the poles on the fabric, you may accidentally damage the shock cord, the poles, or the tent fabric. Most experienced lightweight campers prefer tents with clips.

Poles. In general, poles for backpacking tents can be made from either fiberglass or aluminum, and they can vary in diameter from about six millimeters to about fifteen millimeters. Economy tents typically use small-diameter fiberglass poles that can easily bend and break under the pressure of high wind or accidental misuse—especially if the weather is cool. If you only plan to camp on warm dry summer nights, you could save a lot of money and use one of these economy tents. Mid-priced tents typically use thicker fiberglass or aluminum poles that are more durable. As a result, they will keep you dry and comfortable, even in windy and rainy weather. High-end tents use ultra-strong and lightweight aluminum poles that will protect you from the elements on very stormy nights. For example, Kelty, REI, Sierra Designs, The North Face, and a few other tent makers use DAC feather-light poles made by Dongah Aluminum Corporation. Other tent makers such as Mountain Hardwear use Atlas Scandium aluminum poles from Yunan Aluminum Company to make the frames for their three-season tents. Occasionally you may find tent poles made from carbon or other types of aluminum.

Pockets and gear loft. Some tents have pockets sewn into the wall about twelve inches above the floor, at the point where the bathtub floor and the tent walls meet. Many campers use them to store water bottles, lights, and other gear. I do not think they are necessary. I may use one if it is convenient, but I can just as easily put my glasses and headlight on the floor of the tent in the corner near my head. When I empty my pockets, I put my wallet, keys, knife, change, and other pocket items in a small food storage bag and place the bag near the door. The next morning, after dressing and exiting the tent, I can just grab the plastic bag when I am ready to get my stuff. I do not have to re-enter the tent.

Many tents also offer a gear loft (either as a part of the tent package or as an extra accessory) that attaches to four loops sewn near the top of the tent. Such a gear loft could be used to store water bottles or other items. I do not believe lofts are particularly useful, and I do not use them. Instead I tie a shoestring through the loops around the top of the tent and have a small clothesline if I need it to dry socks or underwear. If a loop has been sewn at the very top center of the tent, I may tie a string to it and use it to hang a micro light.

Vertical walls. About the year 2008, some tent manufacturers began introducing alternatives to the standard sloped-walled dome tents. These alternative tents used innovative design and pole configurations to achieve near vertical walls. These vertical walls provided more interior space that allowed campers to easily sit up, move around, dress, play games, and exit the tent. Some of the first tents with these vertical walls were the Big Agnes Hubba Hubba and the REI Quarterdome. In

2009, several manufacturers introduced lightweight tents with vertical walls. These three-person backpacking tents with vertical walls will usually cost at least three hundred dollars. The tent that won awards from both *Backpacking* and *Outside* magazines was the Nemo Losi 3.

Tent Prices

Tents suitable for motorcycle camping range in price from about thirty-five dollars to over four hundred dollars. The price of a tent is largely determined by the weight of the materials and their durability. Tents made with heavier materials and fiberglass poles will typically be priced less than one hundred dollars. On the other hand, tents made with lightweight fabrics and aluminum poles that are durable enough to withstand strong wind and rain will cost more than one hundred dollars.

To help you decide which tent model best suits your needs and your budget, I will group them according to price and discuss the general strengths and limitations of tents within each price range. The prices quoted in this chapter are manufacturers' suggested retail prices for 2009 models. If you look on the Internet or in some discount stores, you may find some of these tents priced lower than quoted herein. You may also be able to find a previous year's model for a much lower price.

The Ozark Trail Sport Dome is an economy tent sold by Wal-Mart.

Under one hundred dollars. At the bottom of the price range are tents that cost less than a hundred dollars—about the same as a one-night stay in a motel. Several economy models are available. Most discount department stores and many sporting goods stores sell these economy tents. They offer a great entry point if you want to try a short camping trip in fair weather. If you do not like the tent, throw it away after one trip and you will still come out better than if you had stayed in a motel every night. Perhaps the most popular tent in this price range is the Ozark Trail Sport Dome tent sold by Wal-Mart. Another popular model is the Coleman Sun Dome sold in many camping supply stores such as Dick's Sporting Goods.

The main advantage of these tents is their price. If you buy one of these tents along with a fifteen-dollar sleeping bag and a ten-dollar mat, you get your money's worth after two nights. The primary limitations of these tents are their relatively poor wind and rain resistance and their poor ventilation characteristics. They are typically single-wall tents with small rain flies and seams that may leak. As a result, you could get wet if it rains very hard. Another limitation of these tents is their poles, which are typically small-diameter fiberglass poles that may break, especially in cold weather or under the pressure of strong wind coupled with a heavy downpour. A final limitation of these tents is they may be difficult to set up because of having to slide poles through multiple sleeves and other design features.

If you decide to purchase one of these tents, seal the seams with a silicone sealer before your first camping trip and again after every three or four trips. When you arrive at your campsite, be sure to set the tent up properly and stake it securely to the ground to prevent damage that could be caused by moderately high winds. Also leave windows partially open at night, especially if it is raining or if the nighttime low is expected to drop below fifty degrees, to reduce condensation that can accumulate on the walls inside your tent. You could add extra protection by using an inexpensive tarp to make a second, larger rain fly. Handle fiberglass poles with care, especially in cold weather, so they do not break. If you take proper precautions, you may be able to use them for several camping trips.

Recently, while shopping for a tent at REI, I began talking with another customer in the store. When he learned that I was considering a relatively expensive tent, he volunteered that he had bought a forty-dollar backpacking tent a few years ago and had taken it on several camping trips. He claimed that it was a great tent and that it never leaked in rainy weather. This was strong testimony for economy models, but my past experiences with leaky economy tents and my good experience with more expensive tents leads me to conclude that more expensive tents best satisfy my own needs. But you should decide for yourself based upon your budget and the amount of camping you will likely do.

One hundred to two hundred dollars. These tents are a little more expensive, but they typically use a better grade of materials and thereby offer better protection from the weather. To be safe, seal the seams before use. Some have partial rain flies, while others have full-coverage rain flies with vestibules. Some have thicker fiberglass poles, while others have thin aluminum poles. Most of these mid-range tents have a dome design in which two poles are inserted in opposite corners and the tent body is clipped to the poles to form the shape of a dome. A rain fly covers part or all of the tent body. The primary limitations of tents in this price range are that they are a little heavier than more expensive models and they tend to accumulate condensation or water droplets under the rain fly in rainy weather.

By far the most popular tent in this price range is the Eureka Timberline 4. It is different from most other tents suitable for motorcycle camping. It has an A-frame design similar to the old army pup tents. It has a large floor area and aluminum poles and is relatively lightweight. It is also reasonably priced. This tent and others within this price range can usually be purchased in camping specialty stores or on the Web (e.g., Campmor and other retailers). Other popular tents in this range include the Eureka Zeus, Kelty Gunnison 2.1, and REI Camp Dome 2.

Two hundred to four hundred dollars. These tents are typically constructed with modern materials that are lightweight, breathable, and waterproof. Their poles are constructed from aluminum or other strong, lightweight materials, and they frequently have a full-coverage rain fly that provides a vestibule and good ventilation. As such they are very lightweight, pack into a small space, provide excellent weather protection, and offer additional space in the vestibule. This type of tent is preferred by most backpackers and would be a good choice if you plan to take many camping trips.

Several well-known backpacking tents fall within this price range. For example, the Kelty Gunnison 3.1 and 4.1 are good tents if you are riding a touring bike with considerable luggage capacity. They may weigh a little more than others in this price range, but they offer a lot of space—both inside the tent and in the vestibules. Furthermore, they are well ventilated and weather resistant. Other tents recently recognized by *Backpacker* magazine include the Black Diamond Vista, REI Quarter Dome TT UL3, Marmot Aeros 3p, Exped Aries Mesh, REI Hoodoo 2, The North Face Madraque 23, Sierra Designs Vapor Light 2, Nemo Losi 3P, Marmot Crib 3P, and Sierra Designs Zeta 3.

Eureka Timberline 4 is a popular mid-priced tent.

Over four hundred dollars. Several three-season tents cost more than four hundred dollars. These tents are designed for backpackers and other ultra-lightweight campers who take long trips and must be prepared for severe weather conditions. These tents offer excellent space-to-weight ratios and many technical features (such as vertical walls) not found on lower-priced tents. Some examples of these tents include the Nemo Nano OZ ($450), Sierra Designs Lightning XT4 ($450), Big Agnes Slide Mountain SL3 ($500), Big Agnes Copper Spur UL3 ($500), Go Lite Valhalla ($525), and Hilleberg Kaitum 3GT ($895). I have not included these tents in the charts because their prices are too high for most motorcycle campers and their features are not necessary for typical motorcycle camping trips.

Tent Care

To assure that your tent lasts for a long time, you should observe several well-accepted suggestions for tent care. If you buy a good-quality tent and follow these suggestions, your tent should look good and protect you from both bugs and weather for ten years or longer. We have used an REI Family Dome tent on dozens of trips over the past eleven years, and it still looks almost new. In general, treat your tent with care. Move slowly as you enter and exit your tent and as you zip and unzip doors or windows. Here are some other suggestions.

Set up your tent at home before your first trip. There are at least three reasons for setting up your tent at home. First, you want to become familiar with the set-up procedure. If you do not understand how some parts fit, you can read the manual in leisure or you can call a technical expert at the store where you bought it. The second reason for setting up your tent at home is that you want to be sure all of the parts were included in the package and that they are undamaged. The third reason for setting up your tent at home is that you will be able to repack it to include its ground cloth (or footprint) and a doormat.

Use a ground cloth or footprint. Tents rarely come with a ground cloth or footprint. Nevertheless, you should always purchase one and use it. A footprint especially constructed for your particular tent can be joined with your tent at the corners. It usually costs an additional thirty to fifty dollars. One drawback of a manufacturer's footprint is that it usually fits only the inner tent and not the vestibule.

A ground cloth can be made from a tarp and thus is much more economical. It works as well as, if not better than, the manufacturer's footprint. Simply cut a tarp or piece of heavy plastic a little smaller than the floor dimensions of your tent. You may wish to include a floor for your vestibule to provide additional weather protection for your gear. To make your ground cloth, set your tent on top of the tarp, mark the edges of your tent, come in about two inches from the edge, and cut the tarp. If you want a first-class footprint, get some nylon webbing and grommet small pieces to each corner of your tarp. Then insert a second grommet in the webbing for the tent-pole seat. You can find additional instructions for making footprints in the February 2007 issue of *Backpacker* magazine. A floor in the vestibule will help keep it dryer and cleaner. Several tent owners choose to make their own ground cloths rather than buying them.

Ground cloths provide a waterproof barrier that keeps the floor of your tent dry in the rain. By keeping the floor dry, it also keeps you and your gear dry. When you set up your tent, be sure your tent completely covers the ground cloth. In other words, you should not be able to see the edges of your ground cloth after your tent has been properly set up. If part of the ground cloth is exposed, rain will run down the side of your tent, collect on the waterproof ground cloth, and seep under your tent. When water gets under your tent, it may eventually seep into your tent. Ground cloths also provide some degree of protection to your tent floor from accidental damage from sharp rocks or sticks.

Replace your stakes with six-inch galvanized nails. Regardless of price, all tents come with poor-quality tent stakes. When you try to drive these stakes into packed ground or gravel tent pads, they will bend or break. Later, when you try to remove the stakes from the ground, they are further likely to bend. You can buy replacements, but you would have to buy them after almost every trip. The best thing to do is to purchase six-inch galvanized nails from your local hardware store. I got this idea after reading an article on the BMWMOA Web site. The author suggested using gutter nails as tent stakes. The suggestion seemed like a good idea, so I went to the hardware store to buy some. As I was looking, I noticed the six-inch galvanized nails. These nails seemed like a better choice. They are shorter than the gutter nails and are indestructible. They last forever. Set aside your original equipment stakes in case you decide to sell the tent in the future, and use six-inch nails instead. Pack them in your camping tool bag with your ax, pliers, and cord.

Use a doormat. Backpackers and other ultra-light campers would not consider a doormat to be necessary (and would not pack one) because of its extra bulk. However, motorcycle campers can easily justify the few extra ounces and will enjoy the added comfort they provide. A doormat gives you a clean place to put your hands and knees when entering and exiting your tent. It also gives you a clean, dry place to stand in your socks when removing your shoes before bed and when putting them back on in the morning. Furthermore, the doormat provides a dry floor in the vestibule to help keep your gear clean. We have used hand towels as our doormats for several years and believe they should be considered as essential gear. They weigh almost nothing and help to keep the tent clean. When packing your tent before your trip, roll a doormat inside the tent. When you arrive at your campsite and set up your tent, the doormat will be ready for use. When you pack up to go home, use your doormat to dry your tent before packing.

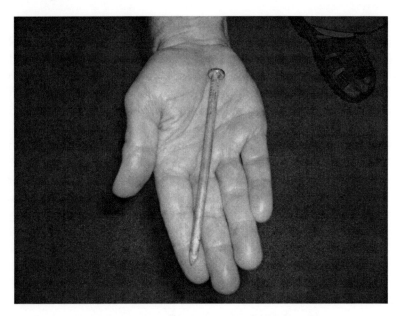

Six-inch galvanized nails make excellent tent stakes.

Set your tent up in a shady spot. Prolonged sunlight will gradually destroy nylon and waterproofing materials used to make most modern tents. To preserve the life of your tent, set it up in shady sites as often as possible. If you cannot find a site with full shade, try to find one with afternoon shade rather than afternoon sun.

Stake the corners of your tent. The main reason for this is to prevent accidental damage from strong winds. I learned this lesson the hard way. One afternoon I set my REI Family Dome tent up in my driveway to dry after returning from a camping trip. It was a warm summer afternoon with no wind, so I turned my attention to other matters. After a while, I heard thunder. When I went out to check on the tent, it was gone. Upon searching for it, I found it upside down about forty yards away, wedged against a line of bushes. I was certain it was ruined. Incredibly, neither the fabric nor the mesh was torn. The only damage was to one aluminum pole section that had become bent. I tried to bend it back but I could not get the kink out. I called Tent Pole Technologies in Washington State and ordered a replacement. The owner, Tom Hegerle, was very personable and immediately shipped my replacement pole section. I received it in a couple of days and easily repaired my pole.

Avoid fire and heat. One winter night several years ago, I was longing for warm camping weather and started browsing the Internet for motorcycle camping tips. I found many good sites and learned several good tips. But I also realized that some of the tips posted on Web sites are not very good. One of the tips suggested using small candles to provide light and warmth in the tent. Another site recommended cooking in your tent during cold weather. I was shocked to see these suggestions, because most tent manufacturers clearly advise against these practices. Using candles and cooking in a tent can be very dangerous! You should never bring fire into or close to your tent. This includes candles, stoves, matches, and cigarettes. A small ember or accidental contact could easily damage your tent and could cause it to catch fire—with you trapped inside. Or you could be exposed to potentially deadly carbon monoxide gas. Such accidental outcomes could easily ruin your camping trip, not to mention your life. Therefore when deciding to follow another person's recommendations, use good judgment. For similar safety reasons, set up your tent several feet away from your campfire, grill, and stove. It should be at least a picnic table's length away from the fire, or further if it is windy.

Never, ever bring food into your tent. Animals will be attracted to the smell of food and will damage your tent to get it. Furthermore, once you bring food into your tent, the smell can linger for a long time and may attract animals for many trips in the future. One afternoon I was relaxing in my campsite at Fort Pickens National Seashore in Pensacola, Florida. I noticed a squirrel walking near my neighbor's tent. In an instant, the squirrel tore the fabric and entered the tent to get some food. By the time I reacted, the squirrel was back in a tree and my neighbor's tent had a big hole in the side. Raccoons and skunks prowl at night and can do as much if not more damage. If you are in bear country such as the Smoky Mountains, your safety and the safety of others could be jeopardized by bringing food into the tent or leaving it unguarded in the campsite.

Remove as much moisture as possible before packing your tent. When you are ready to pack up and leave your campsite, you typically will be packing in the early morning hours and will have a wet tent. It may be wet from the dew or from an overnight shower. Before packing your tent in its stuff sack, remove as much moisture as possible. Water trapped inside the tent and its stuff sack increases the risks of developing mold and mildew. The darkness of the pack plus the heat of a summer day seems to speed up the development of mold. And mold can damage the fabric and shorten the life of your tent. To reduce the chances of mold and mildew problems, shake your tent after taking it down (to remove as much moisture as possible) and then hang it on a clothesline for a few minutes. Use a hand towel to wipe away as much moisture as possible before packing it in its stuff sack. You will not be able to dry it completely, but you will be able to dry it enough to protect it for a few hours. At the end of the day, set it up again and allow it to continue drying. When you arrive back home, open it again and allow it to dry for several days before packing it away for your next trip.

Remove tent loops from stakes before pulling stakes out of the ground. The reason for this practice is to prevent accidental damage to your tent loops and fabric. For hard-to-pull stakes, I have two procedures. I first double a long piece of rope and wrap it around my wrist and arm a couple of times. Then I wrap the loop around the stake head and pull. This procedure will remove most stakes wedged in hard ground. But sometimes the stake is lodged in a tree root and is very difficult to remove. This situation requires the small crowbar, which I always keep in my bag of camping tools. Using rocks or pieces of wood, you can get the proper leverage and easily remove the toughest stakes.

Clean and dry your tent before long-term storage. After returning home, hang your tent on a clothesline or set it up in an open room, wipe dirt away using a damp rag, and allow it to dry for at least three days. If tree sap is stuck on your tent, refer to your manufacturer's recommendations regarding the best way to clean the tent. REI suggests using small amounts of kerosene to remove tree sap from my Camp Dome 4 tent. Drying your tent is necessary so that moisture and mildew cannot grow and damage your tent. Allow ample time for the seams to dry. They are thicker and will require more time. Once it is clean and dry, pack your tent and store it in a dry, cool place such as a closet in your house.

If zippers get sticky, refer to your manufacturer's recommendations. REI suggests removing dirt and sand first and if the zipper is still sticky use a light coat of a silicone lubricant. Try to avoid contact with fabric and mesh.

Tent Packing

After striking your tent and drying it as much as possible, you must pack it for travel. There are two different philosophies regarding the best way to pack a tent—the fold-and-roll method and the stuffing method.

Many campers, including myself, use the fold-and-roll method. First, lay the tent flat on the ground and spread the rain fly on top of it. Then fold the tent a couple of times so that its width is about the same as the width of the stuff sack. For example, if the tent floor is eight feet by five feet, fold the long side in half to make it four feet wide and then fold it again to make it two feet wide. Then fold the ground cloth to the same dimensions and roll the tent poles inside the ground cloth. Finally, roll the ground cloth/tent pole package along with the doormat inside the tent. This procedure yields a compact package that easily fits inside the stuff sack. An article in the March 2008 issue of *Backpacker* magazine (Annual Gear Guide) asserted that this fold-and-roll method may preserve the life of a tent better than the stuff method.

On the other hand, some tent manufacturers recommend the stuff method. Basically, they recommend that you just stuff the tent body, rain fly, and ground cloth into the stuff sack along with the poles. This method certainly is a lot faster than the fold-and-roll method. More importantly, tent manufacturers believe that this method reduces the chance of developing permanent creases in your tent that could weaken the fabric and its waterproof coating. The logic of the stuff method is that each time you pack your tent into its stuff sack it will fold a different way, and thereby you avoid making permanent creases in the material. Furthermore, stuffing your tent will likely include small air pockets that could help reduce the risk of developing mold and mildew.

Conclusion

What is the best shelter for motorcycle camping? Most camping experts would agree that three-season backpacking tents are small enough to easily pack on a motorcycle but provide enough space and protection to camp comfortably in a wide range of weather conditions. Which model is best? The answer to this question depends upon your riding habits and camping plans. If you ride solo or two-up on a touring bike with a luggage rack, you should have room to pack a three- or four-person tent. If you ride two-up on a cruiser, you may have to settle for a two-person tent. If you plan to camp just a few days in good weather, you could buy an inexpensive tent from a discount department store or sporting goods store. If you plan to take many camping trips throughout the year, you should consider investing in a more weather tight (and expensive) tent. When shopping for the right tent, consider five basic criteria. The tent should be relatively long, have a relatively large floor space, weigh less than nine pounds, be weather resistant, and have adequate interior height. Several modern tents satisfy these five criteria.

At the end of this chapter are two summary charts. These charts list the names of several two-, three-, and four-person backpacking tents available in the spring of 2009. Tents for each manufacturer are grouped together and ordered according to average price of their models. To the right of each model you will see basic specifications. Weight is the minimum weight given by the manufacturer. Remember that you should always buy or make a ground cloth, and this ground cloth will add an extra pound to the tent's weight. Floor space measurements were copied from the manufacturer's specifications. Some of the tents (e.g., Black Diamond Vista and Mountain Hardwear LightWedge) have asymmetrical floors. Thus their actual square footage does not match their length by width calculations.

When shopping for a tent, you may discover that some models listed in these charts may no longer be available. Manufacturers change models every year or two. Just look for well-known tent brands such as Big Agnes, Coleman, Eureka, Kelty, Marmot, Mountain Hardware, The North Face, REI, and Sierra Designs. Compare the space, weight, interior height, and price of the newer models with the tents listed in the chart. After reviewing the available tents, select the ones that seem best suited for your needs, and shop for the best price.

When the time comes to buy your tent, do your homework. After reading this chapter, find the most recent *Backpacker* magazine's annual gear guide. It is published every spring. This guide lists many of the tents available for that particular year along with their specifications. Once you get the names of some possible choices, search the Web for sites that describe and sell the particular models you have selected. Also go to the Trail Space Web site (www.trailspace.com) and read reviews of the tents you have selected. Finally, look for the best prices and make your purchase.

Two-Person Tents

Model	Length	Area	Ht	Wt	Vestibules	Price
Coleman Exponent Sun Dome 2	7' 0"	35	4' 0"	7, 0	0	$50
ALPS Mountaineering Meramac 2	7' 6"	38	4' 0"	6, 2	0	$100
Cabela's XPG Ultralight 2	7' 3"	34	3' 6"	4, 9	1 (7)	$150
Cabela's Delux XPG	7' 6"	37	3' 8"	7, 1	2 (7+7)	$180
Eureka Timberline 2	7' 2"	38	3' 6"	5, 13	0	$130
Eureka Pinnacle Pass 2XTA	7' 5"	36	3' 7"	4, 11	2 (3+3)	$170
Eureka Zeus 2	7' 5"	33	3' 6"	3, 14	1 (12)	$160
Eureka Mountain Breeze	7' 0"	30	3' 4"	4, 14	2 (12+12)	$350
Kelty Grand Mesa 2	6' 10"	29	3' 8"	4, 2	1 (6)	$120
Kelty Gunnison 2.1	7' 8"	37	3' 4"	4, 14	2 (12+12)	$190
REI Camp Dome 2	7' 0"	32	3' 6"	4, 15	0	$100
REI Half Dome 2 HC	7' 6"	34	3' 5"	5, 1	2 (9+9)	$170
REI Quarterdome T2	7' 0"	30	3' 4"	3, 12	2 (7+7)	$190
REI Hoodoo 2	7' 6"	32	3' 2"	5, 12	2 (10+10)	$220

L.L. Bean Mountain Light 2	7' 6"	33	3' 10"	5, 14	2 (12+12)	$240
Mountain Hardwear Lightpath 2	6' 8"	30	3' 5"	3, 14	1 (10)	$180
Mountain Hardwear Light Wedge 2	7' 4"	35	3' 7"	5, 6	1 (9)	$235
Mountain Hardwear Viperine 2	7' 1"	25	3' 10"	4, 10	1 (10)	$265
Sierra Designs Clip Flashlight 2	7' 5"	32	3' 7"	3, 11	1 (7)	$200
Sierra Designs Lightning XT2	6' 11"	30	3' 5"	3, 15	2 (14+6)	$260
Sierra Designs Vapor Light 2	6' 11"	25	3' 2"	3, 4	1 (8)	$330
The North Face Rock 22Bx	7' 5"	34	3' 7"	5, 4	2 (9+9)	$190
The North Face Tadpole 23	7' 3"	26	3' 4"	4, 10	1 (9)	$200
The North Face Fat Frog	7' 6"	31	3' 6"	5, 11	1 (14)	$260
The North Face Roadrunner 23	7' 4"	35	3' 6"	4, 13	2 (7+4)	$280
The North Face Manta Ray	7' 2"	42	3' 8"	5, 11	2 (11+11)	$350
Big Agnes Seedhouse 2	7' 0"	28	3' 2"	3, 14	1 (6)	$220
Big Agnes Parkview 2	7' 6"	36	4' 0"	5, 3	2 (10 +10)	$290
Big Agnes Emerald Mountain SL2	7' 6"	29	3' 6"	4, 3	2 (13+10)	$350
Black Diamond Mesa 2	7' 8"	33	3' 8"	4, 9	2 (9+9)	$320

Black Diamond Firstlight 2	6' 10"	27	3' 6"	2, 11	0	$320
Marmot Earlylight 2	7' 4"	30	3' 3"	4, 12	2 (9+9)	$200
Marmot Aeolos	7' 6"	35	3' 4"	5, 5	2 (10+10)	$268
MontBell Thunder Dome	7' 1"	30	3' 6"	3, 8	1 (9)	$300
MSR Hubba Hubba	7' 0"	29	3' 4"	4, 3	2 (9+9)	$300
Exped Aries Mesh	7' 5"	38	3' 7"	4, 14	1 (16)	$377

Notes: Length = feet and inches; Area = square feet; Ht = height in feet and inches; Wt = weight in pounds, ounces; Vestibules = total number and size of each in square feet.

Three- and Four-Person Tents

Model	Length	Area	Ht	Wt	Vestibules	Price
Ozark Trail Sport Dome 4	9' 0"	72	4' 0"	8, 8	0	$ 32
Wenzel Pinon 3	7' 0"	49	4' 2"	5, 9	0	$ 40
Wenzel Timber Ridge 4	9' 0"	63	4' 4"	8, 0	0	$ 50
Coleman Exponent Sundome 4	7' 0"	49	4' 4"	9, 4	0	$ 65
Stansport Astral III	7' 0"	46	4' 0"	5, 5	0	$ 50
Mountainsmith Guardian	7' 10"	45	3' 6"	5, 10	1 (9)	$100
Alps Mountaineering Extreme 3	8' 0"	48	4' 2"	6, 12	2(11+11)	$250
Cabela's XPG Ultralight 3	7' 6"	47	3' 11"	5, 8	1 (8)	$170
Cabela's XPG Ridgelight 3	8' 11"	54	3' 9"	6, 5	2 (5+5)	$300
Eureka Timberline 4	8' 9"	63	4' 10"	7, 13	0	$180
Eureka Pinnacle Pass 3 XTA	7' 6"	49	4' 2"	5, 15	2 (7+7)	$220
Eureka Zeus 3	7' 11"	48	4' 0"	5, 1	1 (13)	$200
Eureka Autumn Wind 3XD	7' 3"	40	4' 4"	7, 9	1 (14)	$280
Kelty Grand Mesa 4	8' 0"	53	4' 8"	7, 4	1 (19)	$190
Kelty Teton 4	8' 2"	54	4' 10"	7, 8	1 (12)	$210

Kelty Gunnison 3.1	7' 6"	48	3' 10"	5, 14	2 (10+10)	$230
Kelty Gunnison 4.1	8' 4"	57	3' 10"	8, 0	2 (16+16)	$250
L.L. Bean Mountain Light 3	7' 6"	42	4' 2"	6, 8	2 (12+12)	$270
The North Face Rock 32	7' 5"	43	4' 0"	5, 15	2 (9+9)	$210
The North Face Roadrunner	7' 3"	44	3' 9"	6, 8	2 (9+9)	$260
Mountain Hardwear LightPath 3	7' 6"	44	4' 1"	5, 5	1 (15)	$220
Mountain Hardwear LightWedge 3	8' 0"	44	3' 11"	5, 15	1 (12)	$260
Mountain Hardwear Hammerhead 3	7' 7"	46	4' 6"	7, 15	2 (5+5)	$295
Mountain Hardwear Viperine 3	7' 10"	43	4' 9"	6, 14	1 (14)	$340
REI Half Dome 4 HC	7' 10"	57	4' 3"	7, 9	2 (11+11)	$250
REI Hoodoo 3	7' 7"	47	3' 9"	6, 6	2 (19+4)	$250
REI Quarter Dome T3	7' 0"	40	3' 7"	4, 7	2 (6+6)	$300
Sierra Designs Sirius 3	7' 0"	41	3' 8"	4, 11	2 (4+4)	$190
Sierra Designs Zeta 3	7' 1"	43	3' 10"	6, 9	2 (18+8)	$250
Sierra Designs Meteor 3	7' 9"	49	3' 9"	7, 1	2 (19+11)	$350
Sierra Designs Lightning XT3	7' 1"	42	3' 10"	5, 10	2 (15+8)	$350

Big Agnes Parkview 3	7' 6"	50	4' 0"	6, 14	1 (22)	$330
Black Diamond Vista 3	8' 0"	51	3' 10"	5, 15	2 (9+9)	$370
Marmot Limelight 3	7' 9"	43	3' 10"	5, 15	2 (10+10)	$230
Marmot Aeros 3	7' 6"	46	3' 5"	5, 3	2 (10+10)	$370
MSR Mutha Hubba	7' 0"	40	3' 10"	6, 2	2 (7+7)	$400

Notes: Length = in feet and inches; Area = square feet; Ht = height in feet and inches; Wt = weight in pounds, ounces; Vestibules = total number and size of each in square feet.

3. Sleeping

After buying a good tent, you must accumulate the gear needed to sleep comfortably during your camping trips. You need five major items: a good sleeping bag, a good sleeping pad, appropriate clothing, a pillow, and a knit cap. These five items constitute your *sleeping system*. This chapter provides the information you should know to buy the best sleeping system, to pack it on your motorcycle, to use it for maximum comfort, and to care for it properly.

I have already described my disastrous first motorcycle camping trip to the Cherokee National Forest in chapter 1. After this trip, I knew that I was not prepared for cool weather camping, but I still thought that I could camp in the summer without having to buy good sleeping gear. During the following summer, Robin and I decided to take a 150-mile camping trip to the Land Between The Lakes National Recreational Area near Clarksville, Tennessee. We were riding two-up on my Harley-Davidson Low Rider and had extremely limited space to pack our gear. The forecast predicted warm daytime temperatures all weekend and mild nighttime temperatures. In other words, it seemed to be perfect riding and camping weather. Since the predicted low temperature was not very cold, I thought we could get by with a couple of cheap air mattresses and a couple of lightweight fleece blankets.

Our first two-up trip:
Piney Campground in the Land Between The Lakes National Recreation Area

After arriving at our campsite and setting up our tent, we rode to the grocery store for some food to cook and returned to our campsite to enjoy our evening meal. Everything seemed to be going well. After supper, we took our showers and went to bed under our blankets. The temperature felt very comfortable. It looked like we were going to stay warm all night. Life seemed perfect. But during the night, the temperature dropped a little. Gradually we felt cooler and cooler, especially our legs and feet. We did not get as cold as I did on my previous Cherokee Forest trip, but neither of us slept very well because we could not get warm. I had obviously miscalculated again. I did not realize that we were unprepared even for summer camping.

I must be a slow learner. A few months later, I convinced Robin to go on a 375-mile trip to Gulf Shores, Alabama, on my recently purchased Harley-Davidson Electra Glide—without adequate sleeping gear. The campground (Gulf State Park, Alabama) was located on the Gulf of Mexico. The summer nighttime temperature was predicted to drop no lower than seventy degrees. I packed two cheap foam pads and one summer sleeping bag to use as a blanket. Cold again! Fortunately a Wal-Mart was located near the campground. After the first night, we rode over and bought a second sleeping bag for less than fifteen dollars. Now we each had our own sleeping bag and pad. Finally, we were able to stay warm during the night and sleep comfortably. The only problem with the new bag was that it did not compress very well and thus was difficult to squeeze on the bike's luggage rack with the rest of our gear when we were ready to head back home.

We learned at least two important lessons from these two trips. First, we learned that, no matter what the predicted temperature, we must always pack sleeping bags. Second, we learned that cheap, fifteen-dollar sleeping bags may be acceptable for summer camping trips but do not compress much at all. Two of them are difficult to pack on a motorcycle along with two sleeping pads and a tent. Getting everything tied securely on our luggage rack was a challenge and a little dangerous.

After the Gulf Shores trip, I decided to do a little homework. I read everything I could find about sleeping bags suited for motorcycle camping. In particular, I wanted to learn how to pick a good sleeping bag that would pack small but would provide a warm night's sleep. I read the motorcycle camping literature, but I found very little information about good-quality sleeping bags. Later I began reading the backpacking literature and found much more helpful information. I learned that we needed lightweight compressible sleeping bags that could be packed into a small space, insulated air mattresses, pillows, thermal underwear, and knit hats. I learned that several good sleeping bags and thermal mats were available but could not be purchased in discount department stores. They could only be found in outdoor gear retail stores and Web sites. Furthermore, I learned that good-quality sleeping gear costs a lot more money than I had realized. But I decided that if I wanted to continue taking motorcycle camping trips and sleep comfortably in a wide range of weather conditions, I had to move up to better gear.

Sleeping Bag Specifications

When you begin shopping for sleeping bags, you will quickly discover that many different sleeping bags are available, each with different features. Prices range from less than fifteen dollars to over seven hundred dollars. How do you determine the bag that best suits your needs?

First you must decide how much you plan to use the bag. If you have never tried motorcycle camping before and want to see whether or not you will like it, you might go to your local discount department store and purchase a cheap bag. If you only plan to ride solo and camp in the hot summer, you could buy a bag rated down to thirty-five or forty degrees. These bags will cost about fifteen dollars. They will keep you as warm as more expensive bags rated at the same temperature but will not compress into a very small space. Two of these bags would be very difficult to pack for a two-up camping trip.

On the other hand, if you ride two-up and plan to take several motorcycle camping trips during the year, you should buy more expensive, three-season bags. Two three-season bags can be compressed into a relatively small space and will be absolutely necessary if you want to extend your camping season from early spring to late fall. To help you decide which bag best suits your needs, consider four basic features: comfort rating, weight, fill material, and fit.

Comfort rating. The first important feature to look for in a sleeping bag is the comfort rating. Most sleeping bags sold in America will have a number ranging from about fifty degrees Fahrenheit to about minus twenty-five degrees. This number is supposedly the lowest temperature at which the bag will keep you comfortably warm when wearing thermal underwear. Bags rated down to about forty degrees are sometimes called summer bags. Bags rated down to about twenty degrees are called three-season bags. Bags rated down to about zero degrees are called winter bags. And bags rated down to about minus fifteen degrees are called severe cold bags.

To test the accuracy of these comfort ratings, gear experts actually take each model out into the wilderness and sleep in it for several nights. After performing these tests, experts have concluded that the accuracy of sleeping bag comfort ratings is frequently overstated and that they vary from one maker to another. In particular, these experts report that comfort ratings of some sleeping bags (especially some American-made bags) are overstated by ten to twenty degrees. In other words, these experts were unable to sleep well when temperatures dropped near the comfort rating of some models. Because of these discrepancies, experts recommend that you mentally add ten or more degrees to the stated comfort rating of most sleeping bags. Bags rated down to twenty-five degrees, for example, should be considered to be thirty-five degree bags—you would likely feel uncomfortably cool if temperatures drop below thirty-five degrees.

In January 2005, European manufacturers began using the European Norm (EN 13537) to calculate their sleeping bag ratings. When manufacturers use this norm, they get more accurate comfort ratings. In other words twenty-degree bags manufactured under EN standards should allow you to sleep comfortably when actual temperatures drop down to twenty degrees or even lower. Moreover, the EN directs manufacturers to specify four different ratings for their sleeping bags. The *upper limit* tells you how low the temperature must drop before you will not sweat in the bag. The *comfort limit* tells you how low the temperature must drop before an average woman will feel cold and be unable to sleep. The *lower limit* tells you how low the temperature must drop before the average experienced male outdoorsman sleeping in the fetal position will feel cold and be unable to sleep. And the *extreme limit* tells you how low the temperature must drop before the average person will begin to develop hypothermia. Some of the companies who now manufacture their bags according to the EN standard include Bergans (Norway), Crux (United Kingdom), Lafuma (France), Mammut (Switzerland), Marmot (Germany), OMM (Poland), and Vaude (United Kingdom). REI, an American company, adopted the EN in the spring of 2009. Before purchasing a particular bag, read more about its comfort rating. The best place to read about comfort ratings of different bags is the Trail Space Web site. Read reviews for the specific model you are considering and reviews for other models made by the same manufacturer.

Backpackers and mountain climbers who camp in cold weather usually purchase winter bags rated down to zero degrees or lower. These cold weather bags typically are higher priced than summer or three-season bags and require more packing space than bags rated for warmer weather. If backpackers like to camp in a wide range of weather conditions, they usually purchase two or more different sleeping bags so that they will have the right bag for any weather condition.

Motorcycle campers, on the other hand, would not need winter or severe cold bags because they probably would not camp when temperatures drop below freezing. Instead motorcycle campers should consider buying good-quality three-season bags if they plan to camp during the spring, summer, and fall. These three-season bags compress into a relatively small space yet are able to keep you warm on cool spring and late fall nights. Motorcycle campers who plan to camp only during the warm summer months and ride bikes with limited packing space could buy good summer bags that pack into a smaller space than do the three-season bags.

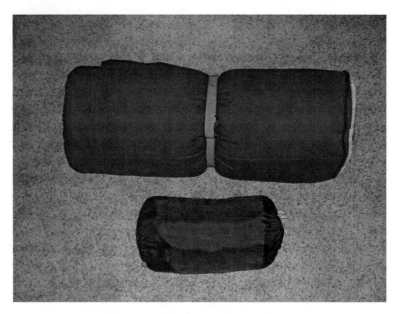

An older cotton-filled bag rated to 40 degrees (top)
compared with a newer synthetic-filled bag rated down to 20 degrees (bottom)

Weight. The weight of a bag is the best indicator of its compressibility. Heavier bags do not compress much at all, while lightweight bags can be compressed into a relatively small space. If you ride solo, you do not have to be as concerned about weight because you will have only have one sleeping bag and can pack it with your tent and sleeping pad on your backseat where the extra bulk and weight will have a negligible effect on your bike's handling.

On the other hand, if you plan to ride two-up, you should select bags that weigh less than four pounds each. You will need these lightweight bags because you will be unable to pack your gear on your back seat. Instead you must pack two sleeping bags along with two sleeping pads and a tent relatively high on the back of the bike. The more weight you pack high and behind your rear axle, the more it will adversely affect your bike's handling, especially at low speeds and when making sharp turns. The lighter your sleeping bags are and the smaller they pack, the less they will affect your bike's handling.

Generally speaking, the weight and compressibility of a bag is inversely correlated with its price. In other words, good lightweight bags that can be packed into a small space will cost more than heavier bags that cannot be compressed much. A very compressible two-pound down-filled bag rated at twenty degrees, for example, will cost over three hundred dollars. A less compressible three-pound synthetic bag rated at twenty degrees will cost between one hundred and three hundred dollars. And a bulky five- to ten-pound economy bag will cost less than fifty dollars. Two-up campers who want to have warm bags that can be packed into a small space must purchase bags that cost at least a hundred dollars.

If you purchase two bags that weigh less than four pounds each, you can easily pack both bags on almost any bike. We stuff them together into a large water-resistant compression sack, compress the sack into a relatively small size, and then tie the sack onto the luggage rack of my touring bike. If you ride a bike with limited packing space, you may be able to stuff two bags together into one stuff sack or you may have to stuff each bag into a smaller stuff sack and pack them separately inside a saddle bag or T-bag.

Fill material. The third feature to consider when shopping for sleeping bags is the thermal insulation material used to fill the bag. In other words, you need to determine whether they are filled with goose down feathers or with synthetic fibers. Backpackers usually prefer down-filled bags because down is lightweight, will compresses into a relatively small space, and has a longer life than synthetic fibers. Unfortunately down-filled bags have at least four limitations: 1) they typically cost more than synthetic bags; 2) they lose their ability to keep you warm if they get wet, 3) they require a relatively long time to dry, and 4) they may slowly lose feathers through their coverings.

Down-filled bags typically are rated in terms of their fill power—a number ranging from about 550 to 850. This number refers to the fluffiness of the feathers used to insulate the bag. Bags with lower fill power (e.g., six hundred) use feathers that are not very fluffy. One ounce of these feathers will only fill six hundred cubic inches of space. On the other hand, bags with higher fill power (e.g., eight hundred) use fluffier feathers. One ounce of these feathers will fill eight hundred cubic inches of space.

Sleeping bags made with higher-fill down require fewer ounces of feathers and thus will weigh less—and require less packing space—than bags made with lower-fill down. A reviewer at the Consumer Search Web site claims that the Marmot Atom 850 down-filled bag rated at forty degrees will compress down to the size of a coffee cup. Unfortunately these higher-fill bags will also be considerably more expensive than bags made with lower-fill power feathers.

Because down-filled bags lose much of their insulation value when wet, manufacturers are constantly striving to develop lightweight waterproof materials to make the linings and covers of these bags. One such material is Pertex micro light—a waterproof material that is soft to the touch. Ultimately manufacturers hope to find ways to design down-filled bags that are completely waterproof so they will keep you warm even if your sleeping gear gets soaked.

Down-filled bags may be your best choice if you ride a bike with limited packing space, such as a Low Rider. But if you decide to purchase a down-filled bag, pack it in a waterproof stuff sack and diligently strive to keep it dry at all times. Also buy a good-quality tent that will not leak to reduce the chances that your bag will get wet on rainy days or nights. If you buy a down bag and it gets soaked, you will likely have a cold and miserable night and risk the possibility of developing dangerous hypothermia.

The first table at the end of this chapter provides a list of three-season down-filled bags rated down to about twenty degrees that were available for sale in the spring of 2009. The three-season down-filled models receiving special recognition in the 2008 *Backpacker* magazine's annual gear guide included the Exped Woodpecker, the GoLite Adrenaline, the Lafuma Pro 950, the MontBell Super Stretch Down Hugger #2, and the Mountain Hardwear Spectra SL. When you read this book, some of these models may no longer be available, but you can use this chart as a guide for comparing whatever models are available when you decide to shop for your bag.

The alternatives to down-filled bags are synthetic-filled bags. Synthetic bags have some advantages over down-filled bags, but they also have some limitations. The primary advantages of synthetic bags are: 1) they usually cost less, 2) they will keep you warm even when wet, and 3) they dry out much faster than down-filled bags. One of the major limitations is that synthetic bags do not compress as much as down bags do. This fact could be an important factor for motorcycle campers who ride bikes with limited packing space. If you ride two-up on a cruiser with limited packing space, two synthetic bags may require more space than you have available. However, if you ride solo or have adequate packing space, the relatively small differences in compression size between down- and synthetic-filled bags will not be particularly significant.

A second limitation of synthetic-filled bags is that they usually lose their *loft* (or fluffiness) faster than do down-filled bags, especially when compressed for long periods of time or when washed several times. Consequently, after a few years, you may notice that your bag does not keep you as warm as it did when you first purchased it; you will have to replace your synthetic bag sooner than you would a down bag.

Several different manufacturers make synthetic insulation materials for sleeping bags, and each manufacturer typically claims that their own propriety thermal material is better than their competitors' products. In fact, each synthetic material differs in its physical appearance and structure from all other materials, but these differences provide little practical information for motorcycle campers. Instead motorcycle campers should focus upon other features such as older versus newer insulation materials, comfort ratings, weight (compressibility), longevity, and price.

Bags made with older synthetic fibers are more economically priced but are heavier and lose their ability to keep you warm faster. Some of these older materials include Cloudloft, Insul-Therm, Hollofil 808, Hollofil II, Quallofill, Slumberloft, Thermolite, and Thermashield. Sleeping bags made with these materials will keep you just as warm as bags made with any other material but are heavier and will not compress as much. Thus they are more difficult to pack. Some newer economy insulation materials include Coletherm by Coleman and Heatshield Optimal Technology (H.O.T. SL) used by The North Face. Twenty-degree bags made with these materials will usually be priced less than a hundred dollars. Bags filled with any of these materials may be acceptable choices for car camping or solo motorcycle camping. But they are poor choices if you must pack two sleeping bags on a motorcycle along with a tent and two sleeping pads.

Each year, manufacturers have developed (and will continue to develop) newer, warmer, more compressible synthetic materials for sleeping bags, but the price of these bags will be much higher than the price of bags made with older materials. Some of these newer materials include Polarguard 3D, Polarguard Delta, and Thermic Micro. In the past five years, Climashield has become a popular synthetic filling material used to insulate high-quality bags by Sierra Designs, L.L. Bean, Big Agnes, The North Face, and other manufacturers. More recently, PrimaLoft Sport has emerged as an excellent thermal insulation material that is lightweight and compressible. Some manufacturers such as Big Agnes, Integral Designs, Marmot, and The North Face now use it to make sleeping bags that rival down-filled bags in weight, compressibility, and longevity. To learn more about each synthetic material, search their names on the Internet or go to REI's and Campmor's Web sites.

The second table at the end of this chapter provides a list of several synthetic-filled sleeping bags available in the spring of 2009, along with their basic specifications. The price listed is based on a man's regular bag that is designed for men who are less than six feet tall. If you are over six feet tall, you will need a long bag, and these typically cost a few dollars more. *Backpacker* magazine's 2008 annual gear guide recognized several synthetic bags as good choices: the Big Agnes Skinny Fish, the Sierra Designs Verde (partly made from coconut shells), and The North Face Fission.

Fit. The final feature to consider is the overall shape and size of the bag. In general, you will find three types of sleeping bags: rectangular bags, semi-rectangular bags, and mummy bags. Select the bag that best fits your stature and sleeping style.

Rectangular bags are very roomy but not very heat efficient. They are quilts folded in half with a zipper that runs along the bottom and up the side. In addition to serving as a spacious one-person sleeping bag, they can be opened as a quilt or they can be zipped together with a second bag to make a large sleeping bag for two. Double sleeping bags can be romantic for couples but are not very warm. If the temperature drops below sixty degrees, couples may feel uncomfortably cool. Semi-rectangular bags are very similar to rectangular bags but have a more contoured shape to improve heat retention. Each year, manufacturers produce fewer and fewer rectangular and semi-rectangular bags because of their inefficient heat-retention properties. Manufacturers may quite possibly stop making lightweight three-season rectangular bags in the next two or three years.

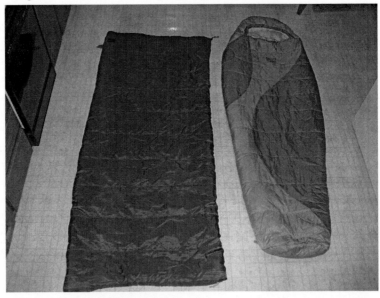

The Kelty Adirondack (rectangular) and a Sierra Designs Rosa (mummy) are both rated down to plus-twenty degrees.

Mummy bags are clearly the most popular three-season bags. They are contoured to fit your body—wide at the shoulder and chest area and tapered around the hips, legs, and feet. This design maximizes their ability to retain heat and keep your body warm with a minimum amount of material. Most of the time, they have hoods that will keep heat from escaping from your head. They sometimes have shorter zippers to further reduce heat loss. (Personally, I prefer bags with long zippers because they are easier to enter and exit, but these bags typically weigh a little more.) Because of their features, mummy bags are much lighter than rectangular bags and more heat efficient. In other words, mummy bags pack into a much smaller space than rectangular bags rated at the same comfort level. The primary limitation of mummy bags is the confined feeling they create, especially if you are a relatively large person.

The standard mummy bag is made for a normal-sized man who is less than six feet tall. These bags—commonly called regular male bags—typically measure about eighty inches long and about sixty to sixty-two inches in shoulder girth. In addition to these regular bags, most manufacturers make long bags for men who are up to six feet, five inches tall. Long bags typically measure about eighty-six inches long and up to sixty-four inches in shoulder girth. They typically will cost about ten dollars more than their regular size counterpart.

If you are an extra-large man, like me, you may find that the long mummy bags are not big enough in the shoulder girth. This tight cut makes it very difficult to sleep comfortably on your back with your arms to the side. Fortunately you have several options if you need more room in the shoulders. Perhaps the best option is an oversized mummy bag that may weigh a little more than the regular size bag. Examples of oversize bags include the Sierra Designs Paul Bunyan long, The North Face Mammoth, the Marmot Trestles long X-wide, and the Integral Designs Renaissance long broad. Other options for big guys are sleeping bag expanders (such as the one made by Mountain Hardwear) that fit most regular or tall bags with long zippers, Montbell Super Stretch Long bags that stretch to seventy-six inches in shoulder girth, or rectangular bags such as The North Face Big B. Finally, you might consider Big Agnes bags. They are much wider in the shoulder than most other bags, but they are not insulated on the bottom and require a twenty-inch-wide air mattress to provide complete protection from the cold. See the summary chart at the end of this chapter for more information about sleeping bags for big guys.

Women have several choices. They could select a regular man's bag if they wanted, or they could select one of many bags specifically designed for women. These women's bags are smaller than regular men's bags and are shaped in ways designed to fit most women's figure. In addition, women's bags typically have extra insulation in certain places to meet the heating needs of the average woman's body and may have some additional comfort features. For example, the Sierra Designs Rosa has a fleece-lined foot bed that Robin loves. Women's bags are usually priced the same as a regular man's bag.

Before purchasing your bag, consider visiting an outdoor-gear store and actually trying on (i.e., getting inside) several different bags. Since sleeping bags vary considerably in their size and features, most stores will be happy to allow you to see how well they suit your body type, sleeping style, and personal needs.

Our choices. Since we are "cold sleepers" (we like lots of blankets even on mild nights), have felt cool on many past camping trips, and have gotten wet on several past trips, we decided to purchase synthetic-filled, three-season, mummy bags. We have been very satisfied with our decision. After using a Kelty Adirondack and Kelty Lightyear bags for several years, I recently decided to move up to an Integral Designs Renaissance long broad mummy bag made in Canada, which weighs three pounds, eight ounces. At first Robin was afraid of the confined feeling of a mummy bag and used a relatively large rectangular bag. But with a little urging, she purchased a Sierra Designs Rosa and is very happy with it. It weighs two pounds, twelve ounces. We are glad we chose these bags rated down to twenty to twenty-five degrees because we frequently camp on cool nights. Both of our bags have kept us warm and comfortable, even on cool nights. On warm nights, we may sleep on top of our bags or use them as blankets or leave them unzipped.

Sleeping Bag Care

Outdoor gear experts and sleeping bag manufacturers recommend a few basic procedures to get the maximum warmth and camping life out of your sleeping bags.

Pack your bags in waterproof or water-resistant stuff sacks. When packing your bag for travel, compress it into a smaller waterproof stuff sack or bag. The stuff bag should be waterproof, because you never know when you will encounter rain. In the past, we used a heavy dry bag but found that it added several additional ounces to our packed weight and required more packing space. Now we use a super (thirteen by thirty inch) water-resistant nylon compressor stuff bag. On solo trips I stuff one sleeping bag in the stuff sack. On two-up trips I stuff both sleeping bags into the compressor sack. Once the sleeping bags have been stuffed into the compressor sack, I cinch the compression straps tight and have a very lightweight package that is approximately thirty inches long and five to eight inches in diameter. As such, the compressor sack—with the sleeping bags—can be easily tied with the tent and sleeping pads on the luggage rack of my Harley-Davidson Ultra. If you ride a bike with limited packing space, you may have to stuff each sleeping bag into its own travel stuff sack and pack them separately.

Air your bag every day during the trip. Each morning, turn your sleeping bag inside out and allow it to air out as long as possible. Airing the bag will dry any moisture absorbed from your body and will help eliminate bacteria and odors. Many years ago, when we used cotton-filled, flannel-lined sleeping bags, we turned them inside out and laid them on top of our car in the sun. The basic philosophy was to leave them in the sun as long as possible to kill odor and bacteria. Today the recommended procedure is different. You still should turn them inside out, but leave them in your tent or hang them on a clothesline in the shade. The reason for drying your bags in the shade is that prolonged direct sunlight will gradually degrade the newer materials used to make sleeping bags. However, if your bag gets soaked, you may have no other option but to leave it in the sun for an hour or so to dry.

Fluff your bag before placing it in the tent. Many manufacturers and camping experts suggest shaking your bag each day to loosen the loft and to be sure the fibers are evenly distributed throughout the entire bag.

Take a shower before going to bed. During the day your body sweats, accumulates dirt, and develops an odor. If you do not take a shower, this dirt, oil, sweat, and odor will transfer to your sleeping bag liner and you will have to wash your bag more often. The combined effect of the dirt and oil being ground into the bag plus the frequent washings will shorten the overall life of your bag.

Wear as much clothing as the temperature permits. The more clothing you wear, the less body oil and sweat will transfer to the bag's lining.

At the very least, wear shorts and a T-shirt. If possible, wear thermal underwear and socks. If it is not very cold, sleep on top of the bag. When the temperature drops, get inside the bag. By wearing clothes, you will be lengthening the life of your bag, you will be ready for the temperature drop, and you will be ready to go to the bathroom if nature calls. More detailed information about selecting and wearing clothing to stay dry, warm, and comfortable will be discussed in chapter 5.

Dry your bag thoroughly after returning home. Once you return home, open your bag, turn it inside out, and allow it to dry for several days before packing it for long term storage.

Store your bags properly. Sleeping bags should be stored so that their feathers or fibers are in a relaxed, non-compressed state. When a bag is compressed, the filling fibers or feathers will gradually weaken and the bag's loft (its ability to keep you warm) will be compromised. Experts recommend that you store your sleeping bags in large cotton bags such as pillowcases or hang them upside down in a closet. In fact, many bags are now sold with their own long-term storage stuff sacks. Regardless of the method you choose, store your bag in a cool place in your home, such as a closet, rather than in the garage.

Clean your bag after several trips. If you use your sleeping bag often, you will eventually need to clean it. When the time comes to clean your bag, first refer to your manufacturer's recommendations. Most of the time, manufacturers recommend that you avoid dry cleaning because dry cleaning chemicals may damage your bag and could leave a residue that could cause an allergic reaction the next time you sleep in it. Instead most manufacturers recommend hand washing with a small amount of mild soap (such as Ivory or Woolite) in a bathtub or washing it in a large *front-loading* washing machine. Top-loading washing machines should be avoided because the agitator could damage the bag's cover and insulation. After washing, manufacturers typically recommend that you first allow the water to drain out of the bag and then tumble dry in a machine set to a gentle, low-heat cycle. When handling a wet sleeping bag, support the entire bag with your hands. Do not allow parts of the wet bag to hang down. If part of the wet bag hangs, the weight of the water may tear or damage the bag's filling material or liner.

Sleeping Pads

If you have ever tried to sleep on the bare ground, you probably had a miserable night and never want to do it again. In addition to being hard and uncomfortable, the ground is cooler than the air temperature and will chill your body by conductive heat loss. Without adequate insulation, your body will quickly feel cold and you will be unable to sleep well. Sleeping bags and warm clothes provide some protection from the cold ground but usually not enough. To assure warm and comfortable nights, you need a good-quality insulated sleeping mattress. The comfort provided by an insulated mattress pad cannot be overstated. In addition to smoothing out the bumps on the ground and providing a soft sleeping surface, they insulate your body from the cold ground and keep you warm.

Many types of sleeping pads and air mattresses are available. You could buy an economy inflatable air mattress, such as those used for floating in the lake, from a discount department store for about five dollars, but these air mattresses will not protect you from the cold ground. You could buy an inexpensive open-cell foam mat such as the ones used for yoga or exercise, but these pads do not provide adequate insulation and will absorb moisture—thus making your body feel colder. You might find other types of air and foam pads in discount department stores, but they each have significant disadvantages. Some must be manually inflated by blowing into an air valve, while others must be inflated with a large pump. None of these pads provide the convenience, warmth, and comfort provided by good-quality backpacker's mattresses. Experienced campers and mountaineers typically agree—forget the economy sleeping pads and buy a good-quality mattress.

Closed-cell sleeping pads. Some backpackers and other campers sleep on closed-cell pads made from dense foam that has been sealed to prevent moisture absorption. These pads are considered to be good options for camping because they insulate your body from the cold ground well, are very durable, and do not absorb water. When you choose this type of pad, you can be assured that you will always have a dry, warm mat to sleep on. The limitations of these pads are that they are bulkier than other options and they do not provide as soft a sleeping surface as do air mattresses.

Self-inflating insulated air mattresses. Most veteran campers seem to prefer insulated, self-inflating air mattresses. These mattresses are superior to more economical products in terms of convenience, warmth, and comfort. Just open the valve and roll out the pad. Within a few minutes the pad will automatically inflate. Sometimes you may have to blow an extra puff of air into the pad to fully inflate it before closing the valve. But within a few minutes after opening, a self-inflating mattress is ready to provide a comfortable and warm sleeping surface.

The most recognized brand of self-inflating mattress is Therm-a-Rest. Therm-a-Rest pads come in over twenty different sizes. To find the best size for your needs, you must understand the basic differences between the models. They are grouped into three general thickness categories. *Camp and Comfort* pads (blue) are very thick and very comfortable but require too much space to be practical for two-up motorcycle camping. *Trek and Travel* pads (green) have a medium thickness and are ideal for motorcycle camping if you have the space to pack them. Within this category is a new ToughSkin pad that resists puncture better than other self-inflating pads. *Fast and Light* pads (orange or pink) are thin and pack into very small spaces so that they can be easily packed on any motorcycle with limited packing space, even when riding two-up. In addition, Therm-a-Rest makes several pads specifically designed for women.

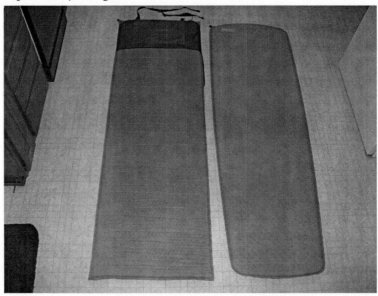

The Therm-a-Rest Expedition (left) is very comfortable,
but the Prolite 4 (right) packs much smaller.

Within each of the three basic categories, pads are available in different lengths and thicknesses. A small pad is designed for the summer backpacker who wants to travel ultra-light. It is only long enough for the upper half of a person's body. A regular pad is long enough for a person who is six feet tall, but it is only twenty inches wide. It would be suitable for a slender to average build person. A large pad is twenty-five inches wide and seems best suited for average-to-large-build people like Robin and me. Therm-a-rest also makes a couple of pads in an extra-large size for even greater comfort. Within each category, pads vary slightly in degrees of thickness. For example, within the Fast and Light category, the ProLite 3 is one inch thick and the ProLite 4 is one and a half inches thick.

After several trips using inferior open-cell pads and air mattresses and after reading so many positive reviews of the Therm-a-Rest pads, we finally bought two of them. We have not regretted our decision. Robin sleeps on a Trail Lite Large (Trek and Travel series). It is over six feet long, over two feet wide, and one and a half inches thick. It weighs two pounds, eleven ounces, which is a little more than some of the other sizes, but the size and weight is not too much to pack on my bike. I sleep on a Prolite 4 Large. It is about the same dimensions as the Trail Lite but weighs only two pounds, one ounce and packs a lot smaller. Both pads are very comfortable and provide an insulating layer of warmth from the cold ground.

In addition to the Therm-a-Rest brand, there are several other high-quality self-inflating mattresses pads. For example, the ECO Thermo 6 sleeping pad made by Pacific Outdoor is an environmentally friendly pad made completely from bamboo (a fast-growing woody plant) rather than from polyester and nylon. Its price ($150) is a little higher than the price of a Therm-a-Rest pad. Big Agnes, Eureka, Exped, Mammut, MontBell, and REI make other high-quality self-inflating sleeping mattresses. You can purchase these pads in camping specialty stores and on the Web. A list of possible retailers was presented at the end of chapter 1.

Therm-a-Rest accessories. The Therm-a-Rest company makes a number of accessories that could help you sleep better on your motorcycle camping trips. One valuable accessory for Therm-a-Rest pads is the repair kit. Although these pads are relatively tough, they can be accidentally punctured by a thorn, stick, or sharp rock. To reduce the risk of an accidental puncture, try to rake away rocks and sticks from the ground before setting up your tent. If your pad is punctured, you will find yourself sleeping on the cold hard ground unless you have a repair kit and know how to use it. The kit requires very little space and thus would be a good accessory to pack.

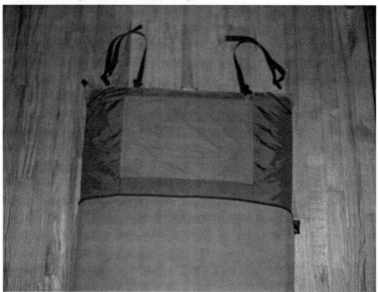

This Therm-a-Rest pad is shown with a Wrap-it pillow cover.

Another accessory for Therm-a-Rest mattresses is a Wrap-it pillow. This attachment slides over the top of a mattress and allows you to slide clothes or jackets between it and your mattress, thereby making a small pillow base that will not slither away in the night. The top side is padded with comfortable fleece. When you are ready to pack up, remove your clothing, leave the Wrap-it pillow in place, and roll the mattress. The pillow cover becomes a protective compression cover with nylon straps and buckles. No other straps are needed to secure the rolled mattress. We used these Wrap-it pillows for two or three years and were generally pleased with the comfort they provided.

Therm-a-rest makes several other accessories that you may wish to consider, if you have the space to pack them. For example, Therm-a-Rest makes fitted sheets that have smooth, non-slip surfaces, rubber non-slip understraps, and snaps that allow you to connect two pads together (making a full-size bed) and attach Tech Blankets that will keep you warm in moderately cool weather. Therm-a-Rest also makes a variety of pillows and stuff sacks.

Clothing

There are at least five good reasons for wearing as much clothing as possible while sleeping. First, clothing will keep you warm on cold nights. Second, clothing will protect your sleeping bag from your body oil and sweat. Third, clothing will allow you to slide easily into the polyester or nylon liner of your bag and comfortably shift your sleeping position; in the morning, it allows you to easily slide out of the bag. Fourth, clothing, especially thermal underwear, gives you a layer of warm clothing when you are ready to exit your bag in the cool morning. And finally, wearing your clothing allows you to get up and walk to the bathroom in the middle of the night without having to find your clothes and put them on in the dark.

Thermal underwear. For maximum warmth and bag protection, wear a thermal shirt and pants as often as possible. Regardless of the weather, I always pack a set of thermal underwear and try to wear it every night unless the weather is unbearably hot. The best thermal underwear is made from wool, polyester, or other moisture-wicking materials.

Insulating garments. When the nighttime low temperature is predicted to drop below forty-five degrees, you may wish to consider wearing additional clothing. For example, wearing a fleece, down, or synthetic jacket and fleece pants in addition to your thermal underwear will provide considerable warmth. Or you might find good polyester athletic garments that would also provide considerable warmth. Combining these garments with a good three-season bag should keep you warm even if the temperature were to drop below twenty degrees.

Wool socks. A pair of socks will also help to stave off the cold on chilly nights and will further protect the liner of your sleeping bag.

Knit cap. Knit caps provide considerable warmth and comfort while sleeping. If you are a little older and have lost some of your hair, like me, you probably learned this lesson many years ago. A bare head allows a considerable amount of body heat to escape into the air and allows the cool air to lower your body temperature—thus making you feel cold. Wool or polyester knit caps help to hold in body heat and keep you warm all night long. Without a cap, you may have difficulty sleeping, even on normal summer nights.

For several years, Robin thought she did not need a cap because she had long hair; but recently we were camping on a cool night and I had packed an extra cap for her, just in case. After wearing it one time, she has become a believer. Now we always keep knit hats in the corner of the tent near our heads. If the temperature gets a little cool, the caps are easily accessible.

Pillows

If you are like most people, you will want a pillow for your head. But pillows, even small ones, ordinarily take a lot of packing space. To have a comfortable pillow you have to get a little creative. For example, if you packed a daypack, one person could use it to make a pillow or a pillow base. If you packed a laundry bag with a drawstring, you could fill it with clothes and use it as a pillow base. Or you could purchase Therm-a-Rest Wrap-it pillows and stuff clothing or jackets under the material to create a small pillow base.

After creating this base, you may want to add another small pillow for a little more support. If you packed some clothes in a small stuff sacks, you could use the stuff sacks as pillows, but they may be a little uncomfortable. You may have to wrap them with a T-shirt or towel to provide a softer surface for your head. By simply adding or removing clothes, you can adjust each pillow's firmness. Better yet, buy soft flannel pillow covers such as those that are typically sold in camping supply stores. Therm-a-Rest and other camping-gear companies make them. They may come with filling material, but you can discard the filling and stuff clothes inside. In particular, you may wish to consider packing an extra pair of pants, a long-sleeved T-shirt, a pair of wool socks, and a set of underwear in your pillow cover. These items constitute the complete set of clothes you will need on the last day of your trip. Cover the pillow with a plastic bag while traveling so it does not get wet in rainy weather. When you arrive at your campsite, just remove your stuffed pillow from the tour pack and toss it into the tent. It is immediately ready for service.

Other Sleeping Gear

Sleep aids. On many trips, both Robin and I may have a little difficulty falling asleep the first night. I do not know if it is the change of environment or if we are just keyed up about the trip. For whatever reason, we expect this problem and plan accordingly. To help us sleep, we each take a warm shower, drink a glass of milk, take an acetaminophen or ibuprofen tablet, and go to bed with music from our personal music players and ear buds. Sometimes we need a little more help and may take a Benadryl or a mild sleeping pill the first night. Robin also keeps earplugs near her head because she is a light sleeper and is easily awakened by noise, which unfortunately occurs fairly often in some campgrounds.

After the first night, we typically have no more sleeping problems. As a result of being tired from too little sleep the first night and adjusting to our camping routine, we typically sleep well the rest of our trip. In fact, I usually sleep better in a tent than I do in my bed at home. I love to smell the fresh air and hear natural sounds of the night, especially owls, whippoorwills, and a gentle rain falling on the tent.

Cots. Some campers like to sleep on cots because they provide more cushion from the hard ground. Some cots pack as small as Therm-a-Rest pads, but they have a few limitations that make them less desirable than sleeping pads or mattresses. First, cot legs could damage the floor of your tent. Second, cots raise you a few inches above the floor in a small tent that already has limited space. Third, cots provide no insulation from the cold and thus would probably make you feel colder than would insulated pads. Finally, cots require more effort to set up. If you insist upon having a cot, you may want to investigate the LuxuryLite UltraLite Cot. Its legs are very short and are designed to produce minimal impact upon the floor of a tent.

Hammocks. A few backpackers prefer to sleep in hammocks supported by two trees. For protection from rain, they tie a tarp between the same two trees and pull the corners down to the ground to make an A-frame rain fly. They prefer sleeping in hammocks rather than tents for several reasons; for example, hammocks and tarps require less packing space than tents and sleeping pads. Another important reason is that hammocks produce less environmental impact than do tents. Tents will likely trample vegetation and pack the ground so that vegetation will have difficulty growing there in the future. Hammocks, on the other hand, do not disturb the ground.

For motorcycle camping, there are at least three limitations of using hammocks as your primary place to sleep. First, many established campsites do not have trees suitable for holding one or two hammocks. Second, hammocks do not provide insulation from the cold and thus will make you feel cold on cool nights unless you use a sleeping pad. Finally, sleeping in hammocks all night may be a little uncomfortable, especially for us big guys. See chapter 7 for more information about hammocks.

Robin is reluctant to exit her warm bag on a cool morning.

Secure Your Campsite

Before going to bed, you must take care of a few details around your campsite to avoid having problems during the night. First, be sure all your food is properly secured so that animals cannot access it. Many animals, such as raccoons, skunks, and bears, scavenge for food during the night. If you fail to secure your food, these animals may visit your campsite, damage some gear looking for food, and possibly injure you or another person in your party. When you register for your campsite, ask the park employee or camp host how to best secure your food during the night. If you have hard saddlebags, you may be able to pack your food items in them. If you only have leather bags, you may have to look for another way to secure the food. Some campgrounds have food storage lockers. If not, you may have to hang your food from a tree limb. Tie a rock to one end of a cord and throw it over a high limb, then tie the end of the cord to a bag with your food and pull it up to a height of about twelve feet. Then tie the cord high on the tree trunk.

After securing your food, gather up all of your garbage and put it in garbage receptacles. Animals may be attracted to the smells of food in your garbage and shred paper and plastic all over the ground looking for scraps. Furthermore, the wind could kick up during the night and blow your garbage around the campground.

The third thing to do before going to bed is to secure all your gear lying on your picnic table and around your campsite to assure that it does not get wet or damaged if a thunderstorm develops during the night. On many occasions, I have gone to sleep in nice calm weather thinking that my utensils, pots, stove, and other gear would be okay only to wake the next morning to find my gear wet or damaged from being blown off the table.

Fourth, inspect your tarp and be sure it is ready for rain and wind. Lower one corner of the tarp away from your tent to allow water to drain. Also be sure all lines are tied securely. If you know that high winds are likely, you may want to untie your tarp for the night, use it to cover your gear on the picnic table, and weight it down with rocks and firewood. You can easily put it back up after the storm has passed.

Finally, be sure your campfire has been completely extinguished. Pour water on the fire, stir the ashes, pour water again, stir again, and repeat until the fire is completely out. You would not want your campfire to accidentally start a forest fire.

Conclusion

What sleeping gear do you need for a motorcycle camping trip? To sleep dry, warm, and comfortable regardless of the temperature and weather conditions, you must assemble a good sleeping system that can be packed into a relatively small space. You and your passenger must have a compressible insulated mattress, a three-season sleeping bag that weighs less than four pounds, a pillow, and warm clothing.

At the end of this chapter are three charts that list over fifty different three-season sleeping bags available in the spring of 2009. The first chart lists many popular down-filled bags, the second chart lists many popular synthetic-filled bags, and the third chart lists many bags made for big guys. If you begin looking for sleeping bags after 2009, some of the models listed in these charts may no longer be available. As with tents, some manufacturers change models every year or two. Just look for well-known sleeping bag brands such as Big Agnes, Integral Designs, Kelty, Lafuma, Mammut, Marmot, MontBell, Mountain Hardware, The North Face, REI, and Sierra Designs. Compare the temperature rating, fill materials, weight, size, and price of the newer models with bags listed in the two charts. Review available bags, select the ones that seem best suited for your needs, and then shop for the best price.

If you assemble a good sleeping system and follow a few basic procedures, you will probably come to enjoy sleeping in your tent as much, if not more, than sleeping at home in your bed. For more information about sleeping gear, get a copy of *Backpacker* magazine's most recent annual gear guide, which is published every spring. Then go to REI (www.rei.com), Campmor (www.campmor.com), and Trail Space (www.trailspace.com) to learn more about current models, their specifications, their strengths, and their limitations.

Down Bags

Model	Material	Temp	Wt	Price
Campmor Mummy	550-fill	+20	2, 4	$120
Campmor Rectangular	550-fill	+20	2, 8	$140
REI Sahara	600-fill	+25	2, 2	$150
Coleman Exponent Cloudcroft	600-fill	+20	2, 9	$155
L.L. Bean Goose Down	650-fill	+20	2, 9	$170
Kelty Lightyear XP	650-fill	+20	2, 6	$180
Kelty Galactic	600-fill	+20	3, 0	$180
ALPS Navajo	650-fill	+20	2, 11	$200
EMS Mountain Light	725-fill	+20	2, 0	$200
Lafuma Warm 'n Light	650-fill	+20	2, 3	$200
The North Face Chrysalis	600-fill	+15	2, 12	$200
Marmot Sawtooth	600-fill	+15	2, 14	$200
Mountain Hardwear Piute	600-fill	+20	2, 10	$205
Marmot Massif Semi-Rec	600-fill	+20	3, 8	$219
MontBell SS Hugger #2	650-fill	+25	2, 6	$225
Bergans Senja Zero	700-fill	+25	2, 6	$230
The North Face Blue Kazoo	600-fill	+15	2, 12	$240
REI Sub Kilo	750-fill	+20	1, 13	$240
Lafuma Pro 950	750-fill	+15	2, 2	$280
Exped Woodpecker	750-fill	+20	2, 3	$280
MontBell UL SS Hugger #2	800-fill	+25	1, 12	$315
GoLite Adrenaline	800-fill	+20	2, 1	$325
Big Agnes Zirkel SI	800-fill	+20	1, 14	$340
Feathered Friends Swift	850-fill	+20	2, 2	$375
Mountain Hardwear Spectra SL	800-fill	+20	2, 12	$390
Western Mountaineering Alpenlite	850-fill	+20	1, 15	$395

Notes: Temp = temperature rating; Wt = weight in pounds, ounces; EMS = Eastern Mountain Sports; SS = Super Stretch.

Synthetic Bags

Model	Material	Temp	Wt	Price
Wenzel Northfork	Insul-Therm	+20	6, 8	$ 28
Eureka Cimarron	Thermashield	+15	4, 1	$ 46
Slumberjack Lattitude	Slumberloft HQ	+20	4, 2	$ 55
Kelty Tundra	Cloudloft	+15	4, 1	$ 65
Coleman Exponent Tasman	Coletherm	+20	4, 11	$ 70
Slumberjack Ultrapacker Magnum	Slumberloft HP	+20	4, 8	$ 75
Marmot Trestles	Spirafil 120	+20	3, 8	$ 80
REI Polar Pod	Polyester fiber	+20	3, 8	$ 80
L.L. Bean Adventure	Climashield CL	+20	3, 0	$ 80
Slumberjack Ultimate	Thermolite Extreme	+20	3, 0	$ 80
Coleman Exponent Emmons	Coletherm XTR	+20	3, 3	$100
Sierra Designs Wild Bill	Climashield HL	+20	3, 1	$110
L.L. Bean Katahdin	Climashield HL	+20	2, 15	$120
The North Face Blaze	Climashield HL	+20	3, 2	$120
Kelty Light Year	Climashield XP	+20	2, 14	$130
Mountain Hardware Switch	Thermolite Extra	+20	3, 10	$135
Coleman Exponent Klickitat	Climashield XP	+20	2, 11	$140
Mountain Hardware Lamina	Thermic Micro	+20	3, 0	$140
The North Face Cat's Meow	Climashield Prism	+20	2, 10	$150
MontBell SS Burrow #2	Exceloft	+25	3, 3	$160
The North Face Orion	Primaloft	+20	2, 8	$180
Sierra Designs Verde	Climashield Green	+20	3, 2	$180

Big Agnes Skinny Fish	Climashield HL	+20	3, 14	$180
Big Agnes Savery SL	Primaloft SB	+20	2, 13	$190
Marmot Pounder Plus	Primaloft	+25	2, 2	$200
Integral Designs Renaissance	Primaloft Sport	+20	2, 14	$220
The North Face Fission	Climashield Neo	+20	2, 4	$240

Notes: Temp = Temperature rating; Wt = weight in pounds, ounces; SS = super stretch.

Bags for Big Guys

Model	Material	Temp	Girth	Wt	Price
Slumberjack Lattitude, Long	Slumberloft HQ	+25	76	3, 8	$ 60
Slumberjack Ultimate, Long	Thermalite Extra	+20	68	3, 4	$ 85
TNF Bighorn Bx, Reg. (6' 4")	HOT SL	+20	66	3, 15	$ 80
TNF Bighorn Bx, Long (6' 8")	HOT SL	+20	68	4, 5	$ 90
Slumberjack Vertex	Climashield XP	+20	68	3, 7	$108
Marmot Trestles, Long X-wide	Spirafil 120	+15	70	3, 14	$110
Slumberjack Bafin, Long	600-fill Down	+20	68	3, 1	$115
TNF Mammoth, Reg. (6' 4")	ClimaShield HL	+20	66	3, 9	$150
Sierra Designs Paul Bunyan	Climashield HL	+10	70	3, 14	$150
MontBell SS #2 Burrow, Long	Exceloft	+25	76	3, 8	$160
TNF Mammoth, X-Long (6' 8")	ClimaShield XP	+20	68	3, 14	$160
TNF Big B (semi-rec), Reg.	ClimaShield	+20	70	3, 12	$170
TNF Big B (semi-rec), Long	ClimaShield	+20	72	3, 15	$180
ID Renaissance, Broad Long	PrimaLoft	+20	68	3, 8	$230

Marmot Sawtooth, Long X-Wide	600-fill Down	+15	70	3, 7	$240
Marmot Massif, Long	600-fill Down	+20	66	3, 14	$240
MontBell SS Hugger #2, Long (6' 4")	650-fill Down	+25	76	2, 6	$245
MontBell UL SS Hugger #2, Long (6' 4")	800-fill Down	+25	76	1, 15	$301

Notes: TNF = The North Face; ID = Integral Designs; SS = Super Stretch; Temp = Temperature Rating; Girth = Shoulder area in inches; Wt = Weight in pounds, ounces.

4. Essentials

Once you have assembled your tent and sleeping system, you must decide what other gear to pack for your motorcycle camping trips. As you consider this question, you will realize that you must confront a basic packing dilemma. You have limited packing space on your motorcycle (especially when riding two-up), but you need to pack enough gear to stay dry, warm, and comfortable in a variety of weather conditions. How can you resolve this dilemma?

Most books and articles on camping suggest that campers prepare a list of the gear that they need to pack on future camping trips. Many books provide examples of such lists and suggest that readers either copy the lists or modify them to suit their particular needs. Once you have a well-prepared list, you can use it before each trip to remember everything you need to pack. Most of these lists offered in other camping books and articles are long and include a wide range of items. Some of the items (e.g., your tent, sleeping bags, clothing, and cooking supplies) are things that you would likely remember without referring to a list. But other items (e.g., medicine, headlight, camera, cord, paper towels, water container, and fire starter) could be easily forgotten when packing in a hurry.

A tarp above the table provides shelter from the rain and shade from the sun.
This was my campsite at Monte Sano State Park, Huntsville, Alabama.

Books and articles about motorcycle camping also offer camping gear lists. Perhaps the best known of these lists is the one found on Bill Johns' Excellent Motorcycle Camping Guide Web site, www. wetleather.com. This list includes 235 items divided into seven categories (camping/sleeping equipment, cooking/eating equipment, riding gear, camp clothes, personal effects, bike paraphernalia, and tools). In addition to the standard camping items, this list also includes knife sharpener, shovel, saw, matches, post-it notes, sewing kit, and electric razor, some of which may not be necessary for most camping trips. Other lists can be found in the book *Motorcycle Camping Made Easy* by Woofter, on the BMW Motorcycle Owners Association Web site, and on Gary Sosnik's personal Web site.

At first these lists seem to tell you what you need to pack for a motorcycle camping trip, but upon further consideration you will realize that these lists still do not provide the guidance needed by people who want to plan camping trips (especially those who have never attempted to camp on their motorcycles before). Most of these lists include so many items that you could not possibly pack all of them on a motorcycle, and many of these items are unnecessary.

In the early stages of my lightweight camping learning curve, I used lists offered by other motorcycle camping experts as a guide and bought several suggested items (e.g., shovel, spare parts, and folding chair) only to discover that these items were never used and required valuable packing space. Furthermore, I realized that I needed other items that I had not packed. I eventually realized that lists suggested by other motorcycle campers are like Christmas wish lists rather than practical guides. They include many more items than anyone could ever pack on a motorcycle (or even in a small car) and include items that are only needed on special occasions. If you want to know the basic list of things you will probably need to pack for a motorcycle camping trip, you may need a little more information regarding gear that is absolutely essential and gear that should be regarded as optional.

Backpackers addressed the question of essential gear over seventy years ago. In the 1930s, a hiking and mountain climbing club in Seattle, Washington, published a list of the ten essentials in a book entitled *Mountaineering: Freedom of the Hills*. This list presumably included the ten things that back-country hikers and campers would need to survive emergencies such as sudden snowstorms or getting lost. The ten essentials were a map, a compass, sunglasses and sunscreen, extra food and water, extra clothes, a headlamp/flashlight, a first-aid kit, a fire starter, matches, and a knife. Over the years, other groups have revised the list to fit different geographic areas and recreational activities. REI recently published a more general list of the ten essentials. The REI list includes gear needed for navigation, sun protection, insulation, illumination, first-aid supplies, fire, repair kit and tools, nutrition, hydration, and emergency shelter.

While these ten essentials provide a good starting point, they do not seem to be ideally suited for motorcycle camping. Motorcycle campers who camp in front-country campsites, for example, would not need topographical maps of the area, compasses, or GPS receivers. Furthermore, motorcycle campers would not need some toilet supplies and water-purification equipment included in the essentials. On the other hand, motorcycle campers have space to pack some other gear (e.g., tarp and tarp support poles) that would assure more comfortable camping experiences.

One Web site has attempted to define essential gear for motorcycle camping. The River City Beemers (www.rcb.org) provides a list of twenty-three essential items. Many of these items (sleeping bag, sleeping pad, tent, ground cloth, pillowcase, and water bottle) would probably be generally accepted by other motorcycle campers. But some of the items on the list could be debated (toilet paper and several cooking/coffee-related items). Furthermore, the list omits several items that are considered to be essential by experienced campers (e.g., first-aid kit, personal items, shower bag, shower shoes, cord, tarp, and ax).

After considering all of the available lists and our past camping experience, we developed our own way to think about camping gear. First we conceptualize our gear as falling into one of three basic categories: 1) essential items needed for any motorcycle camping trip, 2) clothing, and 3) optional items that could be taken if we have the space to pack them. We consider most kitchen gear, such as stoves, pots, and utensils, as optional. We initially used opinions of camping experts as our guide but eventually added and deleted items based upon our personal camping experiences. Some of the items we chose to include on our list of essentials could be debated. As you read this chapter, you can decide for yourself whether or not to accept all of the items on our list.

We define essential gear as those items that are small enough to pack on most motorcycles (even when riding two-up) and functional enough to provide a lot of comfort in the campsite regardless of weather conditions. Our list of the essentials needed for motorcycle camping has thirteen groups of items. Shelter, sleeping system, and clothing are discussed in chapters 2, 3, and 5 respectively. The remaining items on our list of essentials include rain gear, first-aid kit, shower supplies, personal items, camping tools, basic kitchen items, lights, tarp, plastic bags or stuff sacks, and a few miscellaneous items. We pack these essential items on our bike first—before packing any other items. Other than the tent and sleeping system, we pack most of these essentials in our saddlebags. After packing the essentials, we can actually see the amount of remaining space that could be used to pack extra clothing and optional gear.

If you ride a touring bike, you will have lots of room to pack your essentials and will have plenty of space for some optional items. But if you ride a cruiser or if you must pack heavier clothing for cool-weather trips or more clothes for long trips, you may have very little space after packing your essential gear. If you are traveling two-up, do not expect to take many optional items.

Rain Gear

Basic rain gear includes a jacket, a pair of pants, a pair of gloves, and a pair of gaiters. If you wanted to save money, you could purchase rubber-coated ponchos, rain suits, and gloves for ten to twenty dollars in discount department stores. But these items would be hardly worth their price. They may not keep you dry from the rain and, more importantly, they do not *breathe*. In other words, these garments make you sweat, even on cool days, and trap this sweat inside the suit, making your body wet. If you wore one of these suits, your clothes would likely become soaked very quickly—regardless of the temperature. How counterproductive is that? You might as well not wear a rain suit at all.

If you have ridden much at all, you probably have already discovered the value of good-quality rain gear and keep it packed on your bike. Some riders believe that rain gear (or all-weather riding suits) is far more practical than leather chaps and jackets. Riders who hold this opinion typically forgo the leather and buy good-quality waterproof, breathable jackets, pants, gloves, and gaiters instead.

Good-quality, waterproof, breathable rain gear is typically made from nylon or polyester fabric that has been laminated with a thin waterproof, breathable membrane. The membrane has pores that are large enough to allow warm water vapor (steam) to escape and evaporate but are so small that they prevent cool liquid water droplets from penetrating. Furthermore, the nylon exterior of these garments is coated with a durable water repellent (DWR) wax coating to give an extra measure of moisture protection. The best-known waterproof, breathable membrane is Gore-Tex. It has been on the market for several years and is widely used to make breathable rain gear. Some of the many manufacturers who use Gore-Tex include Arc'Teryx, Asolo, Marmot, Merrell, Montrail, Mountain Hardwear, Outdoor Research, The North Face, and Vasque. Recently, several other proprietary waterproof, breathable membranes have appeared on the market. The best known of these newer membranes, eVent, is used by a few manufacturers (Boure Bicycle Clothing, Integral Designs, and REI) to make their rain suits. Other waterproof breathable membranes include Conduit (used by Mountain Hardwear), Elements (REI), H2No (Patagonia), HyVent (The North Face), MemBrain (Marmot), Omni-Tech (Columbia), Pertex Shield (Outdoor Research), and PreCip (Marmot). All of these newer materials seem to perform about the same as Gore-Tex in terms of water protection and breathability.

Jacket and pants. At the high end of the financial continuum are high-quality riding suits, such as the ones sold by AEROstich. This company offers jackets and pants in few different styles and price ranges. Most of these jackets and pants are made from Cordura (a heavy nylon fabric) laminated with a Gore-Tex membrane. These suits are waterproof and breathable, plus they offer protection against abrasions or "road rash" in the unfortunate event of a fall. Extra padding can be added to provide further protection. The price of these suits is much higher than the price of other rain gear but is comparable to the price of good leather garments. Depending upon the options selected, these high-quality riding suits are priced from about five hundred to eight hundred dollars. They seem to be especially popular with BMW and other sport-touring motorcycle riders.

A less-expensive option is a windproof and waterproof breathable hard-shell jacket and pants designed for hikers, backpackers, mountaineers, and other outdoor enthusiasts. These suits are typically made from a much thinner nylon or polyester material and some type of waterproof, breathable membrane. In addition to keeping you dry in the rain, they block the wind well on cool days and offer a small degree of abrasion resistance—thus providing a little protection from road rash in the unlikely event of a spill. These suits are typically lightweight and compress into a very small space. They are ideal for backpackers who do not want to wear their rain gear all the time.

Good-quality hard-shell rain suits also seem to be an excellent choice for motorcycle camping, not only because they are made with breathable waterproof materials but also because they are windproof, they work with insulating garments to retain your body heat in cool weather, and they compress into a small space for packing. Furthermore, they are comfortable enough to wear as an extra set of clothes if all your other clothes get wet or dirty. The one potential problem with these suits around the camp is they are heat sensitive and could be damaged if they come into contact with an ember from the fire or with a hot exhaust pipe. Excessive heat could melt them and possibly burn your skin.

Many different brands of high-quality breathable hard-shell rain jackets and pants are available. During the summer months, I wear a lightweight Precip jacket and pants by Marmot. This suit is very comfortable and compresses into a small space. It has several desirable features such as large pockets, underarm zipper vents, and a hood. Other highly rated hard shells include Alpha SL (Arc'teryx), Beryllium (Mountain Hardwear), eVent Rain Jacket (Integral Designs), Foray (Outdoor Research), Koven Plus (Cloudveil), Kulshan with eVent (REI), Phantom (GoLite), Rain Shadow (Patagonia), and Venture (The North Face). In colder weather, I wear an insulated Titanium parka and a pair of ski pants made by Columbia.

A new type of rainwear—called soft shells—has recently emerged on the market. These garments stretch and are much softer to the touch than the older hard shells. Like the hard shells, they are waterproof, but they breathe much better and they feel more like fleece. Examples of soft-shell rain jackets include Alchemy (Mountain Hardwear), Everest

(The North Face), and Ready Mix (Patagonia). Many backpackers and other outdoor enthusiasts have begun to use such soft-shell rain wear, but motorcycle campers may not find them to be as practical as the hard shells because they do not compress as small.

We have used our rain gear a lot over the years, both on camping trips and on non-camping trips. In fact, we have used our rain gear more often as cold weather suits than as a rain suits. Whenever the weather gets a little cool, we put on an insulated vest or jacket, gaiters, and rain suit and we have a warm, wind-resistant shell that keeps us dry, warm, and comfortable. When the weather warms up and we no longer need our rain gear, we can pack our hard-shell garments into a relatively small space. We sometimes pack them into a saddlebag, but more often we pack them in our daypack tied on the top of our luggage rack.

Rain gloves. For rain gloves, I have tried rubber gloves made for refinishing furniture and leather gloves with a Gore-Tex lining. Neither of these options was acceptable. The rubber gloves made my hands sweat profusely, and the leather gloves quickly became soaked and felt very heavy on my hands. Eventually I tried a pair of Harley-Davidson nylon rain gloves with a Gore-Tex lining and have been very satisfied with them. In cold weather I add a pair of thin glove liners, and together these gloves are as warm as any gloves I have ever worn. Makers of good-quality rain gloves include Black Diamond, Komperdell, Mountain Hardwear, Outdoor Research, REI, and The North Face. These gloves can be purchased in most camping and mountaineering-supply stores.

Gaiters. When riding a motorcycle in the rain, water will sling up from the front tire back onto your boots and socks. If your socks get wet, they will quickly wick the water down to soak the insides of your boots. Your rain pants will not completely protect this area from the water. Therefore motorcycle riders need a pair of gaiters to prevent their socks and boot uppers from getting wet. Gaiters also provide considerable warmth for your ankles in cold weather. In the past, Robin and I both used nylon overboots with open heels. These overboots did a great job of keeping our boots dry, but because of their rubber soles, they required a relatively large amount of packing space. Furthermore, they required considerable effort to put on, which made us reluctant to remove them for each short refueling and eating stop. But we felt uncomfortable walking in them in convenience stores and restaurants. After several years, we changed to a pair of standard gaiters such as those used by many hikers, backpackers, and other outdoor enthusiasts. We are much more satisfied with them.

Several brands and models are available. They all seem to work equally well—both for keeping you dry and for helping you to stay warm. Some models are relatively short, while others are longer. We selected mid-calf length gaiters made by Mountain Hardwear. We like these gaiters because they require very little packing space and are very comfortable when walking around. The one potential problem with these gaiters is they still allow your boot lowers to get wet. In heavy rain, water could soak your boots and feet if you do not have a waterproof liner and have not applied a waterproofing treatment.

First-Aid Kit

Campers should always have a basic first-aid kit available in the event of an emergency. I have used mine on several camping trips. The most common problems I have experienced have been burns from the campfire and insect bites. A basic first-aid kit should include the following items: gauze pads to put pressure on lacerations, tape to hold bandages in place, burn cream or aloe gel, Itch Eraser for insect bites, antibiotic cream (e.g., Neosporin), adhesive bandages, Benadryl to prevent allergic reactions to bee stings, and pain tablets (e.g., ibuprofen, acetaminophen, and aspirin). You can purchase complete kits in nylon bags or you can make your own kit and put it in a one-quart food storage bag. Also consider sunscreen, lip balm, and insect repellent as a part of your first-aid kit.

Sunscreen. Being outdoors, whether riding or camping, exposes you to potentially harmful ultraviolet radiation. The best way to protect yourself from painful sunburn and possible skin cancer is to apply sunscreen. Even on cloudy days, apply sunscreen several times a day. We use a sport cream rated at SPF 30. Some manufacturers sell products that combine sunscreen and insect repellent, but many experts seem to think that these two products should be applied separately.

Insect repellent. When camping, you never know when mosquitoes, ticks, biting flies, redbugs or chiggers, and other insects will show up to make life unpleasant. Be prepared with a can of repellent. There is considerable debate about the best products. Those with DEET seem to offer the best protection and last longer but are considered to be environmentally unfriendly. Other products are more environmentally friendly but have limited usefulness. We prefer to use Off Deep Woods with DEET because this product reportedly offers the best protection against the insects that cause West Nile virus and Lyme disease. We know from personal experience that this product does an excellent job of repelling insects.

Pack first-aid kit, personal items, and paper towels in one-quart food storage bags.

Personal Items

Items selected for your personal-grooming kit should be travel-sized products that can be purchased in your local discount department store. The basic items for a man include razor, toothbrush (I cut a few inches off the handle of a standard toothbrush so it can be packed into a smaller space because I do not like the small travel-sized toothbrushes), floss, toothpaste, hairbrush, deodorant, and prescription medicine. All of these items can be packed in a small one-quart food storage bag.

The list for women may contain a few extra items. Some women may consider a certain amount of makeup to be essential. Try to work together to limit the items so you can minimize the required packing space as much as possible. For example, consider leaving the hair dryer at home. Hand dryers on the walls of many bathrooms can serve as hair dryers, and on warm days, natural air-drying is a viable option.

Shower Supplies

For showers, you need five basic items: shower bag, pair of shower shoes, towel, washcloth, and soap. We typically pack all these items together with our clothes inside a stuff sack or a soft side cooler. Together they require very little packing space.

My shower shoes, soap, washcloth, and towel are shown on top of my shower bag.

Shower bag. The shower bag is useful for holding your soap, washcloth, clean clothes, watch, and glasses while you shower and for holding your dirty clothes as you return to your campsite. Plastic shopping bags serve this purpose well. Perhaps the best option is a heavy-duty plastic shopping bag (approximately eighteen inches square), such as the ones you get from bookstores, upscale department stores, or motorcycle dealerships.

Shower shoes. Shower shoes are important because many campground workers do not clean their shower stalls as well as you might wish, and some campground showers may have standing water and signs of mold and mildew. Moreover, you never know who was in the shower before you and what foot problems they may have left there (e.g., athlete's foot or some other contagious condition). We pack a pair of Crocs for the shower and also wear them around our campsite as casual footwear. If you do not have the room to pack a pair of Crocs, you could substitute a pair of plastic flip-flops.

Washcloth and towel. Washcloths generally pack into a small area, so you can simply use one from your home. Standard bath towels, on the other hand, require much more packing space. The best alternative is a compressible backpacking camp towel. Several brands and sizes are available. Even the largest ones are relatively inexpensive and compress into a small space. They can be purchased from discount department stores or camping supply stores.

Soap. Some campers prefer bar soap, while others prefer liquid soap in a small plastic travel-sized bottle. I have tried both and have not yet decided which I like best. Each has some advantages and disadvantages. For example, liquid soap in plastic bottles is neater because it can be packed in a bag with your clothes and will not get them wet and sticky. But bar soap is convenient to pack and will last longer. If you decide to use bar soap, dry it as much as possible before placing it back into the bag. You may wish to wrap it with your washcloth.

Camp Tools

Several tools are essential to perform various camping tasks necessary for having a comfortable experience. These tools, along with our tent stakes, are all packed in a small nylon tool bag and then packed in the bottom of my left saddlebag.

A small crowbar and an ax have many uses around camp.

Ax. Backpackers and other ultra-light campers usually would not consider an ax to be essential gear and would be reluctant to pack them because they are relatively heavy. When backpackers set up their camp, they use rocks to drive in their tent stakes and they either find small pieces of wood that do not need splitting or they forgo fires altogether and cook on their backpacker's stoves.

On the other hand, most car campers consider an ax to be an essential camping tool. It can be used for several chores around camp, such as driving tent stakes into the ground, shaving kindling from larger logs, and splitting firewood. Occasionally you will find other uses for it, such as moving logs in the fire. The best type of ax is a small steel-handled ax with a molded rubber grip. These axes can be purchased from discount department stores, hardware stores, or camping outfitters.

Before each trip, check the bit, or edge, for nicks and overall sharpness. If the ax is dull or has any nicks, sharpen it by using a grinding wheel or by putting it in a vise and using a metal file on each edge. You will have to push hard enough to shave away small amounts of metal. When packing the ax, cover the bit with a sheath so that it does not accidentally injure someone or damage some of your gear. If you do not have a sheath, use an old washcloth secured with a heavy-duty rubber band. The washcloth will also protect the bit from accidental damage.

Small crowbar. You probably will never see small twelve-inch crowbars on any other camping gear list. Backpackers wouldn't consider them to be essential because of their weight and because they have learned other ways to survive without having one. However, I discovered that a crowbar can be a very useful tool for motorcycle camping and requires minimal packing space. The weight of the crowbar, packed with the ax in a small camping tool bag, is not enough for a motorcycle rider to notice. To pack a crowbar, wrap it in an old washcloth so it will not accidentally damage other objects in your saddlebag.

Small crowbars have many uses around the campsite. They can be used to remove large rocks that are partially buried in the ground where you want to pitch your tent. They can also be used to remove nails driven into trees by other campers. And they can be used to rearrange hot logs in the fire, charcoal, or grills. Perhaps the most important use of a crowbar is to pull tent stakes out of the ground when they cannot be removed by any other means. If you have used heavy-duty galvanized nails for your stakes, you want to get them back out of the ground after every trip, but sometimes they get stuck and are hard to remove. Stakes are especially difficult to remove if they have been inadvertently driven into a tree root. Many campers are unable to remove their stakes from tree roots and just leave them in the ground for the next occupant to deal with. The crowbar will get the stakes out every time. Realizing the usefulness of a small crowbar was one of the most enlightening discoveries of my camping life. It is the perfect tool for resolving a problem that had me baffled for several years—those stuck stakes. Now I do not have to leave any more tent stakes in the ground.

A crowbar also makes an excellent trenching tool, whenever one is needed. Most of the time, you will not need to dig trenches because established campgrounds typically have tent pads made with porous materials that provide good drainage. Furthermore, trenching on bare ground should be avoided as much as possible because it disturbs the natural environment, increases the problem of soil erosion, and creates a negative environmental impact. But when trenching is necessary, the small crowbar does an excellent job. Simply hold the straight end and drag the curved end through the ground like a plow.

Cord. Rope or cord is an important but often-overlooked piece of gear. Car campers usually carry some rope but may not always use it in camp. Backpackers would not pack rope because it requires too much packing space. Furthermore, they may not pack cord because cord also requires valuable packing space and because backpackers typically do not stay in camp long enough to use cord for clotheslines or dining flies. Motorcycle campers, on the other hand, frequently recommend cord as a potentially useful item but usually do not tell you how much to pack or how to use it. After experimenting with various combinations of ropes and cords over the past ten years, I have finally come to some conclusions about what type is best for motorcycle camping, how much to pack, how to pack it, and how to use it to make your camp dry and comfortable.

First, I agree with many other motorcycle campers that small-diameter cord is the best option because it is strong enough to handle most camping chores yet it packs into a relatively small space. When traveling, it can be used to tie your gear securely onto your luggage rack or back seat. In camp, it can be used to set up a tarp as a dining fly over your picnic table (or as a wind break), to tie your tablecloth onto the table on windy days, to make a clothesline, to connect grommets along the edges of a tarp to make a bike cover, to hang a bear bag, or to lash pieces of wood together. Each motorcycle camper seems to have his or her favorite type of cord. Some prefer clothesline cord, while others prefer parachute cord. I like one-eighth-inch-diameter nylon cord that can be purchased in most hardware or discount department stores.

After purchasing a package of cord, I precut the cord into specific lengths that are practical for most camping chores. I begin by cutting several five and a half foot lengths. Each time I cut the cord, I immediately burn the ends with a butane lighter or candle to prevent unraveling. Then I tie a permanent overhand loop at one end. (This is the loop end; the other end of the cord is the free end.) After the loops have been tied, each cord section will be about five feet long. To prevent the cord sections from tangling, I hook the loop ends with a carabineer and then repeatedly fold the cord sections in half until they are about four inches long. Then I secure the cord with a heavy-duty rubber band. The number of five-foot cords to pack will depend upon your camping style. I like to camp in base camps for several days and want to have enough cord to perform several different chores. Therefore I pack fifteen five-foot cords in my tool bag. If most of your camps are overnight camps or if you ride a bike with limited packing space, you could get by with ten or fewer five-foot cords.

After preparing the five-foot cords, I also prepare some ten-foot cords. First, cut each cord about ten-and-a-half feet-long. Burn both ends of each cord to prevent unraveling, tie a permanent overhand loop at one end, hook the loop ends with a carabineer, fold the cord sections until they are about four inches long, and secure them with a heavy-duty rubber band. I pack ten of these cords in my tool bag so that I am prepared for almost any situation. You may not want to pack as many.

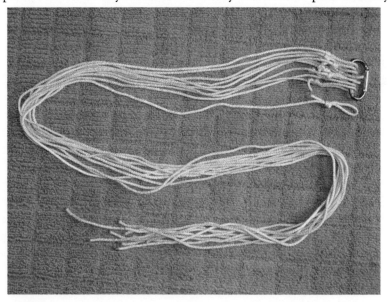

We hook ten five-foot lengths of cord with a carabineer to prevent tangling.

Finally, cut a few shorter sections of cord. In particular, I need two thirty-five-inch sections of cord to secure our rolled sleeping pads (one cord for each pad) when traveling, and I may need a few one-foot sections to tie tarp grommets onto a line or small sapling.

After preparing and packing your pre-cut cord sections, you are ready for almost any campsite scenario you may encounter. If you want to erect a dining fly over your table, you will need at least one cord section to secure each corner of the tarp to a tree. If trees are spread far apart, you may need two or more sections to reach each tree. See chapter 9 for information about knots that can be used to join two or more cord sections. If you use tarp support poles as we do, you will need two ten-foot cord sections for each pole. Two tarp support poles require a total of four ten-foot cord sections.

If you want to keep your tablecloth from blowing away on windy days, you can tie it onto the table with one or two cord sections (five-foot cord sections for smaller tables or ten-foot sections for larger tables). If you want a clothesline to dry your towel, washcloth, dishcloth, and clothes, you will usually need two or more cord sections. A clothesline or two could also be used to dry your tent before packing.

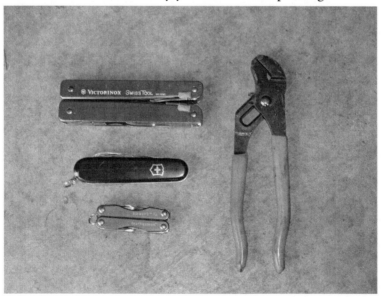

Our tools include a small pair of pliers, a large SwissTool, a medium Swiss Army knife for my pocket, and a small Leatherman Squirt P-4 for my waist pack.

Duct tape. One of the basic principles of camping is to expect something to tear or break on every trip. When something breaks, duct tape can frequently be used to make a temporary repair that will serve until you can make a permanent repair or replace the damaged item. Duct tape can be used to patch torn tablecloths, tarps, ground cloths, backpacks, and tents. It can be used to splice broken poles, to hold down tablecloths on windy days, and to solve many other unexpected problems. If possible, buy a flattened roll that will pack into a smaller space. If you cannot find a flattened roll, make one.

Camp gloves. In addition to any other gloves you may have packed, you need a pair of gloves to use around the campsite. Camp gloves are especially useful for handling wood, hot pots, and foil as well as working around the campfire. At times they may be useful for other camping tasks. The first time I heard someone suggest packing a pair of camp gloves, I did not immediately appreciate the value of the suggestion. I knew that gloves were sometimes useful around the campsite, but I didn't think an extra pair was necessary. I thought I could use my riding gloves for these chores. But one day I grabbed a grill and got grease all over my gloves; despite considerable effort to clean the gloves, they are still stained. So I learned this lesson the hard way. Now I pack a pair of leather gloves for handling firewood and grills and poking around in the fire.

Knife or multi-tool. Veteran campers agree that a good knife is an essential piece of gear. In fact, some experts pack two or more knives to be used for different camp chores, such as opening packages, preparing food, and cutting other objects. Experts differ on which type of knife is the best choice. Some prefer fixed-blade knives because they are stronger for cutting heavy objects such as kindling and opening cans. Others recommend a multi-tool or a Swiss Army knife because they have other potentially useful tools and can be packed into a smaller space.

I prefer multi-tools for three reasons: they have always been adequate to meet all of my camping needs, they have other useful tools (e.g., screwdrivers, can opener, and micro-pliers), and they do not require much packing space. I have used these tools so much that I carry three of them. I pack a heavy-duty SwissTool in my tool bag for most camping chores. I carry a Victorinox Tinker Swiss Army knife in my pants pocket and frequently use it for cutting food and opening bottles. It is a medium-size knife that feels comfortable in my pants pocket but yet has a variety of useful blades. I also carry a Leatherman Squirt P-4 in the side pocket of my waist pack or daypack. It is a tiny micro-tool that can be used to work with delicate wires, hooks, or screws. Its knife blade is not very practical for most camping chores, but its other blades, such as small flat-blade screwdriver tips and micro-pliers, are frequently useful.

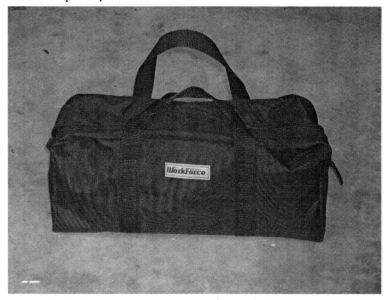

We pack all of our camping tools plus twelve tent stakes in this tool bag.

Before leaving home, inspect your blade edge. If it needs sharpening, use a Smith's knife sharpener (see chapter 1). It works much better than any stones or other sharpening tools I have ever used. First, lay the knife blade on a kitchen counter or tabletop, sharp side up; then grasp the tool in the palm of your hand so that the guard protects your hand and fingers. Pull the tool across the blade edge a couple of times and—magically—your knife is sharp as a razor. This tool makes sharpening a snap and puts a great edge on your blade.

Many campers recommend packing sharpening stones, but stones require extra space and really are not necessary. If you sharpen your knife each time you leave home, you will not need to sharpen it in your campsite. Furthermore, if you do not know how to use a stone, it is of little value. Most people will never be able to get a good sharp edge with a stone because being able to do so takes lots of practice and a special skill.

Small channel-lock pliers. This tool can be used to hold hot pots and grills in addition to making repairs to camping gear.

Small multi-bit screwdriver. Sometimes you may need a screwdriver to make a certain type of repair and the bits on your multi-function tool won't fit the need.

Tent stakes. As discussed in chapter 2, we use six-inch galvanized nails instead of the tent stakes that manufacturers typically provide with their tents. We pack these stakes in our camp tool bag with the ax and other tools so they can be easily located when we are ready to secure our tent and rain fly.

Kitchen Items

We always pack a small cooler, a water bottle for each person, and some paper towels, butane lighters, and garbage bags. We usually need these items regardless of our cooking and eating plans.

Cooler. Although coolers require a relatively large amount of packing space, you need to pack a small one. They come in a variety of sizes. If you were driving a car, you could take a larger one, but since you are riding a motorcycle, you must buy a small six-can, soft-side size. The major reason for including a cooler is so that you can carry a few perishable items such as butter, salad dressing, and cheese. A cooler also allows you to have a couple of cold beverages ready to drink after parking your vehicle for the night.

When shopping for a soft-side cooler, look for a good-quality brand, such as Igloo or Thermos, with good insulation and a continuous inside liner. These coolers typically cost a little more than the economy brands but are usually priced less than twenty dollars. Cheaper brands frequently leak after the ice has melted because their inside liners have sewn seams. When the ice melts, water eventually seeps through the seams and will soak other gear that is packed nearby.

When riding my Electra Glide, we pack this cooler, filled with a few cans of beverage, in our right saddlebag. By packing the relatively heavy cooler in the saddlebag, we keep the weight low and between the two axles, where it has less of an adverse effect upon the bike's handling. If you ride a bike with limited packing space, you could collapse the cooler during travel or pack clothes inside it.

Water bottles. It is always good practice to carry a water container (or two) on your motorcycle, whether you are camping or not. But when you are camping, you definitely need water readily available at your campsite for several reasons: to cook, drink, wash your hands, clean up, brush your teeth, and shave. Having water at your campsite makes all of these chores much easier and keeps you from having to make several trips to the bathhouse or to a water faucet.

Most camping experts recognize the importance of packing water containers and have suggested several different types. Some have recommended military-style or western-style canteens, while others have recommended plastic bottles. Plastic bottles, especially hard plastic bottles such as those made from Lexan, are very durable, convenient, and widely used. However, bottles made with some plastics may pose an environmental hazard. See chapter 10 for more information. One writer recommended a collapsible water bucket because it requires relatively little packing space. Other options include BPA-free plastic bottles such as Nalgene Choice and Camelbak, aluminum water bottles such as those made by SIGG, and stainless steel bottles such as those made by Kleen Kanteen, New Wave Enviro, and L.L. Bean.

Frequently, we just pack one or two twenty-four ounce sports drink bottles (such as those made for Gatorade)—one for each person. They fit in many places, including the drink holders in most cars, the engine guard bags on my Electra Glide, the side pouches of T-Bags, and the side pouches of backpacks. Sometimes when we are staying in a base camp for several days and the water supply is several yards away from our site, we may ride to a nearby store and buy a gallon jug (or two) of drinking water. They cost less than a dollar, and the jugs can be refilled during the length of your camp to reduce the number of trips you will have to make to the water faucet.

Paper towels. Paper towels have a large number of uses around the campsite. When you are cooking, you can use them to dry your hands or soak up grease from fried foods. When you are eating, they can be used as napkins. After the meal they can be used as dishtowels, for general cleanup, or as tissues or emergency toilet paper. We like the Viva brand because it is very strong yet soft enough to be used comfortably as tissues and toilet paper, if necessary. To pack our paper towels, we take individual sheets off the roll, lay about five together, and fold them in half two times. This procedure produces a neat square that packs easily into a waterproof, one-quart food storage bag. We usually pack ten sheets per plastic bag and then pack one bag per person, adding a third bag if we plan to cook in our campsite.

Butane lighters. Be sure to pack a couple of butane lighters. They are handy for starting campfires, lighting stoves, or burning the ends of nylon cord. You need more than one so that you will have a backup when one runs out of fuel. If you are a smoker, you probably pack these automatically, but nonsmokers could easily forget to pack them if they are not on the list of essential items. Do not substitute matches or other fire starters because they typically require more effort and may not work in wet weather.

Garbage bags. Most of the time, you can use grocery bags from your shopping trips as garbage bags. You will typically go to the store soon after setting up your camp and will buy a few groceries and supplies. When you return to your campsite, you will have grocery bags to use as your garbage bags. But occasionally you may need a garbage bag before your shopping trip. To be prepared for these few occasions, stuff a couple of thin plastic grocery bags in with your kitchen items.

Lights

A portable light source is always needed on any camping trip. Perhaps you will need to cook or wash up after dark. Perhaps you will need to find something in your tent. Perhaps you will need to find a small object that dropped on the ground. Perhaps you will have to walk to the bathroom. Or perhaps you want to read a book after dark. All of these tasks would be almost impossible without a good light.

Car campers use a wide variety of light sources such as large fuel-burning lanterns, candle lanterns, and flashlights. But for motorcycle campers, each of these options has important limitations. In general, each of these options is relatively large and would require a considerable amount of packing space. Fuel-burning lanterns and their fuel would require the most packing space and can be messy if they tip over in your saddlebag or have to be refilled. Furthermore, these lanterns should not be used in or around your tent. (Consider the scene in the movie *Wild Hogs.*) Candle lanterns also should not be used in or near tents—plus they don't provide enough light for reading. Flashlights are relatively large and prevent you from using both hands when you are trying to wash dishes, repair a piece of damaged gear, split wood, or read a book. When you have to point the light with one hand, you only have one other hand to hold your book or do your chore.

Without a doubt, headlights are the best choice of lights for motorcycle camping. Miners (who work in total darkness) have used headlights for many years. Headlights allow users to shine light anywhere they look and use both hands. Wearing a headlight in the dark feels so natural that you can easily forget that it is dark.

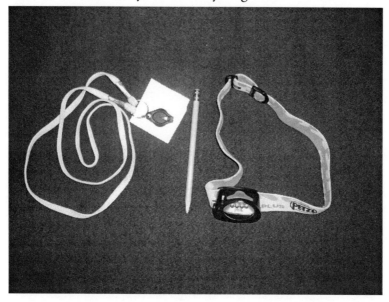

We each wear a micro light on a lanyard and a headlight.

Backpackers have gradually recognized the value of headlights. In fact, headlights have become the choice of most outdoor enthusiasts. Many brands and sizes are available. All of them are preferable to candles and flashlights. Economy lights can be purchased for less than ten dollars but are relatively heavy and provide relatively little light. More-expensive headlights are much brighter and weigh less. Some well-known brands include Black Diamond, CatEye, Petzel, and Princeton Tec. We use Petzel Tikka Plus headlights (thirty-five dollars). They use three AAA size batteries that last for several hours. They are bright enough to read a book or map all night long—if you have difficulty falling asleep. Other brands are even brighter but may cost ten to twenty dollars more.

In addition to our headlights, we each have a backup light in case we need extra light to perform some task (such as replace headlight batteries) or to find something in the dark. Small micro lights with a lock-on switch are excellent choices. They are about the size of two quarters stacked together and provide a considerable amount of light for a considerable length of time. Typically they come attached to a key ring. To make them more practical as a camping light source, get a lightweight lanyard (or a long shoestring) and attach your micro light to the end. Now you can wear the light around your neck and have it handy whenever you need it.

When retiring for the night, place your lights in the corner of the tent next to your head so you can easily find them in the middle of the night and use them to find anything else you may need or walk to the bathroom. Or hang a micro light from the ceiling loop of your tent to have a tent light that will allow you to locate objects in your tent and arrange your gear after dark.

Tarp

Another item on my list of essential gear is a tarp to be used as a dining fly. Many backpackers and other ultra-light campers may not pack a tarp (unless they plan to sleep under the tarp rather than in a tent) because tarps add weight, take up considerable space in their backpacks, and are not absolutely essential. But I believe that a tarp/dining fly should be considered as an essential item for motorcycle camping because it will provide the comfort of having a dry place to sit or stand when it is raining. We have encountered rain on many of our camping trips. A tarp, along with a few sections of cord, a few stakes, and perhaps two eight-foot aluminum poles, can be easily packed on a motorcycle and provide a dry haven for your campsite.

When setting up your camp, tie your tarp to trees and perhaps a pole or two so that it covers your picnic table or so that your table can be moved under it. If it rains, you can sit at the picnic table and read or talk with each other without getting wet. The tarp also provides a handy space where you can stand up to stretch your legs or put on your rain gear or remove it before entering your tent. On sunny days, the tarp provides shade. On windy days, one edge can be dropped to make a windscreen.

A standard eight-by-ten-foot polyethylene (poly) tarp, available in most hardware and discount department stores, costs about five dollars, packs relatively small, and makes a reasonably good dining fly. A better option is to purchase a lightweight nylon tarp from a camping specialty retailer. A nylon tarp will be lighter in weight and will pack smaller than the economy poly tarp. If you buy the ten-by-ten-foot size, you will get a few extra feet of protection. Campmor sells a good ten- by ten-foot nylon tarp for thirty-nine dollars. Other retailers such as Kelty, Equinox, Integral Designs, Moss, and Pacific Outdoor sell much lighter (and more expensive) tarps designed for ultra-light backpacking.

Stuff Sacks

To organize your gear and keep it dry, you will need a few plastic bags or stuff sacks. We pack both of our sleeping bags in a large stuff/compression sack and tie it on the luggage rack with our tent and air mattresses. We sometimes pack our clothes in smaller stuff sacks, especially if we are concerned that they might get wet during the trip. We also need bags to hold our dirty clothes and our clothing and personal items while showering. Other campers use stuff sacks for their air mattresses and other gear. Camping experts have offered many different suggestions regarding the best types of stuff sacks. Some suggest making stuff sacks from old pants legs, while others suggest using plastic garbage bags. Most purchase small nylon stuff sacks sold in most camping supply stores.

We usually pack two different types of bags. We each pack two heavy-duty plastic shopping bags like the ones given by bookstores and up-scale department stores. These bags measure about eighteen inches wide by eighteen inches long but fold into a very small space. We like these shopping bags because they are strong, they have handles, they can be easily replaced when they wear out, and they are free. In camp, we use them as temporary ice coolers, shower bags, dirty clothes bags, and as a means for separating wet and dry clothes when we pack up. Each trip we find different uses for them.

In addition to these shopping bags, we occasionally pack some of our clothing into ultra-lightweight, waterproof, nylon stuff sacks. We like the small sacks made by Outdoor Research. The #1 sack measures six by thirteen inches and sells for twelve dollars. The #2 sack measures seven by fifteen inches and sells for thirteen dollars. Other brands of waterproof stuff sacks include Cabela's, Campmor, Seattle Sports, Sea to Summit, and Therm-a-Rest.

Miscellaneous Items

Several other items may be useful on a camping trip. In some way, each of these items can make your camping trip a little more comfortable or convenient—and they all pack into a very small space. We pack most of these items in our waist pack.

Map and itinerary. Before every trip, prepare a map and itinerary. Then place them in a protective plastic sleeve so they will not get wet if it rains. We use generic one-gallon food storage bags as our map protector, but you can buy better-quality map packets and tank bags from most motorcycle accessory shops.

Cell phone. Do not forget to pack your cell phone. You will need it to touch base with your family and to call for assistance if an emergency situation develops. Be sure it is fully charged before you leave home.

Spare keys. Take a spare set of keys on any long-distance trip. You never know when you may lose your primary set. Without a backup set, you could be stranded for several hours and may even incur the extra expense of a wrecker bill. I like to wear my spare key on a lanyard around my neck.

Spare batteries. Spare batteries do not require much packing space and are nice to have when you need them. We pack an extra set of AAA batteries (for our headlights) and AA batteries (for our camera).

Hand sanitizer. When you are spending a lot of time outdoors, it may not always be easy to find a sink with hand soap to wash your hands. In these cases, a small container of hand sanitizer can be used to clean your hands and prevent many types of bacterial infections.

Lip balm. Constant exposure to sun and wind will make your lips chapped. A small tube of lip balm will make them feel much better.

Sunglasses. Most riders carry or wear a pair of sunglasses, and thus are prepared for long periods outdoors in bright sunlight.

Coffee Supplies

Before concluding, I want to comment on coffee-making supplies. Many campers (including the author of the River City Beemers Web site) consider coffee-making supplies to be essential gear. We, on the other hand, do not consider them to be essential, because we are not coffee drinkers. In fact, we have difficulty relating to the apparent suffering and utter desperation some coffee drinkers seem to experience when they first wake up in the morning. For them, coffee is a necessity of life and coffee-making supplies should be at the top of the list of essential gear. If you are one of these coffee drinkers, ask park rangers or personnel where to find coffee the next morning when you register for your campsite in the afternoon. If necessary, you could add a thermal cup to your list of essential items and pack some coffee bags (similar to tea bags), sugar packs, and cream packs inside. Then all you need to do in the morning is to beg some hot water from a neighbor.

Conclusion

What essential items should be packed for a motorcycle camping trip? Veteran motorcycle campers agree on many items but may disagree about a few specifics. Certainly you need a tent, sleeping system, extra clothing, rain gear, first-aid kit, shower supplies, personal items, tools, sunscreen, insect repellent, lip balm, and some type of light source. Furthermore, I believe you should pack a tarp and few kitchen items, regardless of your cooking and eating plans. Most of these items (except tent, sleeping bag, and mattress) can be packed in your saddlebags with room to spare for a few optional items. My complete list of essential gear for motorcycle camping is presented at the end of this chapter.

After reading this chapter, read other books and articles on camping and motorcycle camping to see how experts agree and disagree. To begin, find a good book on backpacking such as *Lightweight Backpacking and Camping* by Ryan Jordan. Also read *Motorcycle Camping Made Easy* by Bob Woofter and Bill Johns' *Excellent Motorcycle Camping Guide* (www.wetleather.com). Many other books and Web sites on camping provide lists of essential gear with rationale that explains why each item is essential. Find a list you like or make you own personal list and then use it to check off your gear each time you pack for a motorcycle camping trip.

Essential Gear Checklist

Shelter
Tent, ground cloth, doormat, and stakes
Sleeping System
Sleeping bag, mat, pillow, clothes, and stuff sack
Clothing
See clothing checklist.
Rain Gear
Rain jacket, pants, gloves, and gaiters
First-Aid Kit
Large gauze squares (four), elastic bandage, antibiotic cream, and Band-Aids
Burn cream and itch relief product
Ibuprofen, acetaminophen, aspirin, and Benadryl
Sunscreen and insect repellent
Shower Supplies
Shower bag, soap, shampoo, towel, washcloth, and shower shoes
Personal Items
Toothbrush, toothpaste, and dental floss
Razor, hairbrush, deodorant, and cotton swabs
Medicine
Camp Tools
Ax, crowbar, knife/multi-tool, screwdriver, and small channel-lock pliers
Cord (100 feet), duct tape, camp gloves, and tent stakes
Kitchen Items
Small cooler, water bottles, paper towels, butane lighters, and garbage bags
Lights
Headlight and micro-light
Tarp
10 feet by 10 feet (or 8 feet by 10 feet)
Stuff Sacks
Waterproof for sleeping bags, clothes, and gear
Plastic bags (for garbage, shower bag, and dirty or wet items)
Miscellaneous
Map, itinerary, cell phone, spare batteries, and spare keys
Sunglasses, hand sanitizer, and lip balm

5. Clothing

After assembling your essential gear, the next thing to think about is the clothing your companion and you will need for your camping trip. When you begin to address this area, you will be confronted with a major dilemma. You need to pack clothes for two people for several days, and you want to have enough clothes to stay dry, warm, and comfortable during the entire length of your trip. On the other hand, clothing requires a considerable amount of packing space. You want to limit the amount of clothing you pack as much as possible so that you will have space to pack a few optional items such as kitchen gear, a camera, a radio, a hammock, etc.

To resolve this dilemma, you must learn several facts about fabrics and garments. In particular, you must understand the basic set of garments that will allow you to stay dry, warm, and comfortable in a wide range of weather conditions. You must also understand the differences between the various fabrics (e.g., compressibility, drying speed, moisture retention/wicking properties, and heat reflection/absorption) and how these differences should determine your choice of garments selected for any particular trip. And finally, you must understand how weather should guide your choice of garments for a particular trip and how to layer these garments in cool or cold weather to maintain comfort. Once you understand these factors, you will be able to choose your clothing wisely and pack enough to stay dry, warm, and comfortable—regardless of weather—in a relatively small space.

If laundry facilities are unavailable, wash clothes in the bathhouse and hang them on a line. This was our site at the Smokemont Campground, Great Smoky Mountains National Park.

I did not understand the unique properties of different fabrics for many years. One shirt may have been white and another black, but otherwise they seemed pretty much the same. And although I thought I understood the principle of layering, I really did not. As a result, I selected clothes in a random and haphazard manner. Sometimes the clothes I selected for a trip were appropriate, but most of the time they were totally inappropriate for the weather conditions. As it turned out, most of my clothes were made of cotton, and cotton garments are poor choices for most camping trips.

Perhaps the best example of packing the wrong clothes occurred several years ago when I rode my Low Rider up to Wisconsin. It was mid-May and I had a break between spring and summer semesters. The weather had been warm in Alabama for several weeks, so I decided to pack a few clothes and ride up to Wisconsin to visit a friend. I packed about six heavy short-sleeved T-shirts and a couple of long-sleeved T-shirts. I was wearing a pair of jeans, and I packed another pair. I also packed several pair of underwear and socks. I did not pack long underwear because it was May and I thought it was warm enough to leave them at home. I also packed a thirty-dollar rain suit in my saddlebag.

I hit the road early Sunday morning. The weather was beautiful, and everything went smoothly for about 275 miles. But soon after I rode through Evansville, Indiana, it started to rain, and the rain soon became hard and steady. My front wheel slung water from the road up to my chin, and it seeped down inside my rain suit. My clothes were getting soaked. I tried to push on but had to stop several times because the rain was so heavy I could not see. I had picked Danville, Illinois, as my destination for the day and was determined to get there. For a hundred miles I slogged on through alternating waves of light and heavy rain. After I passed through Terre Haute, the rain began to subside, but the temperature dropped dramatically.

Finally, after many hours battling the rain, I arrived at my motel in Danville. All of my clothes were soaked, so I tried to dry them as best as I could. I hung some on the shower rod, some on the towel racks, some on chairs, some on lamps, and some on the TV. I spread a few more items on the second bed. I assumed they would all dry before morning.

The next morning, the temperature had dropped to about forty-five degrees with a strong northerly wind. My clothes were still slightly damp, but I was anxious to get on the road. I did not understand how the dampness of my clothing would combine with the cool weather and the wind to quickly lower my body temperature. I put on two short-sleeved T-shirts, two long-sleeved T-shirts, and my rain suit. I thought the layers would keep me warm. But soon after I got on the highway, my clothes began to feel wet and cold, and my body began to chill. After about thirty minutes on the road, I had to stop at a convenience store to warm up. The bathroom had a hot-air hand dryer, so I opened up my rain suit and used the dryer to blow hot air inside my pants and jacket to dry my clothes. After about fifteen minutes of warming up, I got back on the road but soon began to feel damp and cold again. It seemed like my clothes were getting wetter as I rode. To make a long story short, I had to stop every forty to fifty minutes to re-dry my clothes and warm up during the 350 miles to Wisconsin. What a miserable ride. Even after I arrived in Wisconsin, my clothes continued to feel damp every time I put on my rain suit. At the time, I did not have a clue as to the reasons my clothes felt so damp and my body kept chilling down. I just thought that feeling cold was the normal result of riding in cold weather.

After suffering through this experience, I wondered what I could have done differently. I knew that people in Wisconsin and other northern states camped and rode snowmobiles during the winter and so I was relatively certain there was a way to ride and camp in cool weather conditions while staying dry, warm, and comfortable. I began to read more about clothing designed for outdoor activities. I wanted to learn as much as possible so I could avoid similar experiences in the future. The information presented in this chapter summarizes my findings.

My research led me to the conclusion that my misery stemmed largely from the fact that I made at least three serious mistakes when selecting my clothes for the trip. First, all my garments were made of heavy cotton fabric. Cotton would help me stay cool on hot summer days but was a poor choice for layering in cold weather because it absorbed moisture (rain water and body perspiration) and held the moisture close to my skin. In the cold weather, that moisture chilled my body. In technical terms, heavy cotton fabrics do not *wick* moisture away from the body. After several minutes in cold windy weather, your skin will begin to feel noticeably damp and your body will quickly chill.

The second mistake I made was not packing good thermal underwear. At the time I did not know the difference between good fabrics and poor fabrics, and had I bought a set of long underwear, I probably would have bought cheap cotton underwear from a discount department store. I did not understand that cheap cotton skivvies provide very little warmth in cold weather.

The third mistake I made was using a cheap, *non-breathable* rain suit. Although the suit was waterproof, blocked the wind, and held some body heat in, it also made me sweat and prevented moisture from evaporating. As a result, the moisture from the rain and the moisture from my perspiration were trapped inside the suit and close to my body. The wet clothing combined with the cool temperature and the lack of insulating garments to quickly chill my body.

Desirable Qualities

When selecting clothing for lightweight camping trips, you should look for garments that have several important features.

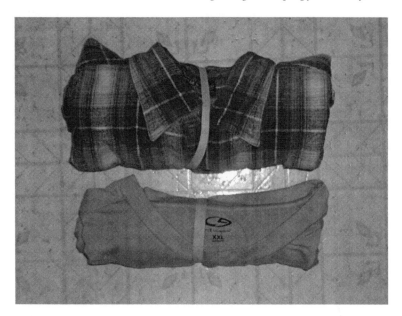

The polyester shirt (bottom) packs into a much smaller space than the cotton shirt (top).

Compressibility. Perhaps your first consideration should be compressibility. When you plan a two-up camping trip, you must pack sufficient clothing for two people into a very small space. To accomplish this task you must look for garments that can be compressed into a small space. When you examine different garments in the store, you will discover that some are made with fabrics that can be compressed into a very small space while others are made with fabrics that cannot be compressed much. For example, shirts and jackets made from polyester compress into a much smaller space than similar garments made from heavy cotton, flannel, or denim. Although these polyester garments may feel much thinner and lighter than cotton garments, they will keep you just as warm—if not warmer—with much less bulk. A pair of pants made from thin nylon will compress into about half the space of a pair of blue jeans made from heavy cotton—and the nylon pants are just as tough and abrasion resistant. Similarly, underwear and thermal underwear made from silk, polyester, or polypropylene will compress into a much smaller space than those made from cotton, and they will keep you warmer than their cotton counterparts. By selecting compressible garments, you and your backseat companion will be able to squeeze a lot of clothing into a relatively small area.

Fast drying. A second important factor to consider when selecting clothing for a motorcycle camping trip is drying speed. Pack as many garments as possible that will dry quickly. Clothing frequently gets wet on motorcycle camping trips. Sometimes it gets wet from the rain; sometimes it gets wet from sweat; sometimes it gets wet from swimming, canoeing, or other water activities; and sometimes it gets wet because you accidentally packed wet items next to dry items. On long trips, you may have to wash some clothes. On almost every camping trip, some clothes will get wet. Therefore you need garments that will dry quickly without having to use a commercial dryer. Garments made from wool, silk, polyester, and nylon will dry much faster than garments made from cotton and rayon. You can hang these fast-drying garments on a clothesline in your campsite and expect them to be dry in a few hours. When you pack fast-drying garments for your trip, you will not have to pack as many garments because you will be able to wash more often.

Moisture wicking. Moisture-wicking garments pull moisture away from the skin and spread it throughout the fabric where it can easily evaporate. Garments with good moisture-wicking properties are made with fibers (usually polyester or nylon) that do not retain moisture (i.e., sweat). The fibers are woven together to make a fabric that will soak up the moisture but not hold it. Once the moisture has been soaked up, it is free to evaporate quickly from the fabric. Since your body moisture evaporates rapidly, you feel dry and warm. Backpackers and other people who enjoy outdoor activities have learned that the best underwear and the best thermal layer garments (i.e., long underwear) have good moisture-wicking properties. In fact, the primary distinction between good thermal-layer garments and poor garments is their relative ability to wick moisture away from the body. In contrast, cotton fibers do absorb moisture and hold it for a relatively long time. When air or wind blows against the moist cotton, it makes your body feel much cooler.

To be comfortable in a wide range of weather conditions, motorcycle campers should look for garments made from fabrics with good moisture-wicking properties. In general, garments made from polyester, nylon, wool, and silk, have good moisture-wicking properties, while garments made from cotton and rayon have poor moisture-wicking properties. As you might expect, garments made from good moisture-wicking fabrics will be more expensive than other clothing and will be more difficult to find. You will probably have to shop at stores that specialize in clothing for outdoor activities or go to the Web.

If you do not have any camping and outdoor specialty stores in your hometown, you can visit my Web site, www.motorcyclecampingtips. com, and look in favorite links for the Web sites of several different vendors. Or you can refer to the end of chapter 1 for a list of well-known Web retailers.

Heat absorption/reflection. Dark-colored garments absorb the sun's radiant energy and make you feel warm, while light-colored garments reflect the energy and help keep you cool. If you are riding on cool days, black or dark garments will make your body feel warmer. If you are riding on hot summer days, white, khaki, or other light-colored outer garments that reflect the sun's radiant energy will make your body feel cooler.

Insulation. Wool, fleece, down, and synthetic fibers are popular materials used to make insulating garments. These garments are usually used to keep your body warm in cool winter weather. When camping in the spring, fall, or winter, consider wearing or packing an insulated vest or jacket that will hold in your body heat if the temperature should drop. Insulated garments can also sometimes help to keep you cool in hot summer weather. For example, wool socks help insulate your feet from the hot pavement in the summer as well as from the cold weather in the winter.

Breathability. The term "breathability" is usually used in reference to rain gear, boots, and tents. Some rain jackets, for example, are said to breathe—they allow body heat and sweat to escape but yet are waterproof. Other rain jackets do not breathe—they trap body heat and sweat inside the garment where it will eventually soak the wearer's clothing. See the rain gear section in chapter 4 for additional information. Similarly some boots breathe, while others do not. And some waterproof tent materials breathe, while others do not. You may occasionally see the term breathability used in reference to other garments, especially outerwear used for insulation from cold weather. For example, many hikers like to wear fleece as an insulating garment because it breathes so well. It retains body heat but allows sweat to quickly escape and evaporate, thus keeping the wearer dry even when engaged in strenuous physical activity.

Fabrics and Their Properties

Many fabrics can be used to make clothing. If you are like most people, you may not pay much attention to the fabric unless it requires special cleaning methods. However, if you want to become proficient in motorcycle camping, you must become familiar with the names of several common fabrics and understand their strengths and limitations as related to staying dry, warm, and comfortable. Once you are familiar with the names of different fabrics and their general properties, begin to look at the tags on clothing so you can learn to recognize garments made of each different fabric.

Cotton. This material grows as a plant in hot dry climates such as the American South. It feels comfortable to the touch and is easy to clean. It readily absorbs and retains moisture and as a result will produce a cooling effect on the body. In hot summer weather, some cotton garments are desirable for their cooling effect, but in cooler weather, cotton garments should be avoided because they do not keep you as warm as garments made with other fabrics.

In hot summer weather, motorcycle campers should consider wearing lightweight, light-colored cotton pants and T-shirts. These garments reflect the sun's radiant heat and hold in body moisture. This moisture, combined with the wind from riding a motorcycle, makes the body feel cooler. Furthermore, some manufacturers are now treating their cotton fabrics with other products to increase their cooling properties. Shirts made with *Cool Max*, for example, are good examples of such garments.

When I am riding or camping on very hot summer days with temperatures in the nineties, I wear a white long-sleeved cotton T-shirt to help protect me from sunburn. Before heading out on a ride, I soak the T-shirt with water from my water bottle. When riding, the wet shirt combined with the wind produces a cooling effect that is comparable to being in an air-conditioned car. When the shirt dries out, I soak it again.

Many motorcycle riders wear heavy cotton garments such as blue jeans, black cotton shirts, flannel shirts, and denim jackets all year long, but these garments are poor choices for motorcycle campers who must spend all day and all night outdoors. In particular, these garments make you hotter on hot days and colder on cold days. They do not retain body heat well, they take a relatively long time to dry when they get wet, they do not wick moisture away from the body very well, they require a lot of packing space, and they provide no protection from the rain. In every respect, these heavy cotton garments that are so popular among many motorcycle riders are poorly suited for long periods of time outdoors and should be avoided in most weather conditions.

Another reason to reduce the number of cotton garments in your wardrobe is their eco-impact. Environmentalists frequently point out that traditional methods used to grow cotton require a considerable amount of chemicals (pesticides and herbicides) that cause disease and even death to farm workers and other people who may inhale or ingest large amounts of them. In fact, environmentalists claim that cotton requires more chemicals than any other plant and have urged consumers to boycott clothing and other products made from cotton. In response to these environmental concerns, a few clothing manufacturers are now making their garments from organic cotton produced without using potentially harmful chemicals. See chapter 10 for more information about this topic.

Silk. Silk comes from threads in cocoons made by silkworm larvae. It is very comfortable, lightweight, warm, and compressible. Furthermore, it has high moisture-wicking properties and thus is a good choice for thermal underwear and other garments.

Wool. This fabric can be made from the fur of several different animals but is usually from sheep. Wool fibers have a crimped nature that creates small air pockets that trap body heat and prevent cool outside air from cooling your skin. In addition to serving as a good insulator, wool is very breathable and can keep the wearer warm even when it is wet. In the past, it has been used to make blankets, sweaters, and military clothing. For many years, wool garments were unpopular because they often felt scratchy.

Today wool and wool blends are much more comfortable to the touch. In particular, merino wool is the softest wool available and claims to have superior heat-retention and moisture-wicking properties. It has become the wool of choice for backpackers and should be strongly considered by motorcycle campers. This wool comes from lambs in a few select countries such as New Zealand. It is available in several different weights and is used to make socks, underwear, thermal layers, and T-shirts. Some backpackers claim that T-shirts made from merino wool are cooler in hot desert weather than shirts made from cotton. Motorcycle campers certainly should consider wearing wool socks regardless of weather conditions and other wool garments in cool weather. Wool undershorts and T-shirts may be more expensive than garments made with other materials but will keep you much warmer in cool weather.

Polyester. This is a synthetic plastic fiber made from petroleum. It is used to make very compressible fast-drying garments, especially underwear and athletic apparel. It can be blended with cotton to produce very comfortable shirts and blouses. Whether blended with cotton or not, polyester garments retain body heat well, dry quickly, and are able to keep the body dry. Polyester can be manufactured to have excellent moisture-wicking properties. It is used to make a broad range of shirts, shorts, and fleece. It is an ideal fabric for camping garments because it requires little packing space, dries quickly, and usually helps to keep your body dry and warm.

Several special polyester fabrics have been created to enhance specific properties. For example, *Dri-Release* is a polyester fabric that is combined with small amounts of cotton or wool to make garments with high moisture-wicking properties that remain after several washings. It is used to make a wide range of athletic apparel. *Capilene* is a polyester fabric made by Patagonia with at least 50 percent recycled polyester. It is very soft and reportedly much warmer than cotton. It is used to make thermal underwear and is available in four weights. Capilene 1 is the lightest weight, designed for warm or mild weather; Capilene 2 and 3 are mid-weights, designed for cool weather; and Capilene 4 is the heaviest weight, designed for the coldest weather. *MTS* is a polyester fabric used by REI to make underwear and thermal underwear. The initials stand for moisture transport system. It is available in three weights: lightweight, mid-weight, and heavyweight. It is very compressible and wicks moisture well. *Power Dry* is a very lightweight polyester fabric made by Polartec and used to make thermal underwear.

Fleece is also made from polyester. Fleece garments are frequently used as insulating layers instead of wool. Polartec is the best-known maker of fleece garments. This company typically manufacturers fleece in three weights: Polartec 100 is relatively lightweight; Polartec 200 is a mid-weight; and Polartec 300 is a heavier weight. Polartec sells the Classic 200 as the standard insulating layer. In addition to holding in body heat well, fleece is water resistant and fast drying, but it is not wind resistant. In cool windy weather, many outdoor enthusiasts wear a wind-resistant jacket (such as your rain suit) over their fleece garments to keep the wind from making the wearer cold. The Gore Company has recently developed a new windproof membrane called

WindStopper that can be added to fleece to make windproof garments that provide all-purpose weather protection without requiring an outer shell. Examples of fleece garments with the WindStopper membrane include the WindStopper Tech jacket or vest by Mountain Hardwear, the Pamir WindStopper jacket by The North Face, and the Crystal jacket by Outdoor Research.

Polypropylene is a synthetic polyester thermoplastic fiber. It is extremely lightweight and consequently very compressible and fast drying. Its makers claim that it is one of the warmest of all fabrics, with the highest moisture-wicking properties. In the past, it had a tendency to develop an odor after brief use, and sometimes it retained the odor even after washing. A new manufacturing process recently developed using silver threads reduced its odor-retention properties. It has many different uses, but the primary use of interest to motorcycle campers is to make sock liners and thermal underwear.

Nylon. This is a thermoplastic thread made from coal, water, and air. It is highly abrasion resistant and dries quickly. Nylon is used to make pants, shorts, and water-resistant or waterproof jackets and pants. It can be made in several degrees of thickness that are designated by graduated denier numbers. The denier number refers to the weight, in grams, of nine thousand meters of fiber. In practical terms, garments with lower denier numbers are made from smaller-diameter yarn and are therefore thinner and more compressible. For example, the Rain Shadow lightweight rain jacket sold by Patagonia is made of fifty-denier, ripstop nylon. Garments with higher denier numbers are thicker and more durable. One limitation of nylon garments, like polyester garments, is that they can melt if exposed to high temperatures. You must be careful around hot exhaust pipes and campfires.

Several different types of nylon fabrics have been developed to enhance certain properties. For example, *Thermax* is a nylon fabric that retains body heat well and wicks moisture away from the body. It is used to make thermal underwear and socks. *Supplex* is a type of nylon developed by DuPont that has a soft cottony feel, is highly abrasion resistant, is breathable, and dries quickly. It can be treated with a thin coat of Teflon to make it windproof. It is used to make shirts, pants, and athletic warm-up suits. REI, for example, makes pants for outdoor recreation from Supplex. *Cordura* is a heavier type of nylon designed to be especially tough and abrasion resistant. It is the tough stuff. It is used to make backpacks, boots, and military equipment. It is also used by AEROstich to make their Darien riding jacket and pants. The Darien light suit uses 160-denier nylon, and the regular suit uses 500-denier nylon.

Spandex. Spandex is a synthetic fiber comprised of at least 85 percent polyurethane. It is reportedly stronger and more elastic than rubber. It also has high moisture-wicking properties and is used to make a wide variety of athletic and outdoor clothing (such as swimsuits, shirts, tank tops, compression shorts, underwear, socks, and jeans) that fit snugly. *Lycra*, made by DuPont, is the best-known brand of spandex. Motorcycle campers who want tight-fitting clothing for hiking, swimming, and other recreational activities may want to consider a few garments made with Spandex.

Rayon. This fiber is made from regenerated cellulose collected from bamboo or pine tree pulp. It is sometimes called artificial silk. It is compressible, smooth, and comfortable, and it holds body heat in well if the wearer is relatively inactive in cool weather. Its primary limitation is that it does not dry as quickly as other fabrics and thus is a poor choice when activity might produce body moisture. The term *Viscose* refers to a procedure for making rayon but frequently is used as a synonym for rayon. It is very soft, comfortable, retains body warmth, and is very compressible. But it is a poor choice for summer riding and camping because it does not dry very fast and it absorbs the sun's radiant energy, making it extremely hot in direct sunlight. It is a poor choice for cool-weather riding and camping because it retains moisture and reacts to wind by chilling the body.

Cocona. This is a new fabric made from coconut shells. It is used to make shirts. According to the manufacturer, this fabric has high moisture-wicking and fast-drying properties, plus it is odor resistant.

Leather. Many motorcycle riders like to wear their leathers because they are abrasion resistant and have the reputation of protecting the wearer from "road rash." But garments made from leather are hot in the summer and provide little warmth in cool weather. In addition they are bulky and difficult to pack, especially on two-up trips. If you feel strongly about wearing your leather jackets and pants, you must accept the fact that you probably will have to wear them the entire trip, regardless of weather conditions.

Fabric Treatments

Most breathable waterproof garments (such as those made with Gore-Tex) are also coated at the factory with a *Durable Water Repellent (DWR)* to help shed water. This factory-applied DWR will gradually lose its water-shedding property after several uses. As the garment is exposed to more dirt and oil, it will begin to feel moist and "clammy" when wet. At first, washing the garment on a gentle cycle and drying it with low heat will restore the water resistant qualities. But after the garments have been repeatedly worn for several months and exposed to additional dirt and oil, washing will no longer restore their waterproof qualities. At this time, you must reapply a DWR product (by washing or spraying) to make it waterproof again. Nickwax is perhaps the best-known DWR product. Nickwax offers several different washes and sprays for different types of clothing and gear. One product, for example, is made for fleece, while another product is made for rain gear and yet another is made for boots. Other brands of DWR treatments include CampDry, Deluge, Rainoff, Rivive-X, Scotchguard, and Techtron.

In addition to DWR treatments, several other special treatments are sometimes applied to cotton, polyester, and nylon garments to enhance certain desirable properties. Some treatments are designed to facilitate cooling effects, while other treatments are designed to facilitate warming effects. Examples of these treatments include *Freshguard* (a treatment applied to Dri-Release garments to reduce odor retention), *VaporWick* (an advanced proprietary finish applied by The North Face to polyester and nylon garments to enhance the moisture-wicking properties of the fabric), *CoolMax* (a fabric treatment specially designed for polyester and nylon yarns to provide comfort and enhance moisture-management properties), and *Teflon* (a treatment applied by some manufacturers such as Ex Officio to make nylon garments more resistant to stains and wrinkles).

Weather Consciousness

An important principle for choosing the best set of clothes for a particular trip is to be aware of the predicted weather conditions and become knowledgeable about how predicted weather should direct your selection of clothing. To begin this discussion, think of camping weather as falling into three general temperature ranges:

- Hot. Daytime high temperature is predicted to be in the eighties or nineties, and nighttime temperature is predicted to be no lower than seventy. This would be typical summer weather in the deep south United States.
- Mild. Daytime high temperature is predicted to be in the seventies or low eighties, and nighttime temperature is predicted to be in the sixties or fifties. This weather would be typical summer weather in the north and mid-western United States.
- Cool. Daytime high temperature is predicted to be in the fifties or sixties, and nighttime temperature is predicted to be in the forties or thirties. This would be typical early spring and late fall weather in many states.

When planning a camping trip, select your garments on the basis of these general weather patterns. If the weather is predicted to fall somewhere between two of these patterns, prepare for the cooler temperature.

Hot-weather camping. Choosing clothing for hot-weather camping is relatively simple. You need several changes of lightweight light-colored cotton shirts, socks, and underwear. Garments made from moisture-wicking materials would be ideal but are not necessary. A pair of lightweight cotton pants could be worn for three days before washing. A pair of quick-drying polyester shorts would be good for casual wear, sleeping, and swimming. Do not forget to pack a set of lightweight thermal pants and shirt for sleeping. Select clothing that compresses into the smallest possible space so that you will have space to pack other gear.

*My typical riding and camping attire includes a loose-fitting Marmot Precip jacket
(under which I can add as many layers as needed), a pair of cotton Columbia ROC
pants (to which I can add thermal underwear and rain pants), and a pair of Wolverine
boots (with a pair of wool socks).*

Mild- and cool-weather camping. Choosing clothing for mild- and
cool-weather camping is a little more complicated. In mild and cool
weather patterns, the best way to keep warm is to wear several layers of
clothing. If you select your clothing with care, you will be able to stay
as warm with a few lightweight layers as you would if you wore a heavy
parka. To help you understand the principle of layering, first think of
clothing as belonging to one of five layers:

- Underwear. These are your shorts (boxers or briefs), your
  underwear T-shirts, your socks, and for women, your bra.
  The primary function of this layer is to control the moisture
  and odor-causing bacteria that can develop between your legs,
  under your arms, and, for women, under your breasts. In cool
  weather, a secondary function of these garments, especially the
  T-shirt, is to help hold in body heat. These garments should be
  snug fitting and, in both cool and hot weather, should be made
  of materials that wick moisture away from your body.
- Thermal layer. This layer goes over your underwear. It is
  commonly known as long underwear, but most outdoor experts
  refer to it as the inner or base layer. It consists of a close-fitting
  pair of pants and a close-fitting long-sleeved shirt. This layer

should hold body heat in and allow moisture, or sweat, to wick away from your body where it can easily evaporate. When buying your thermal underwear, look for garments made from wool, silk, or polyester—not from cotton.

- Middle (or outer) layer. This is the next layer of clothing. In cooler weather this will be your middle layer. Typically it will be a loose-fitting shirt and pair of pants made from materials that wick moisture away from your body. In warm weather it will be your outer layer and will include pants, shorts, short-sleeved T-shirts, and possibly a long-sleeved T-shirt made from light-colored cotton or other materials that trap moisture and thereby provide a cooling effect on the body.
- Insulating layer. These are the garments you will need when the temperature drops. Their primary function is to hold body heat in and to insulate your body from the cool outside air. The best insulating materials are down, wool, fleece, and synthetic insulation. Until recently, wool garments were too bulky for motorcycle camping, so fleece garments have become the primary insulating layer for many riders. One of the most popular insulating jackets is The North Face Denali made from Polartec 300 fleece. If the temperature is predicted to drop down to the low thirties, you may wish to consider wearing a jacket filled with synthetic or down insulation. A synthetic-filled jacket would be the best choice in rainy, wet weather, and the down jacket would be the best choice in very cold weather.
- Outer layer. Your final layer should be a hard-shell jacket and pants that will protect you from rain and wind, especially in cool weather. They should be spacious enough to accommodate several layers of clothing. Rain gear is typically made of nylon with a DWR waterproofing treatment. Ironically, many motorcycle riders purchase cheap thirty-dollar rain suits after spending hundreds of dollars on leather jackets and pants. When it rains, they have a bulky set of leathers that will quickly get soaked, that do not keep them warm, that make them feel miserable when wet, and that cannot be packed because they require so much space. A more practical approach would be to forgo the leathers and spend your money on a good-quality breathable nylon rain suit that you can use as your all-purpose riding suit in a wide range of weather conditions.

Garments Needed

The list of garments needed for a motorcycle camping trip is relatively short. In addition to your rain gear discussed in chapter 4, you will need up to three pairs of socks, underwear, and T-shirts because you will probably want to have a clean pair every day. Packing three sets of these garments will allow you to go four days before having to wash clothes. On the other hand, you may not need to pack a second pair of pants or outer shirts because you can wear these garments two or three days before washing. You will always need a thermal shirt and pants, regardless of the weather. You may not use this thermal layer on many trips, but you definitely want to have it handy whenever the temperature drops. Depending upon the weather and your destination, you may also want to pack a pair of shorts that could be used as a swimsuit. If your trip will last more than three days, pack a small travel-sized plastic bottle of Woolite and wash your clothes as needed. Many campgrounds have laundry facilities, but if they do not, you can always wash your garments in a sink or small basin and dry them either in a commercial dryer or on a clothesline in your campsite. A short checklist of garments you will need is provided at the end of this chapter.

Boots. Most experts recommend a good pair of boots for any type of camping. Boots provide good ankle support when you are walking on uneven surfaces such as the rocks, roots, and landscape timbers that are typically found in campgrounds. They provide more protection from sharp or heavy objects and other hazards that are more likely in an outdoor camping environment. They also provide more warmth in cool weather.

If you ride a motorcycle, you probably already know the importance of wearing boots and probably do so whenever you ride. Unfortunately many motorcycle riders buy boots for their looks rather than for their comfort. As a result, these riders frequently complain that their feet hurt after a few hours of riding or walking.

If you want to camp on your motorcycle trips and be able to walk around the park after setting up your camp, you should buy a pair of good comfortable boots that can serve both as riding boots and as general-purpose camping/hiking boots. After purchasing your boots, and especially after wearing them for a year, consider replacing the insoles with an aftermarket set, such as those made by Superfeet, to make your boots more comfortable.

Good-quality work boots that can be purchased in many local shoe stores frequently are comfortable for camping, walking, and short-distance hiking. They are usually priced between $50 and $150 a pair. I like lightweight, ankle-high work boots that have a non-slip (Vibram) sole. In the hot summer, I want a pair of boots that are not waterproof. I do not want a pair made with a waterproof, breathable membrane because these boots will cost more and will feel hotter than other boots. On the other hand, in the winter I do want boots with a waterproof breathable membrane because they will keep my feet warm and dry. Some well-known brands of work boots include Chippewa, Dunham, Durango, LaCrosse, Red Wing, Thorogood, Timberline, and Wolverine. My favorite summer riding boots are Wolverine Marquette boots. I am very pleased with their comfort. Before taking a camping trip, I apply a waterproof treatment such as Nikwax or CampDry.

Good-quality hiking boots usually cost a little more than work boots but have many additional features. In particular, they usually are very comfortable. They are designed for walking long distances over many hours and for several days in a row. Prices of good hiking boots typically range from about a hundred dollars to over four hundred dollars a pair. Hiking experts usually divide hiking boots into four categories: trail runners are low cut and lightweight; lightweight summer boots can be low or ankle cut and provide more stability on uneven surfaces; mid-weight boots are heavier and provide more stability for carrying heavier packs; and heavyweight mountaineering boots are the heaviest boots. Popular hiking boot makers include Danner, Kayland, Keen, Lafuma, La Sportiva, Lowa, Merrell, Montrail, The North Face, Scarpa, REI, Timberline, and Vasque.

Motorcycle campers probably would enjoy either the lightweight or mid-weight boots. Some are all leather, while others have synthetic fabric in a few areas to enhance breathability. Cool-weather boots typically have a Gore-Tex or similar membrane liner to make them waterproof. Robin bought a pair of Vasque boots about ten years ago and quickly fell in love with them. She wore them as casual everyday wear until they wore out. Recently she bought a pair of Keen boots and is very pleased with them. I frequently wear a pair of Merrell Chameleon Stretch lightweight shoes in the summer and a pair of Keen Growler waterproof boots in the winter. Both are very comfortable.

Occasionally your boots will get soaked. Despite all precautions, it will happen. Although you applied a waterproof product such as Camp Dry or Nikwax and although you have a pair of gaiters, you will get caught in heavy rain or fall into a mountain river or do something else that will soak your boots. To dry them without causing damage to the materials, remove the insoles, stuff them with crumpled newspaper, hang them upside down if possible, and allow them to air dry. Do not attempt to speed up drying by placing them near a campfire, in an oven, or in hot direct sunlight.

Socks. Lightweight wool or polyester hiking socks are the best socks to pack. They compress into a relatively small size, dry quickly, have good moisture-wicking properties, insulate your feet from both hot and cold temperatures, and help keep your feet dry and comfortable. If you are caught in a rain shower, wool socks wick less moisture into your boots and will keep your feet warm even when they are wet. Avoid cotton socks in all weather. They retain moisture, provide little padding for walking, and when wet with sweat or rain, can make your feet very uncomfortable. In addition to the socks you wear the first day of your trip, pack up to three pair of socks and plan to wash them every two to three days. I like socks made by Smartwool, but several other brands (e.g., Columbia and Wigwam) are very popular.

Underwear shorts. Regardless of the predicted temperature, your underwear should be made of compressible, fast-drying, moisture-wicking fabrics. In addition to the shorts you wear the first day, you will need one pair for each day up to three days. If your trip is longer than three days, plan to wash your underwear every two to three days. Good underwear is made from polyester and wool. I like REI MTS underwear and can say that it keeps me dry and provides considerable warmth.

T-Shirts. Use the predicted temperature to guide your selection of T-shirts. If the weather is going to be hot, select shirts or tops made of light-colored lightweight cotton or CoolMax. Do not pack shirts made of heavyweight cotton because they do not compress well and thus require too much space. Avoid black and other dark-colored garments because they absorb heat. If mild weather is predicted, you may want some cotton and some polyester shirts. If cool weather is in the forecast, select shirts and tops made of polyester, polyester/cotton blends, or wool. Some excellent choices for warmth and moisture-wicking properties include shirts by The North Face, Under Armour, REI, and Champion. In addition to the shirt you wear on the first day, you will need one shirt for each day up to three days.

This Champion polyester shirt was reasonably priced and serves as a good mid-layer.

Thermal underwear top and bottom. Always pack a set of thermal underwear—shirt and pants. They should be made from silk, wool, or polyester and not from cotton. If possible, wear them when you sleep to help protect the inner lining of your sleeping bag from absorbing your body oil. Some well-known makers of thermal underwear include Patagonia, REI, and Smartwool.

Long-sleeved shirts. Depending on weather conditions, pack one or two long-sleeved T-shirts. These shirts can be used as a middle layer in cool weather or as outer garments in milder weather. In hot weather you may wish to consider a white long-sleeved cotton shirt to protect you from sunburn, but in mild and cool weather, select polyester garments instead. Polyester garments will be very compressible, will wick moisture better, and will dry faster than cotton. Long-sleeved polyester T-shirts made by Champion (sold by Target Stores) are good choices. These shirts are remarkably warm, compressible, fast drying, and reasonably priced.

Shorts or pants. After arriving at your campsite, you will likely need an extra pair of shorts or pants for casual camp wear and possibly for participating in recreational activities. You may also need clothing for midnight bathroom trips and a change while washing or drying your other pants. The specific garments to pack for a particular trip will depend upon the weather and the activities you will likely undertake. For example, in hot summer weather you might want to pack one or two pair of compressible nylon or polyester shorts—one for casual camp wear and one for swimming. In mild summer weather you may want to pack a second pair of pants. If you wanted to pack a pair of pants, you have several options. Some people prefer nylon hiking pants with legs that zip off; others like military fatigue pants that are roomy and have lots of pockets; others like lightweight painter pants that are cool and roomy; and others like scrub pants that compress into a very small space. In cool early spring or late fall weather, you may want to pack a pair of fleece pants (rather than cotton sweats), which will keep you warm and wick moisture away from your body.

Support top. If your trip is going to last over two days, women should pack a supportive garment that could be worn in a variety of situations. If possible, select a supportive sport halter or shelf bra that could be used for swimming and casual wear. It should be made from compressible, fast-drying, moisture-wicking fabrics such as those used to make athletic tops. Avoid bras made from cotton and those made with excessive padding and wires that make them less compressible.

Knit hat. Regardless of predicted weather, always pack a knit hat for sleeping. You may not need it on hot summer nights, but you never know when the temperature will drop a little more than expected. Putting on a knit hat in the middle of the night is the fastest way to get warm.

Insulated vest or jacket. In cool weather, pack (or wear) an insulation layer over your long-sleeved shirt and under your rain shell. For many years, wool sweaters were used to provide insulation from the cold. They retained body heat well and did not absorb moisture. Then fleece emerged as the preferred insulating material. Fleece had the same desirable properties of wool, plus it felt more comfortable to the skin and it did not require dry cleaning. Polartec is perhaps the best-known maker of fleece. Many companies (e.g., The North Face, Patagonia, and REI) use Polartec fleece to make their insulated shirts and jackets. Some companies have recently begun making extremely compressible insulating vests and jackets with down and synthetic fibers. For example, NAU makes a down shirt ($185) that reportedly compresses to the size of a grapefruit. Other makers of down and synthetic vests and jackets include Arc'teryx, Mamot, Mountain Hardwear, Outdoor Research, Patagonia, and The North Face.

Baseball cap. A cap can be used to shade your eyes on sunny days and keep the rain out of your face and can help you stay warm on cool days.

Assemble Your Wardrobe

Now that you have a better understanding of the specific garments you will need and of various fabrics and their properties, you and your companion should look through your closets to find the garments that are best suited for motorcycle camping trips. Start collecting now, while you still have time to purchase missing garments before your next camping trip. In particular, look for garments made of polyester, polyester blends, and nylon. The odds are that you will find a few garments suited for motorcycle camping, but not all of them. When you find garments suitable for motorcycle camping, pack them together with your camping gear so you can quickly grab them when you decide to take a trip.

Start with your underwear. Do you have compressible, moisture-wicking shorts and T-shirts? Do you have wool socks? You will need one set to wear on the first day of your trip and up to three more sets, depending on the length of your trip. If you don't have these garments, start a list of things to purchase. Once you have inventoried your underwear, move to the thermal layer. Do you have lightweight long thermal underwear—top and bottom—made from a moisture-wicking fabric? If you live in the northern United States, you probably do. But if you live in the South, you likely do not have them. If you do not have them, purchase them. You should pack them for every trip—even in hot weather—and wear them if possible when sleeping. If you want to camp in early spring, late fall, and winter, you may need a heavier set of thermal underwear.

After determining whether you have good thermal underwear, look in your closets for middle (or outer-layer) and insulating garments. Look for garments made from polyester or nylon that can be used in a wide range of weather conditions. Next decide whether you have a good insulating vest or jacket made from fleece, down, or synthetic insulation. If not, consider purchasing one. Finally, take a close look at your rain-and-wind-protection suit. Is it a good breathable suit? If not, consider purchasing one.

You may be able to find a limited selection of compressible, fast-drying, moisture-wicking clothing suitable for motorcycle camping in discount department stores, but a much better selection can only be found in specialty camping or outdoor outfitter stores. In large cities, you should have several stores from which to choose. If you live in a rural area, you may wish to consider mail order retailers. See chapter 1 for a list of well-known retailers or visit my Web site, www. motorcyclecampingtips.com. Some of the better known brands of garments designed for outdoor activities include Arc'Teryx, Campmor, Columbia, Mountain Hardwear, The North Face, Patagonia, prAna, REI, and Sierra Designs. Materials used in these clothes are special blends of cotton, polyester, Lycra spandex, and other micro fiber materials designed to be lightweight, fast drying, moisture wicking, and breathable.

As the date of your trip approaches, check again to be sure you have assembled all the specific garments you will need for your trip. Lay them out on the bed to be sure you have everything you will need. After your trip, wash your clothes and repack them for the next trip.

Packing

When you are ready to pack your clothing, try to squeeze as much into as small a space as possible. To pack your clothes, fold each garment about eight inches wide and then roll it as tightly as possible. Once so rolled, stuff it into a small container. Most backpackers and lightweight campers use small nylon stuff sacks, plastic trash bags, or stuff sacks made from legs of worn-out pants.

We sometimes use stuff sacks, but we usually use containers that have other uses around the campsite. I stuff a lot of my clothes into a small fleece pillow cover and stuff the rest of my clothes along with some of my personal items small soft-side cooler and a small laundry bag. When staying in a base camp, we use the small soft-side cooler to hold additional food, and we use the laundry bags to hold our dirty clothes When Robin rides with me, we stuff her clothes and personal items into her pillow cover and an ultra-light day pack.

Regardless of the container, try to squeeze in as many items as possible. By following this fold, roll, and stuff packing strategy, you will be able to pack all of your clothes plus your shower supplies, medicine, books, personal music players, and personal hygiene kits into a relatively small space.

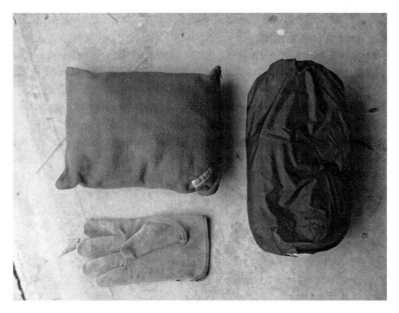

All my clothes for a ten-day trip to Wisconsin were packed into this pillow cover and stuff sack (the glove is pictured to show relative size).

Washing

If your trip will be several days long, you may have to wash your clothes. Be sure to pack a small travel-sized bottle of Woolite. If your campground has a laundry, put a few drops of Woolite into the washing machine. If a washing machine is not available, wash your clothing in a bathroom sink. Regardless of how you wash them, garments made from fast-drying polyester or nylon fabrics can dry on a line in a few hours. Be sure to keep them under a cover, such as your tarp, when you leave your campsite or go to bed so they are protected from a summer shower or nighttime dewfall.

Conclusion

What clothes should be packed for a motorcycle camping trip? Packing all the clothing needed for two people for several days into a relatively small space is one of the most difficult challenges of motorcycle camping. To master this challenge, you must become more knowledgeable and conscious of fabrics and their properties.

I believe that you should pack no more than three sets of basic garments (underwear, T-shirt, and socks) plus a few other garments. Most if not all of your garments should be made from polyester and nylon rather than cotton. If your trip will last longer than three days, pack a small travel-size bottle of Woolite, wash your garments in a bathroom sink, and hang them on a clothesline in your campsite.

After reading this chapter, learn more about clothing that is best suited for outdoor activities such as motorcycle camping. You may want to read *Lightweight Backpacking and Camping* by Ryan Jordan and *The Backpacker's Handbook* by Chris Townsend. Also visit Web sites for REI (www.rei.com), Campmor (www.campmor.com), and Mountain Gear (www.mountaingear.com). Once you have acquired this knowledge and purchased a few items, you will be ready to pack the most appropriate set of clothes for any trip, regardless of its length and predicted weather.

Clothing Checklist

Boots	Worn when riding motorcycle
Socks	1 pair per day; max 3 pair
Underwear shorts	1 pair per day; max 3 pair
Short-sleeved T-shirts	1 per day; max 3
Thermal pants and shirt	1 set
Support top	1 for women
Long-sleeved T-shirt	Max 2, if cool
Shorts or pants	Max 2, depending upon the weather and activities
Knit sleeping cap	1
Baseball cap	1
Rain jacket	1
Rain pants	1 pair
Waterproof gloves	1 pair
Gaiters	1 pair
Insulated shirt or jacket	1, if cool
Neck gaiter	1, if cold

6. Meals

After packing your essential gear and clothes, you now must turn your attention to cooking and eating. You must make decisions regarding the amount of food, kitchen supplies, and kitchen gear you will pack on your bike and the type of meals you want to eat on your trip. The decisions you make in these areas will be very different from the decisions typically made by backpackers.

Backpackers and other ultra-light campers have little choice in this regard. They typically camp in wilderness areas where they have no access to stores. Consequently, they must pack all the food they will need during the entire trip. Typically they pack dehydrated foods that can be mixed with hot water a few minutes before eating. Furthermore, they usually pack the stove, fuel, pots, pans, plates, and utensils needed to prepare and serve the food. When mealtime comes, they collect water from nearby streams and then use special equipment to filter and purify it. Next they boil the water and mix it with their dehydrated food. Sometimes they boil their water on campfires, but most of the time they use ultra-light stoves and pots. Their meal choices are obviously fairly limited.

147

Jim starts a fire to cook our supper at 29 Dreams Motorcycle Resort near Birmingham, Alabama.

Motorcycle campers, on the other hand, camp in state parks or national forests and are able to ride to stores or restaurants anytime to purchase food and supplies. As a result, motorcycle campers have many more options regarding their meals. They can pack less food and kitchenware before leaving home and will typically cook fewer meals in their campsite. Frequently, they ride all day long and eat some, if not all, of their meals in restaurants. After arriving at the campsite and setting up their tent, they can ride to the nearest store or restaurant to buy the food and supplies needed for the next meal or two. When they set up a base camp for a few days, they may wish to buy fresh foods plus a few more supplies and cook several meals in their campsite. Having easy access to stores and restaurants means that motorcycle campers are able to enjoy a wide variety of good-tasting food without having to pack many groceries or a lot of kitchen gear or supplies.

Authors of other references on motorcycle camping have offered many different opinions about the best way to cook on camping trips. Their recommendations include using a wide range of gear such as sterno stoves, alcohol stoves, two-burner stoves, various pots and pans, Sierra cups, military-style mess kits, canteens, thermal cups, tablecloths, pasta strainers, spices, Italian salad dressing, dehydrated foods, and even an inflatable kitchen sink. Some recommend foods that must be prepared and packed at home before departing on the trip. Their meal suggestions include dehydrated foods, pre-portioned meals, jerky, power bars, trail mix, military MREs, and even meals that can be cooked on an exhaust pipe while riding.

Our approach is different. We pack almost no food before leaving home. Instead we prefer to use our valuable space to pack clothes and optional gear. Each day during the trip, we decide what we want to eat and are not constrained by having to eat food packed on the bike. We find this freedom to choose our meals a very enjoyable part of our motorcycle camping vacation. If we feel like eating in a restaurant, we can do so without feeling guilty about wasting food packed on the bike. If we feel like cooking in the campsite, we ride to the nearest grocery store, decide what food appeals to our tastes that particular day, and buy it. Some days we like to cook meat (such as steak, pork chops, or chicken) with potatoes and vegetables. Other days we like to buy packaged meals (such as red beans and rice, spaghetti, or Hamburger Helper) and cook them with a little meat and fresh vegetables.

When we first began camping on motorcycle trips, we experimented with several different combinations of kitchen gear. After a few trips, we formulated a strategy for deciding what to pack for a particular trip. Regardless of the type of trip we are taking, we always pack the basic kitchen items discussed in chapter 4: a small, soft-side cooler, one water bottle per person, a few paper towels, two butane lighters, and a couple of garbage bags.

After packing these basic items, we consider the type of trip we are taking and then decide upon one of three cooking and eating plans. Plan A—usually selected when our trip will be a series of overnight camps or a short base camp trip—is to leave kitchen gear at home and buy all of our meals in restaurants or sometimes buy cold foods, such as fruit, raw vegetables, and sandwiches, in grocery stores. Plan B—usually selected when our trip will be a few days long and good weather is predicted—is to pack a small set of kitchen utensils and cook a few meals on our campfire or charcoal grill. Plan C—usually selected when we plan to stay in a base camp several days—is to pack a backpacker's stove, pots, and pans and cook most of our meals in our campsite. Regardless of the plan we select, we know we must ride to a nearby restaurant or grocery store each day to buy the food and supplies we will need for the next meal or two.

Before embarking on a trip, we discuss the cooking and eating plan we want to adopt. Each plan requires that we pack specific gear on the bike before leaving home. In deciding upon the plan that best suits our trip, Robin and I must consider our space limitations, priorities, and the length of our trip. For example, if we are taking a long weekend trip to the Florida or Alabama Gulf Coast beaches, we do not need any cooking gear. We use our packing space for other items and plan to eat seafood in restaurants as often as possible.

If you ride a bike with limited packing space, like my Low Rider, you will have very little space for packing kitchen gear in your T-Bag after packing your tent, sleeping bags, and most of your clothes. You probably would adopt either Plan A or Plan B. On the other hand, if you ride a touring bike, like my Ultra, you would have much more room to pack kitchen supplies in your saddlebag and could adopt Plan C if you wanted to cook several meals in your campsite.

Restaurants and Grocery Stores

If you are unable to pack food and kitchen gear or if you do not want to cook in your campsite, you can still eat good meals on your trip. During the day, you will likely to be on the road and will probably buy your food in convenience stores, grocery stores, and restaurants. In the evening, after setting up your campsite, you will have several options. For example, you could find a good restaurant located near your campsite and have a hot, well-prepared meal without having to worry about cooking and cleanup. Or you could pick up a pizza, fried chicken, hamburgers, or other fast food and bring it back to your campsite and relax with a beer or two. If you prefer eating healthy foods, you could go to a local grocery store and purchase foods that require no cooking. Examples include fresh fruit, fruit cups, fresh vegetables with dip, pre-packaged salad, cheese, yogurt, granola bars, potato chips, pudding, yogurt, rolls, and cookies. You could buy chicken salad, tuna salad, or deli sliced meats such as ham or turkey and add some lettuce, pickles, and cheese to make sandwiches.

If your campsite has a grill, you could buy a bag of charcoal and some steaks, bratwurst, hamburger meat, pork chops, chicken breasts, or fish and grill them. You would not need anything other than your camp gloves, a pocketknife, a couple of forks, and perhaps some aluminum foil to prepare and eat these foods cooked on the grill. If you think you might cook bratwurst or hamburgers on your trip, pick up a few individual servings of ketchup, mustard, and mayonnaise, such as the ones available in fast food restaurants.

If you do not have enough room in your small cooler for milk, juice, pop, or beer overnight, just use your bag of ice. Discard some of it and place your beverages in the bag of ice. Your plastic bag cooler should keep your beverages and food cool until the next morning.

If you typically need a cup of coffee to get you going in the morning you should determine the best place to find morning coffee the night before, when you are thinking clearly. One way to get such information is to ask the ranger or clerk at the campground registration desk. Some campgrounds make coffee each morning for campers. If not, you may have to ride to a convenience store or restaurant.

Utensils

If you want to cook a few meals in your campsite (plan B or C), you will need some utensils to assist with food preparation and eating.

Cooking utensils. A few basic tools will allow you to cook a wide range of meals on a campfire or stove. The first important tool is a pair of tongs. Tongs pack into a very small space and can be used to pick up meat on the grill and aluminum foil packets in the coals and to flip pancakes. A second useful tool is a nylon mixing spoon. It can be used to stir food in disposable aluminum pans or pots and to serve food when fully heated. Mixing spoons are preferable to serving spoons because they pack into a smaller space: they are smaller and flatter. I prefer nylon spoons rather than wood or metal spoons because they are durable, lightweight, and will not damage nonstick surfaces on pots and pans. A third useful tool is a small can opener. A good one for motorcycle camping is a military style can opener that folds into the size of a comb (some are even smaller). It requires a little effort and skill but opens cans efficiently. These can openers can be purchased for a few cents in any camping gear store or discount department store. Some campers prefer to use large knives to open cans, but we prefer a can opener because it is safe and easy.

Eating utensils. You will need a spoon and perhaps a fork to eat your food. Normally, you will not need an extra knife if you carry a pocketknife. You could use inexpensive metal utensils purchased from discount department stores or you could use lightweight backpacking utensils found in camping specialty stores. Backpacking utensils are typically made from Lexan, stainless steel, or titanium. For example, Tekk makes Lexan utensils that are small and lightweight. Snow Peak makes a titanium spoon with three or four fork tines called a *spork*. GSI makes a similar Lexan utensil called a *foon*. For several years, we used cheap metal spoons and forks, but we eventually converted over to Lexan backpacking utensils.

Our utensil set includes tongs, a can opener, and a nylon mixing spoon.

Dinnerware

If you plan to eat a few meals in your campsite, you could pack a few dinnerware items before departing or purchase disposable items in a store after setting up your campsite.

Cups. Good items to add to your kitchen gear, if possible, are cups or mugs that can be used for drinking both hot and cold beverages and for measuring water to mix with packaged foods (spaghetti sauce or red beans and rice). We probably use our mugs more than any other item of kitchenware. We use them to discretely drink a beer or two after parking the bike for the night, to drink a glass of milk before going to bed, to drink a cup of hot chocolate in the morning, and to drink our milk or juice for breakfast. Many people will need their cups to consume coffee or tea.

As you begin to look for camping cups, you will find many different designs. Some are made from polypropylene (plastic) while others are made from acrylics, Lexan, stainless steel, or titanium. Before selecting one particular design, you should consider five important questions. First, will the cups accommodate both hot and cold beverages? Many do, but hot beverages can damage some cups. Second, will they hold a reasonable amount of beverage? We prefer cups that hold at least twelve fluid ounces (one and a half cups) of liquid. Third, can they be packed into a reasonably small space? Ideally one cup should nest inside the other so that together they only require the space of one cup. Fourth, are they designed to keep beverages hot or cold for a reasonable length of time? In other words, are they insulated? And finally, are they comfortable to use? Cups should be cool enough to hold in your hand and to sip from—even when filled with a hot beverage.

Sierra cups are very popular among backpackers. They typically are made from stainless steel or titanium and have wire handles that can be attached to the outside of backpacks with carabiners. They are smaller at the bottom than at the top and thus nest together well. However, they have at least three important limitations. They are relatively small and typically hold only six to eight fluid ounces; they are not insulated and thus do not keep beverages hot or cold very long; and they are sometimes too hot to hold when filled with a hot beverage.

Plastic or metal-lined thermal cups designed like tumblers without handles would be another choice. These cups typically hold at least twelve fluid ounces. They also keep beverages hot or cold for a relatively long time and are comfortable to hold even when filled with hot beverages. We used this type of cup for several years. The main problem with them is that they are large and bulky. They do not nest together and thus require a considerable amount of valuable packing space.

In 2008, Snow Peak produced a double-wall Titanium mug that holds sixteen fluid ounces and has a folding handle. Two of these mugs will not nest together, but we discovered that one of them can be combined with a tall, insulated thermal mug and the two mugs will nest together well. Together they only occupy the space of one thermal mug. REI has a similar titanium mug that holds ten fluid ounces. The one limitation of these titanium mugs is their price. They cost about forty dollars.

Several other types of cup designs can be found in outdoor outfitter stores. For example, Flatworld makes Orikaso cups and dinnerware that fold flat when traveling. Guyot Designs makes Squishy cups and bowls from food-grade silicone that can squeeze into very small spaces.

Bowls and plates. You will also need some bowls and/or plates to hold your personal serving of food. You could go to the store after setting up camp and buy some inexpensive paper or Styrofoam bowls or plates that could be thrown away after your meals. Or you could pack some dinnerware and plan to wash it after every meal.

You can purchase inexpensive durable plastic dinnerware from discount department stores or wedding supply stores. Better yet, buy backpacking plates or bowls in camping supply stores. Examples of such dinnerware include Sea-to-Summit X-Bowl made from food-grade silicone with walls that collapse for travel, REI Chefware made from Lexan, GSI dinnerware made with baked enamel, Seattle Sports nylon pocket bowls, Flatworld Orikaso plates and bowls that fold flat, Snow Peak dinnerware made from titanium, and several different brands of stainless steel plates or bowls.

Food Staples

If you plan to cook any meals in your campsite, you will also need a few basic staples. For example, you will need some salt, pepper, and perhaps garlic salt. These basic seasonings help to flavor many different foods. If you wanted to pack these spices before leaving home, you could pick up a few individual serving packs, such as those available in many fast food restaurants, or you could purchase a small backpacker's salt/pepper shaker that requires very little packing space. Or you could wait until you have set up your campsite and then purchase picnic-sized salt and pepper shakers when you purchase your food and supplies.

Butter (margarine or olive oil) is a useful cooking item. It can be used to prepare aluminum packet meals and to make other casseroles or sandwiches. We prefer real butter and use a lot of it when we cook. When we decide to take some butter on a trip, we pack one and a half sticks in a small clean soap dish and then pack the soap dish in our small cooler. If we need more butter during the trip, we can buy small amounts in most grocery stores.

As many cooks have noted, Italian dressing is a useful cooking staple. It can be used as a dressing for prepackaged salad and as a seasoning for foods such as grilled chicken or fish. If possible, pack this item at home before departing. You can purchase small servings of dressing in grocery stores that have delis or you could pour a small amount into a medium-sized plastic travel container and pack it in the small cooler. The reason you want to pack it at home is because Italian salad dressing is typically sold in large containers that cannot be easily packed on a motorcycle. If you bought such a bottle after setting up camp, you probably will have to throw away a lot of dressing when the time comes to pack up and continue your trip.

Other staples you may want to pack for motorcycle camping trips include ketchup, mustard, and mayonnaise. You may need these items if you are cooking hamburgers, bratwurst, or other sandwiches. Try to find small individual serving packets like the ones available in fast foods restaurants. They require very little packing space.

You may want to consider packing some hot chocolate, tea, or coffee packs. We like hot chocolate, especially on cool evenings and mornings, so we usually pack a few packets along with a few small packets of creamer. If you prefer tea or coffee, you may want to pack individual tea bags or coffee bags that can be steeped in hot water, along with some sugar and creamer packets. If you do not have a pot, you can pour some water into a disposable aluminum loaf pan and place it on the grill or near the fire. Or you can just beg some hot water from a neighbor.

Finally, do not forget liquid soap for cleanup. You will not need much, because you will likely cook few meals and will have only a small amount of dishes to wash. So pack a small travel-sized bottle of liquid dish soap to wash your utensils and perhaps your hands. In a pinch, you can use it to wash your bike.

After setting up your campsite, you will probably ride to the nearest store and purchase a few more supplies with your food items. The specific supplies you will purchase depends upon what you want to eat and whether or not you will be staying in your campsite for a few days or packing up the next day and moving on.

First of all, you will always need ice to chill beverages, butter, and salad oil. We buy ice every afternoon and use it to chill food for the evening and next morning. If we buy several items that cannot fit into our small cooler, we can use the ice bag to make a temporary cooler. We empty a little ice from the bag and place our food and drinks in the bag. The plastic ice bag will keep drinks and food cool until the next morning.

Most of the time, we will also buy a small or medium bag of Match Light charcoal by Kingsford. If we are staying in our site for several days, we will buy a larger bag. We prefer this specific brand because it lights very easily without having to use lighter fuel. It may be a little more expensive than other brands, but we believe it is worth the extra expense. It can be found in most grocery stores, discount department stores, and convenience stores. It packs smaller than a bundle or two of wood, it cooks more efficiently, and it makes your food taste better. We use the charcoal for cooking meals and sometimes for starting our campfires.

Finally, you may want to consider firewood. If you plan to cook food requiring a hot fire or a long cooking time, you may need to buy firewood and cook on a campfire. Few things smell better than food or coffee cooking on a campfire. And if the nights and mornings are cool, nothing feels better than sitting or standing by a warm campfire. You may occasionally be able to scavenge enough wood for a campfire around the campground. Most of the time, you will not be able to find enough wood for a fire and will need to buy your firewood from the campground office or from a nearby store. If you plan to have a good fire for several hours, you will need two or three bundles and may have to make two or three trips to get them all back to your campsite. On warm summer nights, you may decide to forgo your campfire since it will not be necessary and requires a lot of effort. Some environmentally conscious campers forgo campfires altogether because gathering wood from the forest and repeatedly scorching the ground can cause a cumulative negative environmental impact.

Aluminum Foil Cooking

If you would like to cook in your campsite but do not have much space to pack kitchen gear, you still can cook a wide range of food with a few utensils and some aluminum foil or disposable aluminum pans.

The basic items needed for foil cooking are sheets of aluminum foil (we prefer twelve-inch, heavy-duty aluminum foil), a pair of tongs, spoons, butter, salt, and pepper. Sometimes we also purchase one or more disposable aluminum pans. These items require virtually no packing space but allow you to cook and eat an unbelievable number of delicious meals over hot charcoal or a campfire.

Robin places potatoes, onions, butter, salt, pepper, and a little water on the foil.

Sometimes we pack a few sheets of foil before leaving home, but most of the time we purchase a small roll in a grocery store after setting up our campsite. When packing foil, tear off sheets approximately sixteen inches long, lay groups of four together, and fold them into six by eight-inch squares. This size is perfect for cooking a single serving of food, and you will need four sheets to cook for two people.

Disposable aluminum pans come in a variety of sizes and can be purchased in almost any grocery store. They are economical and have lots of uses around the campsite. Small loaf pans can be used to heat water for hot chocolate, tea, or coffee. They can be used to warm up canned vegetables, chili, beef stew, and soups. Furthermore, they can also be used to heat water for cleaning up after a meal. A pie pan can be used as a frying pan for bacon and eggs in the morning. You could use disposable pie pans as plates or bowls to hold your individual food serving.

If you cannot find disposable aluminum loaf pans and want to warm up canned food, you can shape four sheets of foil together to make a leak-proof boat or tub. Fold the edges of the two sheets together around the top. Place the boat on the grill, open a can of your favorite food, such as vegetables, chili, or beef stew, pour the contents into the boat, and heat. When it is warm, serve your food from the grill. Be careful. The boat is flimsy and could easily spill if you try to pick it up.

Once you have served one portion, use your camp gloves to carefully pick up the boat and use it as a bowl for the remaining portion.

A simple way to cook with foil is to put a sheet on the grill and cook foods such as bacon, eggs, or fish. Another way to cook with foil is to make "packet meals." The packet-meal method allows you to cook many different foods, including potatoes, onions, squash, broccoli, carrots, zucchini, rice, apples, shrimp, and even eggs. Simply cut the food into small bite-sized pieces, place single pieces of foil on a flat surface shiny side up, place individual portions of the food in the middle of the foil, and add several pats of butter or margarine, salt and pepper, and two spoonfuls of water or a couple of medium ice cubes. For corn on the cob, soak the corn in water, add butter and a little salt, and wrap it in the foil. For ground beef and potatoes, omit the butter.

Several Web sites (e.g., Reynolds Aluminum, Kraft foods, and the U.S. Scouting Service) describe aluminum-foil cooking and provide dozens of recipes. When you find an appealing recipe, print a copy and stash it with your camping gear. When you start packing for your next trip, you will see the recipe and it will serve as a reminder. The more you cook with foil, the easier it gets.

Most Web sites recommend the "drugstore fold" for wrapping food. The steps are relatively simple: 1) bring the sides of the foil up over the food and hold together, 2) tightly fold the two sides together three or four times, and 3) at each end, bring the two side edges together and fold three or four times. When finished, you should have a tightly sealed packet that does not leak. Once the packet has been sealed, reinforce it by rolling a second piece of foil around it. When placed on hot charcoal or wood coals, the packet serves as a pressure cooker to cook the food quickly and seal in its flavor.

To cook the food, place the packet on the coals or on a grill above a low campfire and wait until the food begins to sizzle. When it begins to sizzle, start your cooking time. Broccoli takes about five minutes to steam, so turn it after three minutes. Corn takes about eight to ten minutes, so turn it after about five minutes. Potatoes and onions take about forty minutes, so turn them three or four times.

Once the food has been cooked, open the package very carefully. The metallic foil will be hot. The steam inside will be even hotter and can easily burn you. You may wish to use your camp gloves, tongs, and a spoon to help open the packets. If the food is not fully cooked, reseal the packet and cook it a little longer. Once it is cooked, you can eat the food right out of the foil. No plate or bowl is necessary. When finished, cleanup is a snap. Just throw the foil in the trash and wash your spoons.

The Reynolds Company also makes a product called Hot Bags. If you find Hot Bags in the store, you may want to buy them. They make campfire cooking much easier than cooking with regular foil because the bags are specifically designed for charcoal or campfire cooking. One large bag holds enough food for two people. A package of bags comes with directions and recipe suggestions.

A complete meal includes meat, potatoes, onions, and butter peas in a disposable loaf pan.

Cookware

If you want to cook some meals with a backpacker's stove, you will need at least one pot and perhaps a small frying pan. Over the past several years, I have used army mess kit and several different backpackers' pots only to discover that the pots were impractical for cooking many meals—especially when riding with a companion. One day, I noticed a one-and-a-half-quart pot sitting on a friend's stove and realized that this size would be perfect for two-up motorcycle camping. It is relatively small to pack but large enough to cook food portions for two. Shortly thereafter, I went to a local discount department store and bought an aluminum pot with a nonstick surface and removed the handle. We used this pot on several camping trips and were generally satisfied with its usefulness.

After a few years, we decided to invest in more compact backpackers' cookware. Eventually we purchased a GSI aluminum cook set with two relatively large pots from a camping supply store, and we have been very pleased with them. These backpacker's pots are better suited for motorcycle camping than my discount department store pot because backpacker pots weigh less, nest together to make a relatively small set, and distribute the heat from a backpacker's stove more efficiently.

Pots. In general, pots are made from stainless steel, aluminum, or titanium. Each material has its strengths and limitations. For example, stainless steel is usually cheaper than the other materials but does not distribute heat very efficiently. Thus these pots can easily scorch your food. Aluminum distributes heat well but is relatively heavy and not very durable; it adds to your packed weight and may be easily dented or scratched. Titanium is extremely lightweight and allows water to boil rapidly, but it is more expensive than the other materials and does not distribute heat as well as aluminum. Although titanium is great for boiling water for dehydrated meals, it is a poor choice for meals that require long simmering times. Food will easily scorch in titanium pots.

Backpackers prefer titanium because of the weight savings, but we prefer aluminum because it allows us to simmer food without scorching and sticking. We especially like pots with nonstick surfaces because they are easy to clean.

The size of a pot is an important factor to consider. Backpackers typically prefer small one-quart pots that can be packed into a small space. These pots can boil water for dehydrated foods but are not large enough to prepare larger meals, especially for two people. Several years ago, I bought a small boiler (one-quart) and pan (two-and-a-half cups) set because it could be packed into a small space. But after a few trips, I realized that this set was too small to cook many foods, especially when riding two-up. Now I occasionally pack it when riding solo if I only want to boil water for hot chocolate, oatmeal, or ramen noodle soup.

This small cook set allows you to boil water to re-hydrate backpacker's meals, oatmeal, hot chocolate, or coffee. The two pots and fuel canister nest together to make a small package.

Frying pans. To increase the diversity of foods you can cook, you will also need a small frying pan—one that is large enough for cooking portions for two but small enough to pack. We concluded that we needed a nine-inch nonstick frying pan. This size is large enough to brown ground beef for spaghetti or to cook several pieces of bacon but small enough to pack in my saddlebag. Our first frying pan was an aluminum pan purchased from a discount department store. We removed the handle and used a dishtowel or a small pair of pliers from my tool set to handle it when it was hot. Later we decided to purchase a complete camping cook set that included two frying pans.

Complete cook sets. Several manufacturers now offer backpacker's cook sets with a combination of pots, pans, and dinnerware that all nest together into a small space. A good example is the GSI Extreme cook set. It has two relatively large pots and two relatively large lids that can be used as frying pans. The entire set fits into a mesh bag that packs neatly into a saddlebag. We selected this set for our trips and believe that it suits our needs better than any other set we have used.

Several other kitchen sets are available depending upon your particular cooking and eating style. For example, the GSI Dualist Cook

System seems like a good choice for motorcycle campers who do not need a frying pan. This set includes a 1.8-liter pot, two insulated cups, and two bowls. It also has space to pack a fuel canister and a small stove. Another good set is the MSR BlackLite Gourmet Cook Set, which includes two pots (1.5-liter and 2-liter), and a frying pan. And yet another set is the GSI Backpacking Cook System, which includes a 2-liter pot, an 8-inch frying pan, two bowls, and two insulated mugs. Other good sets that include cups and bowls are the GSI Bugaboo Camper cook set, the GSI Pinnacle, and the MSR Quick2 System.

Our GSI set with MSR plates and bowls nests together and makes a compact set.

Additional items. In addition to your stove, cup, pot, and frying pan, you will need a few other items to make your camp kitchen complete. For example, you will need a dishcloth and one or two dishtowels. We use these to wash and dry our dishes and also to hold hot pots. We pack these items with our motorcycle camping gear so they are handy when we begin packing for our next trip. Another item that will make your kitchen set complete is a plastic tablecloth. We usually pack our tablecloth, regardless of our cooking and eating plans. Many campground picnic tables have splinters that could injure you or damage your gear. Furthermore, tables may be covered with dirt, mildew, or bird droppings. A tablecloth gives your table a much smoother, cleaner, and more inviting surface. We tie the tablecloth on to our table with one of our five- or ten-foot cords.

Finally, you may want to consider a cutting board. You could survive without one, but a cutting board helps you cut meat, vegetables, and fruit without cutting your tablecloth. A recent article in *Backpacker* magazine suggested using the flexible plastic cover from a three-ring binder as a cutting board. You can cut it to any size that fits your packing scheme. If you plan to cook often, you should consider this small luxury for your cook set.

Unnecessary items. When you read other books, magazine articles, and Web sites on camping, you will see that other authors recommend several kitchen items that we have omitted. Some authors recommend clamps to hold your tablecloth in place on windy days, but clamps require valuable packing space and are unnecessary. Instead use heavy objects to weight down the corners of the tablecloth. On windy days, tie one or two long cords around your tablecloth. If necessary, use duct tape. Other authors frequently recommend packing spatulas, but we have discovered that we can cook anything including hamburgers and pancakes without a spatula. Granted, having a spatula would be nice, but you can flip burgers and pancakes with your tongs or with a spoon or two. The list of other unnecessary items includes waterproof matches (pack butane lighters), pot grippers (use your dishcloths or the pair of pliers from your tool set), SOS pads (use non-stick cook wear), pasta strainer (use a pot lid), fire starter (use Match Light charcoal), and an inflatable kitchen sink (use a pot from your cook set). You might have room to pack some of these items if you are riding solo or pulling a trailer, but you probably will not have space to pack them if you are riding two-up—and they really are not necessary.

Backpacker Stoves

Backpackers and other ultra-light campers with extremely limited packing space frequently pack extremely small, lightweight stoves. Some ultra-light stoves specifically made for backpackers include titanium alcohol stoves that weigh as little as one ounce (but also require relatively heavy fuel containers) and wood stoves that weigh about a pound and burn small amounts of twigs and leaves that can be found near the campsite. The major limitation of these stoves is their relatively low heat output and relatively longer boils times. Since these stoves require longer time to prepare meals, many backpackers prefer to pack more efficient propane or multi-fuel stoves.

When I first started motorcycle camping, I bought a single-burner Coleman propane stove from a discount department store. I was familiar with Coleman stoves because I had owned four of them over my lifetime and knew that they were reliable stoves. The stove I bought was relatively large but at the time, I did not know that smaller stoves were available. At first it seemed small enough to pack. Most of my trips at the time were solo trips and I did not have to pack clothing and gear for a second person. I just had to pack the burner and base. Later, after setting up camp, I could purchase small propane bottles in almost any store. This stove was reasonably priced, convenient, and worked well.

When I began riding two-up, I realized that the burner plus the cylinder base required too much valuable packing space. I began looking for other options and quickly discovered backpacking stoves that pack into a much smaller space. Generally speaking, there are two types of backpacking stoves: multi-fuel stoves and canister stoves.

Multi-fuel stoves. Multi-fuel stoves are designed to burn white gas but also burn gasoline or kerosene. They have small refillable bottles. Whenever the gas runs out, just refill the bottle, preferably with Coleman lantern fuel that can be purchased in most discount department, grocery, or convenience store. You will also need a small funnel to fill the bottle. Frequently you will spill a little gas when you refill the bottle. After filling the bottle, you must pump air into it before you can light the stove. If other fuels are unavailable, you can use gasoline from your motorcycle gas tank. A simple way to get the gasoline out of your gas tank is to buy a turkey baster from a grocery store and use it to draw the fuel and put it into your fuel bottle.

There are three primary advantages of these multi-fuel stoves: 1) they use fuel that is easy to find, 2) they work well in cold weather, and 3) they work well at high altitudes. But they also have their limitations: 1) they can be messy because of accidental fuel spillage, 2) they need to cool before refilling the bottle—which could be a small problem if you run out of fuel in the middle of cooking, 3) they typically are more expensive, and 4) they require regular cleaning and maintenance. Typically they range in price from $80 to $160. One example of this type stove is the MSR WhisperLite. Other examples of multi-fuel stoves are the Coleman Exponent Fyrestorm Ti, which can also burn canister fuel and the MSR Simmerlight.

The MSR WhisperLite backpacker's stove can burn several different fuels.

We use a MSR Pocket Rocket stove attached to a fuel canister.

Canister stoves. The second type of backpacker's stove burns a propane mixture that comes in a pre-filled canister. When you want to use the stove, simply screw the canister onto the stove and light it. When the fuel runs out, unscrew the empty canister and screw on the new canister. There is no mess. These stoves are typically less expensive, ranging in price from forty to ninety dollars. One example of this type of stove is the MSR Pocket Rocket. This stove folds into a package that is smaller than a twelve-ounce drink can, but it works like a small blowtorch. It can boil water in a few minutes. A small four-ounce fuel canister sells for about four dollars and lasts for several hours. Other examples of canister stoves include the Coleman Exponent F1 Ultra-light, the Snow Peak Lite Max, the Primus ETA Power system, which includes a boil pot and windscreen, the MSR Reactor system, and the Jetboil GCS system.

The primary limitation of canister stoves is the difficulty of finding replacement fuel canisters. Fuel canisters are not sold in most grocery stores or discount department stores. They can only be found in a few stores that specialize in camping gear. So if you use this type of stove, you must always pack a second canister of fuel or you could run out in the middle of a trip and be unable to continue cooking. Another limitation of these stoves is that they typically work poorly in cool weather and at high altitudes.

Regardless of the stove you decide to purchase, its cooking efficiency will be adversely affected by wind. On windy days, you should make a windscreen. One way to make a windscreen is to shape two sheets of aluminum foil into a circle around the burner.

Cooking with a backpacker's stove. Having a backpacker's stove, a pot, and a frying pan makes it easy to cook almost anything you want, except baked items. For example, you can quickly boil water for hot chocolate, tea, or coffee. You can boil water to heat a variety of frozen foods, and you can cook macaroni, spaghetti, or any other pasta. Other food items that can be prepared with a backpacker's stove and pot are chili, soup, and beef stew. You could also use the stove to warm up a variety of canned foods.

One of our favorite meals is red beans and rice. We buy a box of red beans and rice and then add some butter, one medium chopped onion, one large chopped green bell pepper, and about a half package of Polish Kielbasa cut into small bite-sized pieces. We simmer all the ingredients for about twenty minutes and have a great tasting meal. Another favorite meal is fettuccini alfredo. We boil water to cook the noodles and then add milk, butter, and McCormick's seasonings. After the fettuccini has been prepared, we make garlic bread by frying bread in a pan with butter and garlic salt.

For other meals, we use the frying pan to brown ground beef for spaghetti, Hamburger Helper, or a variety of other hamburger-based dishes. Or you can fry a variety of Italian pasta skillet meals. For breakfast you can cook bacon, hash brown potatoes, scrambled eggs, or pancakes.

Baking

Several backpackers and outdoor enthusiasts have devised ways to bake food such as breads and desserts in their campsite. Some of these methods (e.g., using cast iron skillets and Dutch ovens) are not practical for motorcycle riders, but a few methods could be incorporated into your camping routine, especially if you are riding a touring bike. For example, you could purchase an E-Z camping reflector oven for baking breads, desserts, and even pizza. This oven, designed to be used next to a large campfire, folds down to a very small flat package for travel. Or you could purchase the Backpacker's Pantry Outback Oven, which is designed to be used with some backpacker's stoves.

After reading a book describing campsite baking, we decided to try baking brownies on a campfire using two large disposable aluminum pans clipped together to make a Dutch oven. We bought two giant lasagna pans, one eight-inch square cake pan, and a box of brownie mix. We followed the directions and mixed the brownie mix with two eggs, some oil, and some water in the cake pan. Then we placed several stones in the bottom of one lasagna pan so there was about a half-inch of air space between the lasagna pan and the cake pan. Then we placed the second lasagna pan upside down on top of the first and clipped the two pans together with two small binder clips to make a Dutch oven.

Our campfire was a hot wood fire with lots of coals. When it was ready for cooking, we arranged the large flaming logs into a one-and-a-half-foot square with the hot coals in the center. We placed the disposable Dutch oven on a grill about twelve inches above the hot coal bed and added a few hot embers on top of the top pan. The box directed us to cook it for fifty-five minutes at 325 degrees, but we did not have a thermometer and had to guess how hot our fire was. We began checking the brownies with a wooden toothpick after forty-five minutes and could see that they were baking well and not burning—they needed a little more time. We checked them again a few times more until we could stick the toothpick in and pull it out clean. The total cooking time was one hour and five minutes. We were pleased with our ability to cook something else in disposable aluminum pans, but we probably will not do it again: it was too much trouble. In the future, we will just buy our brownies or other baked items in a store.

Food Hygiene

When camping out, you frequently may not have ready access to soap and running water, and you may have to collect a small amount of water in a container or two and bring it back to your campsite. Once you have it in your campsite, there is a tendency to conserve water as much as possible so you don't have to walk back to get more water too often. Because of limited access to soap and water, some campers (especially backpackers) may not wash their hands as thoroughly as they would if they were at home. Furthermore, they may not wash their foods as thoroughly in the campsite as they would at home. One consequence of not washing hands and food is intestinal illnesses. Backpackers and other outdoor enthusiasts report that severe intestinal problems are relatively common on wilderness camping trips.

To be safe, you should strive to follow good hygiene practices. Thoroughly wash your hands with soap after each bathroom visit and again before preparing or eating food. Always be sure your food-preparation surface has been cleaned before placing food on it. Wash your hands again after handling chicken, pork, and other meats. Also wash the cutting surface and the knife with soap and water after cutting meat. Wash all fruits and vegetables before cutting or eating them. If you want to save leftovers, seal them in a food storage bag and place them in an ice cooler immediately after finishing your meal. Discard them if you do not eat them the next day.

Cleanup

After cooking and eating in your campsite, you must clean up all the remaining food and garbage before leaving your site or going to sleep. Food and garbage attracts many different animals. Raccoons and skunks are common in many campgrounds. Bears may be found in a few campgrounds. Leaving food or garbage in your site invites these animals to visit, and they can damage your property or injure your companion or you. Furthermore, feeding animals or allowing access to your food is forbidden in all state and national parks because it will make animals less fearful of people, more aggressive in taking food from future campers, and less able to find food in their natural habitat.

Place any food items remaining after your meal in food storage bags or other containers and store them in such a way as to prevent animal access. If you were driving a car, you could store your food in the trunk, but since you are riding a motorcycle, you must be more resourceful. We usually ride an Ultra with hard saddlebags and a tour pack. Thus we can sometimes pack our food in food storage bags and store them in a small cooler inside our hard luggage. People who ride cruisers with leather bags should consider other options. They should ask park rangers as to the best method of food storage. If they are camping in bear country, they can store their food in the metal lockers that can be found in every established campground. If these lockers are not available, they can hang their food from a tree limb twelve feet above the ground and several yards away from the tent. When in doubt, ask a park ranger.

After storing your leftovers, dispose of all garbage containing food smells before leaving your campsite or going to sleep. Most campgrounds have trash receptacles designed to prevent animal access. Bathe to remove food smells from your body, and put on clean clothing. Consider washing your clothes in a bathroom sink or storing them away from your tent overnight so that animals are not attracted to the food smells on them.

Robin prepares our meal on a cool rainy afternoon. We camped at a private campground near the south entrance station, Land Between The Lakes National Recreation Area.

Conclusion

What cooking and eating gear should be packed for a motorcycle camping trip? Regardless of the type of trip you are taking or its length, you should pack a small cooler, a water bottle for each person, a couple of butane lighters, and a few plastic garbage bags. After packing these items, you must consider the amount of packing space you have available and your meal plans. Will you be eating most of your meals in restaurants? Do you want to buy ready-to-eat foods in grocery stores? Do you want to cook a few meals on the grill? Do you want to cook most of your meals in your base camp? If riding with a companion, discuss these plans with him or her. Once you have made your plans, you can decide what cooking gear, eating gear, and food staples to pack.

If you ride a touring bike with a tour pack, have plenty of packing space, plan to stay in a base camp for several days, and really enjoy cooking (like Robin and I do), you may wish to buy a complete backpacker's kitchen set that nests together to conserve packing space and a backpackers' stove. A complete kitchen set should include a can opener, cooking utensils, eating utensils, two insulated cups, two small bowls, two small plates, at least one pot, at least one frying pan, a dishcloth, and a dishtowel. With a complete kitchen set, you could cook almost any food you would want, with the possible exception of pizza and other baked foods.

Since the items for a complete kitchen set are relatively heavy, pack them in a saddlebag if possible. If you ride a touring bike and if all items of your kitchen set nest together well, you will be able to squeeze everything into one saddlebag. If you ride a bike with limited packing space, you may have to pack a few items in your luggage.

Once you have unloaded your gear from the motorcycle and set up your camp, you can ride to the nearest restaurant or store each afternoon or evening to purchase the food and supplies you will need for the next meal or two. In addition to your food, you may want to purchase ice, charcoal, aluminum foil, disposable aluminum pans, and firewood.

After reading this chapter, you may want to read other books and articles on camp cooking. Some suggestions are *Foil Cookery* by Lori Herod and *Basic Essentials of Cooking in the Outdoors* by Cliff Jacobson. These books present several good recipes and discuss a variety of cooking methods, including using aluminum foil and Jell-O molds to make ovens for baking breads and desserts. If you really enjoy cooking and want some more creative ideas, read *Cooking the One Burner Way* by Melissa Gray and Buck Tilton. For more recipes read issues of *Backpacker* magazine. Finally, search the Web using the phrase "camp cooking" or "aluminum foil cooking." With a little gear and practice, you will be able to cook great-tasting meals in your campsite.

Kitchen Gear, Grocery Items, and Supplies Checklist

Basic Kitchen Items
  Cooler and water bottles
  Paper towels, butane lighters, and garbage bags
Utensil Set
  Tongs, nylon spoon, and eating utensils
  Can opener and dish detergent
Complete Kitchen Set
  Basic kitchen items, utensil set, and the following items:
  Thermal cups, bowls, and plates
  Stove, fuel, pot, and frying pan
  Dishcloths, dishtowels, and tablecloth
Basic Food Staples
  Salt, pepper, and garlic salt
  Butter (or oil) and Italian dressing
  Ketchup, mustard, and mayonnaise
  Hot chocolate (coffee bags or tea bags)
  Oatmeal
  Packaged rice or pasta meal
Supplies to Buy After Camp Setup
  Ice and charcoal
  Aluminum foil and disposable aluminum pans
  Paper products
  Firewood

7. Optionals

If you read magazine articles, Web sites, and other books about motorcycle camping or touring, you will quickly see that other authors recommend a number of items that I have not discussed thus far in this book. For example, if you read *Motorcycle Camping Made Easy* by Woofter or *The Essential Guide for Motorcycle Travel* by Coyner you will find many items I have not included in my chapters on essential gear. Some of these items include cameras, sneakers, backpacks, hammocks, water-purification equipment, GPS receivers, repair kits, spare motorcycle parts, and so forth. The reason I have not discussed these items yet is because I consider them to be optional. Some of these items might make your trip a little more comfortable, but you could easily live without them or buy them in most any store near your campsite. Other items serve no function that could not be performed by one of the essential items discussed in chapter 4. Furthermore, all of these items require valuable packing space that could be better used to pack other gear.

If you have space after packing all your essentials, you could pack a few of these items. For example, if you are taking a solo trip on a touring bike (or driving a car), you could pack a relatively large number of these optional items. But if you are riding two-up on a cruiser, you will have very little space to pack optional items. Even when you do not have space, you know you will be able to camp comfortably without them.

Lounging in a hammock can be very relaxing. This photo was taken in the South Nicolet Bay Campground in Peninsula State Park (Door County, Wisconsin).

Before each trip, you and your traveling companion will have to make decisions regarding the optional gear you will be able to pack. You must consider the length of the trip, the type of trip you will be taking, your personal needs, and the amount of packing space available. My suggestion is to pack all of your essential gear and clothing first and then divide the remaining space in half. Each person can then decide what optional items he or she would like to fit into the remaining space.

Since the list of items recommended by other campers is relatively long, I have divided it into three categories: high-priority items, second-priority items, and low-priority items. High-priority items are the things we try to pack for almost every two-up trip. Second-priority items are the things that cannot be packed for our two-up trips but could be packed for solo trips. Low-priority items are the things we never pack because they require valuable packing space and are unnecessary. As I list each item, I will give a brief explanation as to the reasons why other campers think it is desirable and why we think it is unnecessary. My classification and opinions are admittedly arbitrary. You may disagree with my system and might have sound reasons for classifying a few items differently.

High-Priority Items

Since we usually ride a touring bike with lots of packing space, we usually pack several optional items on most trips we take. We almost assume that these items are essential, but we could live without them if we had to.

Camera. We enjoy taking pictures on every trip we take. Many years later, these pictures help us remember the places we have visited, the things we have done, and the good times we have shared together. They also remind us of the problems we encountered and the solutions we devised. On each trip, we take several pictures, from different angles, of our campsite, the main campground sign, entrance-registration station, unique buildings, landscape, and any special activities we engaged in while camping there.

In the past we used a compact thirty-five-millimeter camera and packed a few rolls of film for our trip. After several trips, we invested in a compact digital camera that requires no film and holds a large number of pictures on a small disc. We love this camera because it requires very little packing space and yet takes excellent pictures. In fact, we used it to take most of the photos shown in this book. We also bought a small padded case with a belt loop so that we can carry the camera on our fanny pack belt. You may decide to pack it elsewhere, but try to pack it where it is easily accessible during the entire trip. Sometimes you may want to take a quick photo on the road. If you forget to pack a camera or do not have the room to pack it, you can purchase a small disposable camera that takes good photos in almost any convenience store, discount department store, or grocery store, or at a souvenir shop near your campsite.

Personal music players. One of the primary objectives of a vacation trip is to relax and do the things you enjoy. Robin and I both enjoy listening to music—but we like different styles of music. Robin likes country and religious music—I like rock and Latin music. Therefore on most of our trips we each pack a personal music player. In the past we used small Walkman-type cassette players/radios or CD players with good-quality ear buds, but we quickly realized that these items required a considerable amount of packing space.

Then we discovered small MP3 players and really love them. We each bought an iPod Shuffle that is about the size of a matchbook and holds fifteen to twenty full albums of music. We can load our favorite songs or albums from our CDs or download songs from the Internet for a small fee. After we have loaded songs onto our MP3 players, we can program our players to play songs in sequential order or to shuffle them much like a radio station would. Having these players allows us to enjoy our favorite music anywhere and anytime during our trips, but we especially enjoy our music at night when we have difficulty falling asleep. Being able to listen to our favorite songs provides a relaxing ambiance that helps us fall asleep or at least pass a sleepless night more pleasantly.

Hammock. When staying in a base camp for a few days, we like to bring our hammocks. We like to relax in them and read our books, listen to our music, and sometimes take naps. Several different styles and brands of hammocks are available. Small fishnet hammocks pack into a small space and can be purchased at many discount department stores, camping-supply stores, and military surplus stores for about ten dollars. We used these fishnet hammocks for several years and were relatively satisfied with them.

After a few years of motorcycle camping with these economy hammocks, we decided to move up to better-quality hammocks because we enjoy relaxing in our hammocks so much. As we began to investigate the types of hammocks that might be suitable for motorcycle camping, we learned that hammocks are very popular among backpackers. In fact, some backpackers prefer sleeping in hammocks with overhead tarps rather than in tents. Some of the best-known brands available include Clark, Crazy Creek, Eagle's Nest, Hennessy, Lawson, Speer, and Trek Light. We eventually decided to purchase two Eagle's Nest hammocks. We purchased one single nest and one double nest (which is presumably designed to hold two people). These hammocks are made from parachute nylon and are more comfortable than the fishnet models. They require a little more packing space compared with fishnet hammocks, but not much more. We think that they are worth the extra space.

The easiest way to tie a hammock to two trees is to use a pair of nylon hammock straps that can be purchased at any backpacker's supply store. These straps have loops at one end that allow you to lasso them around a tree. They also have loops spaced about every ten inches that allow you to attach your hammock in a comfortable position regardless of the distance between two trees.

If you are unable to find these straps (or if you prefer to use a more economical method), you can easily make your own hammock ropes. Simply purchase about thirty feet of non-stretch rope rated to hold about four hundred pounds. You can buy this rope in most discount department stores or hardware stores. Cut the rope into two fifteen-foot sections, burn the ends to prevent unraveling, and then tie a simple overhand loop knot at one end of each rope. When you arrive at your campsite, select two trees that are about twelve to twenty feet apart. Lasso one rope around each tree and tie a bowline knot (discussed in chapter 9) at the place in each rope that will allow you to set your hammock in a comfortable position. The bowline knot is best suited for this purpose because it will not give under the pressure of your body weight in the hammock and will be easy to untie when you need to adjust the rope length or break camp.

When initially looking for a good campsite in a campground, we look for a site that has three trees positioned as corners of a triangle. This configuration allows us to tie the heads of each hammock to one tree and the foot to separate trees. When our hammocks are set up in this manner, we are close enough to have quiet conversations yet we have space to rock our separate hammocks if we so desire.

Bike cover. Although motorcycles and their controls are designed to be weather resistant and although a rain cover is not absolutely necessary, I seem to have more peace of mind when I am able to cover my bike at night—especially if it rains. I purchased a cover made by Exigent. I like it because it packs relatively small. Since then, I have learned that other manufacturers make half covers that pack even smaller. If you get caught in a rainstorm on the road and you can't find a place to get out of the rain, you can use your bike cover to protect your tent, sleeping bags and sleeping pads tied on the back of your bike and your gear packed in the saddlebags. Furthermore, if you decide to spend a night in a motel, your bike cover may reduce the risk of someone vandalizing your bike.

Daypack. Backpackers and other ultra-light campers consider backpacks to be essential. These ultra-light campers typically need relatively large backpacks that can hold all of their camping gear and clothes. Weekend packs typically hold between 1,800 cubic inches and 3,500 cubic inches of gear, and week-long packs typically hold more than 3,500 cubic inches of gear. These packs have a number of features such as internal frames, hip belts, sternum straps, adjustable shoulder straps, and load lifters to make them easier to carry. These features increase the cost of the pack. Prices for these larger packs typically range between $150 and $650, depending upon their features.

Motorcycle campers do not need large backpacks with all these features but may want to pack a small daypack, if possible. We like to have a daypack to carry some of our gear while we engage in activities near our campsite. For example, when we go to the Gulf Coast we like to take our towels, sunscreen, and books down to the beach. When we go to the Smoky Mountains, we like to hike a few of the shorter trails and take our rain gear, water, and a few snacks. We may occasionally want to camp in a hike-in or boat-in site and we need a daypack to carry our small items. Several parks (Fort Pickens Campground in the Gulf Islands National Seashore in Florida, Unicoi State Park in Georgia, Fall Creek Falls State Park in Tennessee, and Rock Island State Park in Wisconsin) now offer walk-in sites. So we pack a small daypack for most of our trips.

Daypacks range in load capacity from about 500 cubic inches to 1,800 cubic inches. Some just hang on your shoulders, while others have features and adjustments that make them reasonably comfortable to wear for longer hikes, even with lots of gear packed inside. Some have several small compartments, while others only have one main compartment. Some are packed through one main top opening, while others (called panel loaders) are packed by opening one of several horseshoe-shaped zippers. Small basic packs can be purchased at any discount department store for about ten dollars. Larger and more comfortable daypacks are sold in camping or backpacking specialty stores or on Web sites such as Campmor, REI, or Mountain Gear. They typically cost between fifty and a hundred dollars. For example, the Lightweight Travel Pack by Patagonia holds 1,200 cubic inches of gear and packs as small as a softball. Other well-known makers of daypacks include GoLite, Gregory, Deuter, Kelty, L.L. Bean, Lowe, Marmot, The North Face, Osprey, and REI. Before buying a daypack, go to REI's online gear shop and Trail Space Web site to read reviews and recommendations. Then go to a camping supply store and try on a few different packs to feel the differences between them.

When traveling on the motorcycle, we tie our daypack on top of our tent, sleeping bags, and sleeping pads, which have been tied on the luggage rack. We use the daypack to hold our rain gear when not wearing it. When we set up camp, I use the daypack to make a pillow base.

Tarp support poles. Car campers frequently use relatively heavy poles to set up large dining (or kitchen) tents or tarps over their picnic table for protection from rain, sun, and wind. Backpackers, on the other hand, typically do not pack poles to support their dining fly and many times do not even pack a dining fly. Since backpackers have very limited packing space in their backpack and don't want to carry the unnecessary weight of poles, they frequently are willing to forgo the comforts that dining flies provide. These ultra-light campers have to rely upon their tent and rain gear to keep them dry during rainy periods.

Motorcycle campers are different from both of these extremes in that they have a few more choices regarding dining flies and poles. They could elect to leave the dining fly and poles at home like backpackers do and use their space to pack other gear. Or they could pack a tarp but no poles and rely on trees in the campsite to set up the tarp. If one site does not have trees, they can easily ride to another. Or they could pack a few poles and use the poles along with the available trees to set up their dining fly.

Over the past ten years, we have experimented with several different tarp poles combinations. For much of this time we only had stainless steel poles that extended to six feet and collapsed to three and a half feet. When riding two-up, we found it difficult to pack any of these poles. Occasionally we could pack one or two. When riding solo, I tried packing more. On one trip, I packed five poles, but I quickly realized that was too many. After several trips, experimenting with different numbers of poles, I realized that these poles were not suitable for motorcycle camping. They were too heavy and required an excessive amount of packing space. Since they were three and a half feet long, we had to pack them on the luggage rack where they stuck out on each side of the bike and made the bike feel awkwardly top-heavy. Just when I was about to give up on poles forever, I discovered some lighter aluminum poles, made by Eureka, that have four sections that nest inside each other. We decided to try using these poles and bought two from Campmor. When collapsed, these poles are only twenty-seven inches long and were easy to pack for travel. In the campsite they can be extended to eight feet and can support two corners of our dining fly. If we can find a site with at least one tree (two would be better), we can easily set up a tarp over our picnic table.

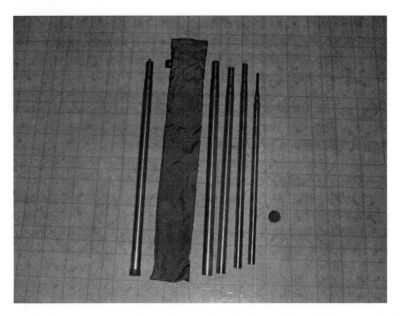

Two eight-foot tarp support poles with a pole bag: the four sections of the pole on the left are nested inside each other for easy packing.

Tablecloth. Although it really is not necessary, we like to have a plastic or vinyl tablecloth to cover our picnic table. As noted in chapter 6, tables in many campsites are dirty and may have splinters that could injure you or damage your gear. A tablecloth gives you a smooth clean table surface for cooking, eating, reading, repairing gear, or doing any other activity.

Empty gallon jug. Car campers usually bring containers that hold between three and five gallons of water. When they arrive at their campsite, they fill the containers with water and bring them back to their site. With these containers they have a source of fresh water at their table for cooking, drinking, and cleaning that usually will last two or three days before having to refill the container. On the other hand, backpackers and other ultra-light campers could not carry such large containers of water on their back for several hours a day. Therefore, they have learned to survive with small water bottles that carry only enough water to last for an hour or two. When they need more water, they catch it from lakes and rivers along their trail or near their campsite and then purify it before drinking it.

Motorcycle campers fall between these two extremes. They can't pack the larger containers that family campers typically use, but they could easily pack or purchase one-gallon jugs that would make their camp life more comfortable. After setting up camp, they can fill the jugs with water and have water readily available at their table whenever they need it. Some campgrounds have water at the campsite, but many others only have a central water supply that is located several yards away from your site. For example, several sites in Governor Dodge State Park near Dodgeville, Wisconsin, and Peninsula State Park near Fish Creek, Wisconsin, are situated several yards away from one of the wells located around the campground. In these campgrounds, you need one or two clear plastic gallon jugs to transport water back to your site.

When traveling, you could attach an empty jug to your daypack on top of your luggage rack with a carabineer. An empty plastic jug weighs almost nothing. Or you could wait until you have arrived at your campsite and unloaded your gear and then ride to a store where you can buy water in one of these jugs.

Chargers for cell phone and MP3 player. If we plan a trip that will last several days, we each take our cell phone chargers. Most campgrounds have electrical outlets near the campsites that can be used to charge your cell phone when necessary. We may also pack chargers for our MP3 players.

Games. Family campers frequently bring games on their camping trips. When they have no other activities to do, they pull out a game to pass the time and have fun. We may occasionally pack a deck of cards, a set of dominoes, or some other small game if we will be staying in a base camp for several days. If we run out of things to do or we are waiting for the rain to stop, we pull out our game to pass a little time.

Hair dryer. Robin considers a hair dryer to be an essential item, but theoretically she could survive without one by either drying hair with the wall-mounted hand dryers in most bathrooms or by natural air drying. Nevertheless, having a hair dryer does make it easier to get ready and get on the road or start doing whatever activity has been planned for the day. A small travel-sized hair dryer requires relatively little packing space.

Second-Priority Items

When I travel solo, I may occasionally pack one or more of the following items. For example, I may pack a small portable TV if I will be camping near a large metropolitan area or a small DVD player if I will be camping in a remote state park with electricity near the site.

Navigation receiver. Navigation receivers that use GPS have become very popular among backpackers, motorcycle tourers, and the general public. Once you buy one of these receivers and become accustomed to its features, you will want to take it on every trip. They show you the major streets, intersections, and geographic features that lie ahead on your route. They also give you information about your speed, your travel time, and the number of miles to your destination. Having a GPS receiver reduces your dependency on maps and allows you to easily find specific addresses, restaurants, gas stations, and other locations along your route. You can buy these receivers in many different stores (including discount department stores) but you may wish to buy one that can be mounted on your motorcycle handle bar. Rider Wearhouse (www.aerostich.com) sells several different models for motorcycles, ranging in price from $270 to $1,000 along with the accessories needed to mount them on your motorcycle.

Books. On many trips I may pack a small paperback book or two. Reading books can be entertaining way to relax around the campsite. A good book can also help pass time while you are waiting for the rain to stop. Furthermore, it can help you fall asleep at night. If we were riding two-up and did not have space to pack books, we could buy some, or a newspaper or magazine, after setting up our camp.

Fleece blanket. When I travel solo in the cold weather, I like to pack a lightweight fleece blanket. I pack the blanket rolled up in the stuff sack along with my sleeping bag. After setting up my tent, I place the blanket flat on the floor before opening my air mattress and bringing my sleeping bag into the tent. The blanket makes the floor softer, warmer, and cozier. Furthermore, fleece does not absorb water and thus can make the floor drier in the event of a water leak.

Binoculars. Many outdoor enthusiasts—especially bird watchers—want to have a pair of binoculars. A few motorcycle campers have also included binoculars on their lists. One Web site author, for example, suggested carrying them in an accessible location while riding your bike to read distant road signs—after stopping the bike, of course. If you were inclined to pack some binoculars, you could purchase a good pair that packs into a very small space. Occasionally I may pack a small pair to watch birds.

Hobby items. Family campers frequently bring a variety of hobby items to pass time or to relax. For example, I may want to learn more about trees, birds, and wildflowers. On past camping trips, I have packed field-identification guides that can be used to identify different species. On other trips, I have packed water shoes for rafting or tubing. Some motorcycle campers may want to bring basic fishing gear. If you enjoy some other activity, you may occasionally have room to pack some of the gear needed to pursue your hobby.

TV. If I will be camping near a large city and have a little extra space, I may sometimes pack a small seven-inch portable television. Sometimes we will take the TV even when riding two-up. We are especially likely to pack it during the fall baseball playoffs and the World Series. Ideally the TV should operate on batteries as well as the standard 120-volt electrical current because many parks do not have electricity available in each campsite.

DVD player. If we are camping several miles away from a big city and will likely have no television reception, we may pack a portable DVD player and entertain ourselves by watching a few movies during the camping trip. The DVD player operates on a rechargeable battery, a twelve-volt car battery, or 120-volt electric current.

Chair. Having a chair in your campsite certainly would make camp life more comfortable. If you ride solo, you could easily pack a folding chair because you would not have to pack a second sleeping bag and mattress. Furthermore, you could pack heavier items such as the chair on your passenger seat and still preserve your bike's handling properties. In this case, a small metal-framed folding chair would be very easy to pack.

However, when riding two-up, packing chairs is very difficult. We have attempted to cram folding chairs onto our luggage rack along with our tent, sleeping bags, and sleeping pads on a few trips but quickly realized that we were dangerously overloading the motorcycle. On one trip we tried packing chairs instead of our sleeping bags, but we did not sleep well on that trip because we were so cold. On another trip we tried packing sleeping bags in the tour pack, but they took so much space we had no room to pack other important items. We soon realized that when riding two-up we cannot pack folding chairs on the motorcycle. No matter how we tried to pack them, the chairs required too much space, adversely affected my rear vision, and adversely affected the balance of my bike.

Other motorcycle campers who ride solo—in particular BMW riders who camp in large open fields during motorcycle rallies—like to carry Kermit's Kamping Chairs. These chairs are specifically designed for motorcycle riders. They pack smaller and lighter than other folding chairs and are strong enough to hold hefty people. These chairs are relatively expensive (about $130 each) and their legs are short. But if you were riding solo and camping in an open field with no benches or tables near your site, they would be more comfortable than sitting on the ground. They can be purchased from Kermit's Camping Company and from Rider Wearhouse. Both vendors can be easily found on the Internet by entering "kermit's kamping chair" into your search engine.

If you cannot pack chairs on your bike, you could sit on the benches of your picnic table, lie or sit in your tent, or lie in a hammock to read and relax. Some campgrounds, especially motorcycle-only campgrounds, may have comfortable rocking chairs near the office or clubhouse. If you were staying for several nights in a base camp, you could go to a discount department store or grocery store and buy a couple of cheap folding chairs. You can usually find them for five to ten dollars. Tie them onto your luggage rack to get them back to your campsite. Enjoy them during the week. On the day you leave, offer them to your neighbors or just leave them near the garbage pickup area where other campers might be inclined to adopt them.

Extra pairs of shoes. Many motorcycle campers suggest packing an extra pair of sneakers or shoes for walking around the campground or for hiking. These authors argue that most motorcycle riders want to remove their riding boots and put on comfortable shoes as soon as possible. However, these authors seem to forget that motorcycle campers must pack many other items (including their shower shoes) and may not have space to pack an extra pair of sneakers. When riding solo, you might be able to squeeze in an extra pair of shoes, but when riding two-up with clothing and gear for two people, you probably will not have space to pack two extra pair of sneakers.

Having inadequate space to pack extra shoes is not a unique problem for motorcycle campers. Many backpackers must also deal with this problem. Backpackers typically have very little room to pack an extra pair of shoes. Most of the time, they must walk several miles in their boots and wear them all day long for several days in a row.

One possible solution to the problem of suffering with uncomfortable boots is to purchase a better pair of boots that are more comfortable (and perhaps waterproof) and insert good insoles in them. These boots will provide comfort when riding and when walking around. At the end of the day, you can slip on your shower shoes. Crocs are great shoes for the shower and for relaxing around the campground.

Grill. Motorcycle riders who camp in large open fields at rallies suggest packing a grill. If you had a trailer or chase vehicle you could pack a complete grill. But if you must pack all your gear on your motorcycle, you could pack a grill top (about twelve inches square). To make this grill top, you could buy a standard grill top and cut it down with a hacksaw. After setting up your camp, you could use rocks or other materials to build the sides of your grill. Or you could ride to the nearest grocery store and buy a large disposable aluminum lasagna pan to make the base for your grill. With a little charcoal you will be able to cook steaks, chicken, Polish Kielbasa, potatoes and other vegetables in foil, vegetable skewers, and many other foods.

Low-Priority Items

If you read other materials on motorcycle camping, you will probably see many other items listed as things to pack for your trips. These lists frequently include many items that require considerable packing space and are unnecessary. Let me comment on a few of these items.

Security chain. Several motorcycle riders have recommended a security chain and padlock because a significant number of bikes are reportedly stolen every year at large motorcycle rallies. After first learning this, I kept a heavy chain and padlock in my saddlebag for several years. At first I used it often, but putting the chain on and taking it off was a hassle. Over time, I used it less and less until I just left it in my saddlebag all the time. Eventually it dawned on me that I rode an old, ordinary motorcycle and had good insurance. Furthermore, I realized that the chain stayed in my saddlebag all the time and occupied valuable space that could be used to pack other items. I also noticed that most other riders did not use security chains. Today we no longer pack the security chain.

Fat pine or another fire starter. This item takes space and is unnecessary for starting a campfire. Instead buy a small bag of Match Light charcoal after arriving at your campsite and use about twenty briquettes to start your fire. This brand of charcoal can be purchased in almost any grocery or convenience store.

Bear canister. Many camping books, magazine articles, and Web sites recommend bear-proof bags, barrels, or containers. The reasoning used to justify this recommendation is that you may camp in a bear habitat where, for your own personal safety—and for the long-term benefit of the bears living in the vicinity—you must keep your food and garbage secured.

When camping in a bear habitat, you must secure your food and garbage whenever you leave your site and when you retire for the night. However, you do not need to purchase or pack a large bear canister for most of your camping trips. When you register for your campsite, inquire as to the best way to protect your food. Most established campgrounds in bear habitats provide other options for securing your food and garbage. In many campgrounds you can store your cooler and other food items in a metal locker located near the ranger station. If such a locker is not available, ask a park ranger how to best safeguard your food.

Pepper spray for bears. Backpackers frequently carry a can of pepper spray in case they happen to encounter an aggressive bear. In such a situation, they would be many miles and many hours away from assistance and thus must be prepared for the worst-case scenario. However, if you camp in established campgrounds and exercise proper care in your food-handling procedures, you usually will never have to worry about bears. Although bears have caused problems in a few campgrounds, 99 percent of the time park rangers are able to keep the bears away from the campers. If you happen to camp in a park where bears live, you will see signs regarding your personal safety. When you register for your campsite, ask the ranger at the registration desk what precautions you need to take. The rangers will usually advise you to place all your food and fruity smelling personal items in a metal locker or hang them from a high cable. Rarely will they tell you that you may need to purchase a can of pepper spray.

Bug net. Bugs, flies, and mosquitoes pose a serious inconvenience certain times during the year in certain locations, especially in the boundary waters between the northern United States and Canada. As a result, some wilderness campers recommend packing bug nets to cover your head. Personally, we have never encountered mosquitoes, flies, or bugs so bad as to require a net. We have camped in many different places in the continental United States including northern Wisconsin. Whenever we had a bug problem, we applied an insect repellent, such as Deep Woods Off. It has been all we have ever needed. If the bugs or flies ever got so bad that our repellent did not work, we would pack up and ride to another location or to a motel.

Snakebite kit. First of all, let me say that I have never seen a snake, venomous or non-venomous, in a designated campground. I have seen plenty of them in my yard and in the woods while walking, but not in established campgrounds. Not that you might not see one, but snakes rarely hang around campgrounds that are used by lots of people. Most snakes are shy and try to avoid human contact. They usually retreat from areas where lots of human noise and activity is present. If a snake ventures into a campground, campers will usually tell a park ranger and the ranger will usually remove the snake to a remote area of the park. The bottom line is that campers staying in established campgrounds probably will never see a venomous snake and thus will never have the occasion to use a snakebite kit. Therefore there is no reason to pack one, especially since it would take space needed for more useful gear.

If you packed a snakebite kit and the unlikely event of a snakebite occurred, you probably would not use the kit. Rather than taking time to find the kit, opening it, and trying to use it, you should evacuate the victim to a medical facility. Furthermore, unless you have been trained in how to use a kit, you could actually make the injury worse. The most prudent thing to do for a snakebite victim is to get a good description of the snake (head shape, color, length, and diameter) and take the person to a medical facility as quickly as possible. Do not try to kill or capture the snake, because doing so could cause you to become a second victim.

Snakebite kits are intended for backpackers and other wilderness campers who camp in remote areas many hours (or days) away from medical treatment and for those who have training in the proper application of these kits.

We pack light when we travel to Gulf State Park, Alabama. After setting up our tent and sleeping quarters, we head to the beach or our favorite restaurant.

Shovel. Backpackers need shovels to dig cat holes for their toilets. Motorcycle campers might occasionally find a use for shovels. For example, you could use it to clean ashes from your campfire ring before starting a fire. But other than in a few rare situations, I cannot think of many reasons why lightweight campers would need a shovel. If you packed a shovel, it would take space that could be used to pack more useful items and you probably would never use it. If you need to remove ashes from a fire ring and did not have a shovel, you could use your crowbar to loosen the ashes and dirt and then either borrow a shovel from park staff or use some other object, such as an aluminum pie pan, to shovel the ashes.

Saw. Backpackers frequently suggest packing saws to cut firewood, but there are almost no situations in which lightweight campers would need one. A few motorcycle campers have also included saws on their lists, but it would be unusual to find a large dead log lying on the ground that could be cut into firewood lengths with a small saw. Furthermore, many parks forbid cutting large logs because they may provide food and habitat for animals and other wildlife. Even if there are no rules forbidding cutting and removing large fallen logs, doing so could have a negative impact upon the park.

Instead of trying to cut logs, look around the park for small fallen branches or buy pre-cut firewood at the camp office or a nearby store.

Never use a saw (or your ax) to cut live saplings or limbs. Green wood from live plants does not make good fire fuel, and most park rules forbid it. Furthermore, cutting living plants would be destructive to the park's animal habitat and would be contrary to fundamental conservation principles.

Plastic mallet. Many economy tents are sold with plastic tent pegs that are very brittle. To avoid breaking them, tent manufacturers recommend using plastic mallets to drive the pegs into the ground. These plastic stakes may work well in loose sandy soil that is typically found in campgrounds near the Gulf Coast but are impractical for tent pads and other durable surfaces that are typically found in most established campgrounds. Furthermore, plastic tent stakes and a plastic mallet require much more packing space than do metal stakes. In sum, if you use six-inch galvanized nails (as recommended in chapter 2), you will not need a plastic mallet. All you need for driving the stakes is the side of your ax.

Sharpening stone. A few motorcycle campers have suggested packing a stone for sharpening your knives. We never need a stone because I sharpen my knives before leaving home. Once sharpened, the edges will hold for several weeks.

Extra tarp. Several campers recommend packing a second tarp or a plastic sheet. One possible use for the second tarp is to cover the floor inside your tent. The tarp inside your tent could provide an extra layer of protection against damage to your tent floor from rocks and sticks and could provide extra protection from ground moisture. Other possible uses for a tarp are to increase your dining fly area, to make a windscreen, and to cover your bike in the rain. We typically do not pack an extra tarp because we pack a bike cover and do not need the tarp for any other reason. If we did need a tarp on a particular trip, we would buy one in a nearby store.

Tent/tarp repair kit. Some motorcycle campers have suggested packing tent repair kits. I was a little surprised to see this suggestion because I have never damaged a tent or tarp during a camping trip so badly that it required immediate repair. One time I got a small tear in the fabric, but I was able to use it the rest of my trip and repair it after I returned home. If a tent or tarp needs immediate repair, slap a piece of duct tape on it to hold it until a permanent repair can be made. If a grommet pulls out, wrap a small stone in the tarp corner, tie a string around the rock inside the material, and use it to attach your cord. If a tarp is severely damaged, buy a new one in a discount department store. They only cost a few dollars.

Water-purification equipment. Backpackers must pack this equipment, but motorcycle campers staying in established campgrounds do not need it. All established national, state, and private campgrounds have clean drinking (potable) water in the campground. In some campgrounds, it may be available at your site. If not, it can be found within a few feet of your campsite.

Stove repair kit. In thirty-some odd years of camping, I have never had to repair a stove in the field. One spring many years ago, I realized that an old stove was no longer working as well as it had when I first bought it. I used it as best as possible during the camping trip and replaced the generator after returning home from the trip. If you have a small multi-fuel backpacker's stove, you must occasionally clean it at home before leaving on your trip to get the optimum service out of it. If a stove fails to work properly in camp, you can easily ride to a store or restaurant. So omit the stove repair kit and use your limited space to pack more useful items.

Sewing kit. Sewing kits are rarely needed and take space that could be used to pack more useful items. If you need a sewing kit on a particular trip, ride to a nearby store and buy it.

Lantern. Family campers frequently use lanterns to provide light around the campsite. But lanterns require a considerable amount of packing space and are limited in terms of providing focused light at specific places where you need it. If a lantern is gas powered, it is of no value in your tent. Instead of using lanterns, the more practical way to have useful light is to use headlights. They are brighter, safer, and require much less packing space.

Collapsible bucket. One motorcycle camper has recommended a collapsible bucket. This item may first sound like a good suggestion, but upon further scrutiny you'll realize it would require a considerable amount of packing space and is unnecessary. There are other ways to get water to your campsite. For example, use your canteens or water bottles. If you need a washbasin, use one of your pots or buy a disposable aluminum pan for a dollar when you go to the store for supplies. If water is located several yards away from your site, go to a local store and buy a one-gallon jug of water and then continue using the empty jug to bring more water to your site as needed.

Glue. I have never needed to stick things together on a camping trip, but if I did, I would first try duct tape. If it failed to solve the problem, I would ride to the nearest store to buy some glue.

Emergency blankets. If you feel strongly about this item you may be able to justify it because it is so small, but they are intended for backwoods and wilderness hikers who may get lost and have to survive a cold night in the woods. I have never used one and prefer to buy good-quality clothing and sleeping gear that will keep me warm. If it gets too cold, just ride to a motel.

Side-stand support. The logic for packing this item is that if you park your bike on soft ground, your side stand could easily sink into the ground and cause your bike to fall over. However, most established campgrounds have hard packed gravel or asphalt parking pads and thus virtually eliminate the risk of your bike falling over. I have never had a problem in an established campground. If you are concerned that the ground at a particular campsite may not support the weight of your bike, find a flat rock, a flattened beer or pop can, or a piece of wood. If all else fails, park in another spot.

Umbrella. Some backpackers and motorcycle campers pack small umbrellas. They use the umbrellas to cover their cooking/eating area in the rain and to provide temporary covers in front of the doors of their shelters or small tents. But motorcycle campers who have larger tents, rain gear, and rain flies over their picnic tables do not need umbrellas. Furthermore, umbrellas require valuable packing space. Although an umbrella would be nice to have in the rain, it is unnecessary for dry and comfortable motorcycle camping.

Tire pump. Some motorcycle riders have suggested packing a tire pump in case of a flat tire. In the past, I packed a pump and tire repair supplies. Eventually I realized that I never used this gear and that it was just taking space that could be used to pack more useful gear. I finally decided to leave it at home. I do carry a can of Fix-A-Flat in one engine guard bag, but I believe that replacing your tires when the tread wears down or the sidewalls begin to show signs of dry rot is the best way to prevent tire failure on your trips. It is extremely unlikely that tire repairs will be required on the road, but if they were, you could call a local motorcycle repair shop.

Spare parts. Many books and articles on motorcycle touring have recommended packing spare motorcycle parts. Perhaps having a good selection of spare parts would be necessary if you were riding in South America or Africa or some other undeveloped area but is unnecessary if you ride in the United States or other countries with plenty of repair shops. Many years ago, I packed a few parts, like spark plugs, in my saddlebags, but eventually I realized that I never needed them. If you ride a late-model bike that has been properly serviced, you should be able to ride thousands of miles without the fear of breaking down on the road. In the unlikely event of a problem on the road, you can easily call a repair shop on your cell phone and use your credit card to pay the bill.

Voltmeter. Many years ago, the voltage regulator on my Low Rider went bad and burned up my stator and battery. There had been some warning signs that I had an electrical problem, but I failed to take timely action and thus was stranded at a restaurant one night. I could have prevented my problem had I had my bike properly serviced and had I taken it to the repair shop when the early warning signs first appeared. Who knows if I will ever have the same problem again, but I have conclude that a voltmeter is unnecessary if your bike has been properly serviced.

Emergency warning lights. One article on motorcycle camping recommended that you pack these warning lights. The rationale behind this recommendation is that if you broke down after dark you could use the lights to warn other drivers. Personally, I do not think these lights are needed. I have my bike serviced at proper intervals and I try to avoid riding after dark. As a result, I have never broken down after dark—and I hope I never will. When camping, you should usually be back in your campsite before dark. If you do ride after dark and need a light, use your camping headlight. Emergency warning lights require valuable packing space and will rarely, if ever, be needed. Consider leaving them at home.

On one trip I packed five long aluminum poles to support the dining fly. This was our campsite at 29 Dreams Motorcycle Resort near Birmingham, Alabama.

Surveyor's tape. One motorcycle camper suggested packing a roll of surveyor's tape to prevent other arriving campers from selecting your site before you can get back to set up your tent. Personally, I have never had a problem in this regard. When you check into your campground, you will typically be allowed to ride around the campground and look for an unoccupied site. Pick out your first, second, and third choices and then promptly return to the ranger station to register for your site. Surely one of your choices will be available. If another camper arrived before you and selected a particular site, they will get that site, regardless of whether you have put up tape. If other campers arrive after you, they should still be riding in the campground when you get back to the registration counter to claim your site. Therefore, leave the tape at home. Use the space to pack more useful gear.

Candles. Don't even think about them. They could damage your tent, cause carbon monoxide poisoning, or injure you if your flame accidentally contacts nearby fabrics. Use headlights instead. If you get cold, put on more layers of clothing.

Pistol. They are illegal in most state and national parks, but this regulation may change in 2010. If you avoid rough places and treat other people with respect, you should never need one.

Conclusion

What optional gear should be packed for a motorcycle camping trip? It depends upon the amount of space available after your essentials have been packed. If you ride two-up on a cruiser or another motorcycle with limited packing space, you probably will not have much room for optional items. But if you ride solo or ride a touring motorcycle, you will likely have room for several optional items. My highest priority items are a camera, an iPod, a daypack, a hammock, a tablecloth, two tarp support poles, an empty gallon jug, and a bike cover. Many other campers include coffee-making supplies as one of their high-priority items.

After reading this chapter, read other books, magazine articles, and Web sites on motorcycle camping to see how other campers rank optional items. Every person has a different opinion as to the optional items they want to take on their camping trips. Once you read these other references and determine the amount of packing space you have available, you can decide for yourself which optional items you can pack.

Optional Gear Checklist

High-Priority Items
- Camera, backpack, and hammock
- Tablecloth and empty gallon jug
- Personal music player
- Bike cover and hair dryer
- Tarp support poles

Second-Priority Items
- GPS receiver, phone charger, or MP3 charger
- Book, cards, games, hobby items, or binoculars
- Fleece blanket
- TV or DVD player
- Extra pair of shoes
- Chair
- Grill

Low-Priority Items
- Security chain
- Fire starter, shovel, candles, and lanterns
- Extra tarp
- Bear spray and canisters
- Bug net and snakebite kit
- Shovel, saw, mallet, and sharpening stone
- Tent, tarp, and stove repair kits
- Sewing kit, glue, emergency blanket, and umbrella
- Water-purification gear
- Tire pump, spare parts, voltmeter, and emergency warning lights
- Surveyor's tape

8. Packing

After accumulating all the gear and clothing you need for your motorcycle camping trip, you must turn your thoughts to packing this gear on your bike. You will have a lot of camping equipment, clothing, and personal items to pack. As you think about this packing process, you should have two primary concerns. First, you want to be able to remember everything you will need for a comfortable camping trip. Second, you must figure out how to pack everything safely in a limited amount of space. When you first attempt camping trips on your motorcycle, you may have to experiment with different combinations of gear and different ways to pack it. Eventually you must devise a system that allows you to pack everything you will need so that it does not substantially affect your particular motorcycle's handling or your own personal safely.

Our packing strategy has evolved over the past ten years. When we first started motorcycle camping, we packed whatever stuff we had in whatever space we could find. We had no system and no understanding of how packing could impact our personal safety. On each trip we attempted to take different gear, and we packed it with no plan.

My tent, tarp support poles, mattress, and sleeping bag are tied on my luggage rack.
If Robin had joined me, we would have tied her sleeping pad with the other gear and
packed her sleeping bag inside the stuff sack with mine.

On our early trips, we rode my Low Rider. We packed our tent, rain fly, stakes, poles, doormat, and ground cloth in separate locations. We thought we had good reasons for using this system: 1) we knew the whole package was too big to fit into one saddlebag; 2) we knew that heavy items should be packed low; and 3) we wanted to even our load between the left and right side. So we packed the tent in the bottom of one saddlebag and the ground cloth and rain fly in the other bag, we placed two folded hand towels (used as doormats) in one saddlebag, we packed our tent stakes wherever they would fit, and we rolled our tent poles inside one sleeping pad and tied them on top of the sissy bar bag. We packed our clothing, shower supplies, and personal items in both saddlebags and in the sissy bar bag—wherever they would fit.

Later, after buying the Electra Glide, we still packed the tent in pieces on a few early trips, rolling our tent poles inside an air mattress and tying it, along with our tent and blankets, on the luggage rack. When we arrived at the campsite, we had to empty both saddlebags and unroll our air mattress to get all the tent parts together before we could set it up.

We did not pack sleeping bags because the only bags we owned were large, cotton-filled, flannel bags that were too big. So we tried other methods for staying warm at night. As fate would have it, we were never successful, and we eventually concluded that we had to buy more compressible (and more expensive) sleeping bags. We also tried packing several optional items, only to discover that these items required too much packing space, adversely affected my bike's handling characteristics, and/or were not needed after all. For example, on a few trips we packed four relatively long stainless steel poles on the luggage rack and used them to set up our dining fly. At first they seemed small and light enough to pack. After all, they collapsed to a length of about three and a half feet. But after a few trips, we realized that they were too long, too heavy, and too awkward to carry on the motorcycle. They were considerably wider than the rest of the bike and had a noticeable effect on my bike's handling. We quickly came to the conclusion that we should leave them at home and either find smaller poles or depend upon trees in the campsite for setting up our dining fly.

Another large, awkward, heavy item we tried to pack was a folding chair. Once we tried to pack two of them, but we realized that two chairs weighed too much, required too much space, and made my bike feel top-heavy. Then we thought we could pack one chair, but it also was too large and too heavy. Eventually we realized that we would have to depend upon the picnic table benches in our campsite to provide a place for sitting or ride to a local store after setting up our base camp and buy a couple of inexpensive folding chairs.

We also experimented with various combinations of kitchen gear before finally deciding upon the basic items we needed. On our first few trips, we bought and used a variety of small backpacker pots—stainless steel and aluminum—but discovered that they were not large enough to cook meals for two people. Although they could be used to boil water for coffee, hot chocolate, or dehydrated backpacker meals, they were useless for cooking eggs, bacon, macaroni casserole, red beans and rice, and other foods we wanted to eat. On one trip, we bought an inexpensive pot and frying pan in a grocery store after setting up our base camp. Then we experimented with a variety of larger pots and pans (with handles removed), packing them wherever they would fit. Eventually we decided that when riding my Low Rider we should forgo cooking gear so that we have more space to pack other items. We just have to eat in restaurants or buy food and supplies in grocery stores. We could occasionally cook a steak, burger, or bratwurst on a charcoal grill or campfire. After buying the Electra Glide, we gained more packing space that allowed us to pack a small backpacker's stove and cook set. Now we can cook more meals in our campsite.

Thankfully, we survived all those early trial-and-error trips and gradually learned some basic principles of motorcycle packing. The secret to packing is to purchase gear that packs as small as possible but yet is very functional in the campsite. The best places to buy this gear are camping specialty stores or Web sites such as those listed at the end of chapter 1.

Today our packing system is relatively simple. When riding the Electra Glide, we first pack the left saddlebag. We tightly roll one tarp and a bike cover about twenty-two inches long and place each in the bottom of the saddlebag; then we place a tablecloth folded the width of the saddlebag and about twenty-two inches long on top of the tarps. Next we place our camping tool bag (containing an ax, a crowbar, pliers, a multifunction tool, camp gloves, tent stakes, and a cord) on top of the tablecloth. We are able to fit a hammock with straps, the passenger's rain gear, and a few personal items into the saddlebag. We avoid packing things in this saddlebag, such as our camera, that could be damaged by moisture. The total weight in the left saddlebag is approximately eighteen pounds. In addition to the saddlebags, I have added a pair of saddlebag guard bags to my motorcycle and use them to carry a few extra items. In the left saddlebag guard bag we pack a can of Fix-A-Flat and one water bottle.

Next we move to the right saddlebag. In this bag we usually pack our kitchen items, a small soft-side cooler (containing three canned beverages, Italian salad dressing, butter, and a little ice), and first-aid kit. Our kitchen items includes two cups, two plates, two bowls, cooking utensils, eating utensils, dish towel, dish cloth, paper towels, dish detergent, backpacker cook set, backpacker stove, and two fuel canisters. It would be much easier to pack the complete set together in a medium soft-side cooler in the tour pack, but the complete set, plus a cooler, is one of our heaviest items. Safe packing strategy dictates that we pack it low in a saddlebag. In addition to the kitchen items, we usually pack our camera in this saddlebag unless our gear is very wet. The total weight in the right saddlebag is approximately seventeen pounds. In the right saddlebag guard bag we pack a small spray bottle of insect repellent, a small tube of sunscreen, a small plastic bottle of Woolite, and one water bottle.

The next step is to pack our tour pack. These are items that must stay dry. First, we each pack a day's worth of clothes (underwear, T-shirt, and socks) plus a few extra items in a small flannel pillow cover and use a plastic bag to keep it dry. Next we pack the rest of my clothing and personal items in a medium soft-side cooler. On short overnight camps, we may leave the clothing in the cooler. But when we stay several days in a base camp, we empty the cooler and use it for additional food storage. If Robin is riding with me, we pack her clothes and personal items into a pillow cover and her ultra-light day pack (REI Flash 18). Once these individual items have been packed, we place our pillow covers, cooler, shower shoes, and other personal items in the tour pack. The total weight packed in the tour pack is about twenty pounds.

Finally, we turn our attention to the luggage rack on top of the tour pack. First, we place the tent (with ground cloth, poles, and doormat rolled together), two tarp support poles, and one sleeping mat on the luggage rack (the tent, which weighs more, is positioned forward, and the tarp support poles are positioned between it and the sleeping pad). Then we stuff both sleeping bags into a large water-resistant nylon compression sack, compress it as tightly as possible, and place these sleeping bags along with the second sleeping mat on top of the tent.

We hold everything in place with three ten-foot lengths of cord from our camping tools bag. See chapter 4 for more details. To tie the gear on the luggage rack, we first start with a cord in the middle of the load. We run the cord around the forward bar of the luggage rack, then over the gear, then under the rear bar of the luggage rack, and then back up over the gear. Next we run the free end of the cord through the loop at the opposite end and cinch everything tight using a simple bowknot. After the center cord has been tied, we tie the left and right sides in a similar manner. This system provides a super secure pack that almost never needs readjustment. We have ridden all day and never had to retie the cords.

After the tent and sleeping gear have been securely tied on the luggage rack, we tie a lightweight daypack on top of the gear. One shoulder strap of the daypack is attached to the forward bar of the luggage rack with a one-foot section of cord, and the other shoulder strap is attached to the rear bar with two more sections of cord. Once the daypack is secure, we use it to hold my cap, rain gear, and map when I do not need them. Although this may sound like a lot of gear on the luggage rack, each of these items is relatively lightweight and their total weight is about twenty-three pounds.

When we arrive at our campsite, we unpack the bike in stages. First, we unpack the luggage rack, set up the tent, open the air mattresses, and put sleeping bags in the tent. Once the tent and sleeping quarters have been set up, we unpack the left saddlebag. In particular, we want to unpack the tool bag so we can stake the tent. Then we unpack the tour pack. We place our clothes, pillows, shower supplies, and personal items inside the tent. If our camp is just an overnight stop and we want to get on the road early the next morning, we do not have to unpack the right saddlebag. If we want a beverage, we can get it any time, because the cooler is packed at the top of the saddlebag bag.

When we are ready to pack up and leave the site, we first pack all our gear in its respective containers and place it on the ground near the bike where it will be packed. After we are sure everything has been accounted for, we pack the gear in its designated location.

This packing plan works well for an Electra Glide, but it may not work as well for your particular bike. For example, if you ride solo on a motorcycle with limited packing space, like my Low Rider, you could pack almost everything you need for a camping trip in a thirty-inch duffle bag and tie it on your back seat.

If you ride two-up on a motorcycle with limited packing space, you will have to add some accessories such as a sissy bar, a pair of saddlebags, a luggage rack, and a sissy bar bag. Some well-known brands of motorcycle luggage include T-Bag, Tourmaster, Willie and Max, and Rev Pack. Some Web sites for buying motorcycle luggage include www.motorcycle-luggage.com, www.motorcycle-superstore.com, and www.cycleluggage.com.

Once you have purchased your luggage, you could pack as much essential gear as possible in the saddlebags and pack your tent, minus its poles, along with your clothes and personal items inside the T-Bag. Roll your poles inside one sleeping mat and tie both mats on top of your T-Bag. If you wanted to pack a cook set, you would have to purchase a small pot in which you could nest two fuel canisters. Lighter items such as sleeping bags could be packed in (or tied high on) the sissy bar bag. If you ride a sport bike, you may have a tank bag for packing some gear. In general, you will have to experiment to find the best packing plan for your bike and luggage capability.

Several other factors will also determine the gear you will need and therefore your packing system. Some of factors such as the length of your trip and the expected weather determine what clothes you must pack. Other factors, such as how much you want to cook in your campsite, will determine the optional gear you will be able to pack. To formulate a safe and efficient packing plan for your particular bike, you should become familiar with several general packing principles.

Packed Weight

Car campers typically do not concern themselves with the weight of their gear. They usually have large trucks or trailers that have plenty of room to haul a lot of gear. The only time car campers might become somewhat concerned is if they buy so much gear that it does not fit into their vehicle.

Backpackers and other ultra-light campers, on the other hand, are very concerned about the total weight of their gear and constantly strive to reduce this weight as much as possible. They will often be walking between three and ten miles a day with their shelter, sleeping gear, toilet supplies, water-treatment gear, rain gear, clothing, cooking gear, and food strapped to their back. For them, every ounce of weight will have an effect upon their endurance. Most backpackers who take weekend trips try to keep the weight of their gear under thirty-five to forty-five pounds. Some ultra-light backpackers claim that they are able to reduce the weight of their gear to less than twenty pounds and thus are able to hike as many as twenty miles a day.

Motorcycle campers fall between these two extremes. They should take the time to weigh their gear and consider alternatives to their heaviest items, but they do not have to spend a lot of money buying the lightest and most expensive gear available. To determine the weight of your gear, purchase a fish scale rated to about fifty pounds. I purchased a digital scale several years ago and tied it to the hanger bar in my closet. Whenever I want to check the weight of a particular item, I just hang it on the fish scale.

I have learned that all of my gear and clothing for a typical solo trip weighs about sixty pounds. Some of the heavier items include my clothing for three extra days plus personal items packed in a soft-side cooler (nine pounds, three ounces), kitchen gear including a small soft-side cooler with five cans of beer (nine pounds, two ounces), my tent with its footprint and doormat (eight pounds, one ounce), and my tool kit (seven pounds, seven ounces). If Robin were joining me, we would add about ten more pounds for her clothing and personal items and about five more pounds for her sleeping gear.

As you begin to assemble the gear for your trip, consider weighing everything to see how close you come to my figures. If, for example, your clothing and personal gear weigh considerably more than nine pounds, consider purchasing lighter, more compressible garments.

Gross Vehicle Weight Rating (GVWR)

Perhaps the most fundamental rule of packing is do not overload your motorcycle. This basic rule is discussed in all operators' manuals, in many books, and in magazine articles on motorcycle touring. However, despite the fact that it is frequently discussed, few motorcycle riders seem to have a clear understanding of this important concept. I confess that for many years of riding I did not really understand this principle. I had heard the admonition "Don't overload your bike" many times, but I never heard an exact explanation and therefore never knew exactly what it meant—until recently.

Basically, this principle means that you should know your bike's Gross Vehicle Weight Rating (GVWR) and try to keep the total weight of your bike and its load under this value. Most people who ride solo do not need to be concerned about overloading the bike because they would rarely be able to pack enough gear to come close to their bike's GVWR. On the other hand, people who ride two-up should become knowledgeable about their GVWR and determine how close they come to exceeding it. For some motorcycles, two relatively large people could exceed the GVWR before packing the first item of camping gear.

Here are the basic facts about the GVWR. For every motorcycle, the manufacturer specifies a gross vehicle weight rating. This value represents the maximum amount of weight, in pounds, the bike is designed to safely carry. This GVWR is printed in the bike's owner's manual and on the bike's frame near the forks. All motorcycle riders, especially if riding two-up, should know their GVWR and try not to load the bike above this specified limit.

The best way to determine how close you are to your bike's GVWR is to weigh it, with your camping load, your passenger, and yourself on a large commercial scale. The sum of your bike, accessories, gear, and riders should not exceed the GVWR.

But most people do not have access to such commercial scales, and so they must estimate their weight. To estimate the weight you are carrying on your bike, first look in your motorcycle owner's manual for the "dry weight" of the bike. This figure is usually stated near the GVWR. Once you have found the dry weight, add the weight of gasoline, oil, and other fluids to estimate the bike's "wet weight." Several experts estimate the additional weight of these fluids to be about fifty pounds. Then add the approximate weight of all the accessories, such as saddlebags, windshields, crash bars, and lights you have added to your bike. Then add your weight, your passenger's weight, and the weight of your clothing and camping gear. If you are like many people, the total weight of your bike packed for a two-up camping trip will exceed its GVWR.

For example, my 1988 FXRS Low Rider has a GVWR of 1,085 pounds and a dry weight of 575 pounds. Its estimated wet weight would be 625 pounds, plus I have added saddlebags, a windshield, a luggage rack, crash bars, and crash bar lights (an estimated 50 pounds). This means that the combined weight of my companion, our gear, our clothing, and me should not exceed about 360 pounds. I weigh about 250 pounds, and Robin weighs ... Whoops. I could get into trouble if I continue this line of reasoning, so let me use a different approach to explain this concept.

If you start with the motorcycle's GVWR (1,085 pounds) and then subtract the bike's estimated wet weight (625 pounds) and accessories (50 pounds), you have a difference of 410 pounds. Then subtract my weight and the weight of our clothing and gear (about 75 pounds) from 410 pounds, and you have a difference of 85 pounds. In other words, if my passenger weighs more than 85 pounds, we would exceed the bike's GVWR. Obviously I need to lose a lot of weight.

Since we now take all of our two-up camping trips on my Electra Glide, let's examine those numbers. You might think (as I did) that it would have as much, if not more, carrying capacity than my Low Rider, but you would be wrong. The GVWR of this bike is 1,179 pounds and its dry weight is 765 pounds with an estimated wet weight of 815 pounds. I removed the leg fairings (10 pounds) and have not added many accessories—so we have about 375 pounds of load-carrying capacity. Using the weights of gear and clothing listed above, you can see that my companion would have to weigh less than 50 pounds to stay under the bike's GVWR. Obviously we exceed the safe weight rating by several pounds.

Three negative consequences can result from exceeding your bike's GVWR. First, your bike will be more difficult to handle and thus more dangerous to ride. It will be more sluggish on the open road and require much more time and space to accelerate and to pass other vehicles. It will be more difficult to stop and will require a longer stopping distance. Its front tire will have less weight bearing on it and thus will skid more easily, especially in gravel, on wet pavement, on grass, and on leaves or other road debris. And perhaps most importantly, it will be more off balance or top-heavy, which will make it overreact when leaning and will make it especially difficult to handle in low-speed leans and turns. From personal experience, let me warn you that even if you know how to make sharp U-turns when riding solo, avoid making them when riding two-up. You can easily lose control of your bike and spill your passenger in the road.

The second possible consequence of exceeding your bike's GVWR is premature tire failure. Carrying an excessive amount of weight on your bike will make its tires ride flatter, especially if they are under-inflated. If you carry this weight for long distances at high speeds on hot pavement, the flatter tire surface, spinning at high speeds on a hot asphalt highway, will produce excessive heat in the tires and could lead to tire failure. Having tire failure on the interstate highway at sixty-five miles per hour could be catastrophic. To reduce your risk of tire failure, you must pay attention to your tires. First, check your tires before departing on a trip. If they show signs of dry rot or other damage or if they have excessive wear, replace them. As a general rule, rear tires on my bikes should be replaced about every ten thousand miles and front tires about every fifteen thousand miles. Second, inflate your tires before your trip—when cold—to the maximum pressure. Finally, make frequent stops during your trip to allow your tires to cool.

The third possible consequence of exceeding your bike's GVWR is accelerated wear and tear on your bike's chain or drive mechanism and brakes and shocks. If you frequently overload your bike and ride many miles, have your motorcycle checked at proper service intervals by factory-trained technicians, and expect frequent repairs.

MSF Principles for Carrying Loads

The Motorcycle Safety Foundation (MSF) has suggested thirteen principles for carrying loads on a motorcycle. Five of the more important principles are published in most state motorcycle operator's manuals. This is the manual that you probably read before taking the written test for your motorcycle license. Toward the back of the manual is a section entitled "Carrying Loads," which briefly discusses each of the five principles. To the five principles listed in state operator's manuals, the MSF has eight more suggestions for carrying loads. To pack your bike safely for a camping trip, you should be familiar with all thirteen principles and understand how they apply to your motorcycle and your packing system.

Keep the load low. Weight has much less effect on a bike's handling when it is packed low, near the bike's center of gravity. It will have a more noticeable effect when packed high. When the weight is packed low you probably will not notice much of a change in turning and low-speed riding. But if the same weight is packed high on a luggage rack or sissy bar bag, you will probably notice that your bike feels more top-heavy, more unstable, and more difficult to control when you are coming to a stop, riding around curves, making U-turns, and especially when you are maneuvering in parking lots. The principle of keeping loads low suggests that you should pack your heavier items, such as your ax, your tool set, and your kitchen gear, in your saddlebags.

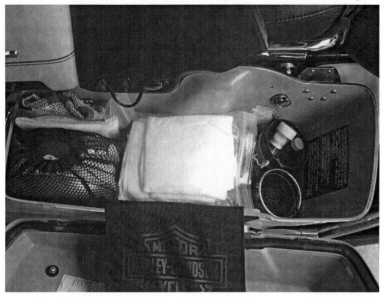

Our cook set with fuel canisters is packed in the right saddlebag. A small cooler can be placed on top.

Keep the load forward of the rear axle. In effect, this principle suggests that you should avoid packing a lot of weight on the luggage rack, if possible. When a load is forward of the rear axle, it is supported by both front and rear wheels and thus is less noticeable. If it is packed behind the rear axle, it puts more weight on the rear wheel and tends to lift the front wheel, like a seesaw. This makes the bike more difficult to handle, especially at low speeds and in turns. If you ride two-up, you will automatically satisfy this principle. Your weight, your passenger's weight, and the weight of your gear packed in the saddlebags will all be forward of the rear axle. If you ride solo, pack heavier gear, such as your tent, on the passenger seat rather than on a luggage rack and, as before, pack heavier items in your saddlebags to keep the weight forward of the rear axle. Heavier items include your tool kit, ax, crowbar, and canned beverages. Heavy kitchen gear like pots and fuel canisters should also be packed in the saddlebags if possible. Lighter items like sleeping bags, mattresses, hats, and jackets, can be packed on the luggage rack.

Distribute the load evenly on each side. The basic logic behind this principle is to preserve the bike's original balance. Some riders believe that unequally weighted saddlebags will make a bike veer or weave on the highway. This instability could increase your risk of crashing and increase the wear and tear on your bike. Motorcycle riders have suggested different ways to pack saddlebags. One writer, for example, recommended packing tools and any other items you might need during the day in the right saddlebag. His logic was that the right saddlebag is more accessible when the bike is leaning on its side stand and that, if you have to stop beside a busy highway, your right saddlebag is further away from traffic.

I prefer to have a little more weight in my left saddlebag. When I come to a routine stop, I want my bike to fall naturally to the left side because that is the first foot I put down to hold the bike during the stop. If my load was evenly balanced or favored the right side, I am afraid that my bike could accidentally fall to the right when my right foot was on the brake and my left foot was ready to support it. And I have not noticed any decrease in the overall stability or handling of the motorcycle.

Secure the load. Be sure your duffle bags, T-Bags, tents, mattresses, and sleeping bags are securely attached to the bike so that they will not come loose during your trip. You certainly do not want to lose your gear in the middle of the highway. More importantly, you do not want your load to suddenly shift in such a way that it could cause you to lose control of your motorcycle. And you do not want any of your gear to become entangled in your wheels or drive mechanism. If your gear gets tangled, you and your passenger will likely have a serious crash.

Many years ago, I used bungee cords and bungee nets to secure gear to my bike. After all, many other motorcycle riders use bungee cords and nets. Although I was never able to secure my gear as tight as I would like, I continued to use them until I had a near calamity. One day I rode to a store to buy some beer and ice. I placed the beer and ice in a small, hard-side cooler and secured the cooler to the luggage rack of my Low Rider with a bungee net. As I was riding back to the campsite, I went around a curve and the cooler slipped off the luggage rack—but it was still attached to my bike by the bungee net. I was suddenly dragging a cooler of beer down a major U.S. highway.

Fortunately I was able to pull off the side of the road before the net became entangled in my spokes or drive mechanism. After that experience, I decided to stop using bungee products and to use strong, non-stretching cord for securing gear to my bike. As it turns out, cord is also a good choice for motorcycle camping because it can be used for many chores in the campsite.

On another camping trip, a friend used bungee cords to secure his camping gear to his bike. I assumed that he knew how to pack his bike and did not offer any advice. About twenty miles down the road we had to stop because his gear was falling off the side of the bike. Even though he secured the load at his house, it shifted considerably in a short time period due to ordinary leaning and riding. Bungee cords may be okay for holding lightweight items like jackets but are unsuited for holding heavier camping gear. A motorcycle safety expert, David Hough, agrees with this conclusion. In his book *Proficient Motorcycling,* he describes his experiences with stretching bungee cords and recommends using straps or ropes rather than bungee cords to secure gear to a motorcycle.

We use one-eighth-inch nylon cord as was discussed in chapter 4. I prefer to use cord (rather than straps) because it provides a more secure package and because it can be used for other camping tasks (such as setting up a tarp or clothesline) once we arrive at our campsite.

In addition to securely tying gear to your motorcycle, you should check all saddlebags and other luggage before departing and check them again during your trip. You want to make sure they are securely fastened. One day I put a baseball cap in the backseat roll bag of my Low Rider. For some reason, my attention was diverted to another matter before securing the cover. When I came back to the bike, I hopped on and failed to check the bag before departing. The cover fell open during my trip and I lost one of my favorite hats on the highway.

Check the load often. During your trip, you should stop every hour or so to buy gas, eat a snack, go to the bathroom, stretch your legs, get your blood circulating, and regain your alertness. Before getting back on your bike, check the tightness of your load and check to see if any straps or cord ends have worked loose. If your load was well secured before you left your home, it should never come loose. But if it does, re-cinch and retie the cords. If some cord ends are loose, tuck them back into your load so they do not damage your paint finish or accidentally tangle in your bike's drive mechanism.

Use a luggage rack for large loads. This seems obvious, but many people who tour on their motorcycles do not have luggage racks. They pack their gear on almost any part of the motorcycle you can imagine. Perhaps you have seen sleeping bags, leather jackets, leather chaps, or other gear tied on the handlebars, on front and rear fenders, on the front forks, and so on. While these applications may look creative, they are potentially dangerous because the gear may alter the bike's handling in a particular situation. And it could come loose and tangle in the bike's drive or steering mechanisms. In either case, it could cause a crash. Instead of packing gear all over your bike, purchase a luggage rack and use it, along with a compatible sissy bar bag, to carry your larger items. Luggage racks are essential because, along with the sissy bar, they support a bag filled with gear and keep it from sagging down where it could obscure the bike's taillights and turn signals or could tangle in the rear wheel.

Store gear behind you rather than in front of you. Secure most of your gear behind you so it does not obstruct your view or interfere with your ability to handle your bike. If you are riding solo, you should tie the gear on the passenger seat. If you are riding two-up, you should store it in a tour pack or in a sissy bar bag. One possible exception to this recommendation would be tank bags such as the ones frequently used by sport bike riders. As a Harley rider, I have never used a tank bag, but riders of sport bikes and sport-touring bikes consider their tank bags to be one of their most useful pieces of luggage. Apparently, tank bags do not create additional handling problems for them.

Become familiar with handling differences of a loaded bike. When you first start your trip, take it easy for several miles until you get a feeling for changes in your bike's handling characteristics due to the heavy load. Be aware of differences in your bike's acceleration, braking, leaning, and steering characteristics. When coming to a stop, put both feet down. You may wish to ask your backseat companion to look over your left shoulder when you are coming to a stop and to refrain from shifting her body position until both of your feet are squarely planted on the ground and the bike is under control.

Do not leave loose rope or strap ends hanging. Tie loops in long ropes and tuck all loose ends into your load. Some riders use duct tape to secure the loose ends. If you fail to tuck them in or secure them, the constant flapping from the wind could damage the end of the rope and your paint finish. Furthermore, if the ends are long, they could tangle in your chain or drive mechanism and cause you to crash.

Be sure brake lights and turn signals are visible. If you are riding a touring bike and have packed most of your gear in your hard saddlebags and tour pack, you should easily comply with this principle. However, if you are riding a sport bike or a cruiser and are using soft luggage, you need to be sure your load does not obscure your rear lights. You want to be sure that other drivers can easily see your taillight, your brake lights, and your turn signals.

Understand that extra weight adds to wear and tear of your bike. If you ride two-up most of the time, you should have your bike serviced often and you should be sensitive to any changes in its handling characteristics. If you notice a problem, get it checked out immediately. Do not put it off or you could have a serious problem that could ruin your trip.

Do not pack gear on front fender or fork. If you go to motorcycle rallies, you probably have seen jackets, tents, and blankets tied on the front handlebars or forks of some bikes. Although many riders frequently pack gear in these places, they are risking a serious accident. The load could alter the steering characteristics of their bike, or it could work loose and become tangled in the front wheel. Furthermore, the load could block fresh air from cooling your motor and thus lead to engine overheating. Any of these consequences could cause you to break down or crash.

Be careful when packing gear inside fairings. Most touring motorcycles have fairings with some storage areas. These areas are intended only for small lightweight items. Heavy items could alter the steering and leaning characteristics of the bike and should be packed in saddlebags. If you were unable to fit heavier items in a saddlebag, your tour pack or sissy bar bag would be a better location than your fairing pockets.

Additional Packing Tips

In addition to the MSF principles for packing a motorcycle, I would like to add a few more suggestions. Most of these suggestions can be found in other motorcycle camping references, but a few reflect my own personal opinions.

Be sure saddlebags (and other luggage) have been installed properly and are clear of exhaust pipes, drive mechanism, and wheels. Several crashes are reportedly caused every year by gear becoming entangled in a bike's wheels, chains, or drive belts. To prevent such problems, be sure saddlebag guards are properly installed before adding saddlebags as an accessory to your bike. When packing, check the saddlebags and the guards to be sure your luggage cannot come into contact with moving parts. Be sure your luggage is clear of your exhaust pipes. If a bag accidentally contacts a pipe, it could cause a fire that can be accelerated by your bike's oil or gasoline. A bag touching a hot pipe will likely burn a hole in the saddlebag and could burn your gear inside the bag. Furthermore, bags touching an exhaust pipe could produce an unsightly black scorched spot on your pipe that will be difficult to remove.

Use a checklist to guide your packing. Most experienced campers know the importance of preparing camping gear checklists. The reason for a list is that, in the excitement and confusion of preparing for your trip, you could easily forget to pack important items unless you have a list of items to check off. Some of these items would be difficult to find on the road and may be expensive. On past trips, we have occasionally forgotten important items and spent a lot time trying to replace them or trying to compensate for their absence. Several camping books and Web sites offer comprehensive camping checklists. We use several lists to guide our packing. I have presented these lists throughout this book. The list at the end of this chapter gives an overview of the items we take on a camping trip and the place on my touring bike where we pack them. You could photocopy these lists or use them to make your own list. Save your list and store it with your camping gear.

Pack as few clothes as possible. Clothing can take a considerable amount of packing space, especially when riding two up. When packing for a camping trip, pack only what you will absolutely need, and plan to wash your clothes every three to four days. Although you will be able to pack up to three changes of socks and underwear, you can live comfortably with only one extra pair of pants and a long-sleeved shirt. You can usually wear these later items two or three days before washing. To further reduce the overall amount of space needed for clothing, be sure to pack clothes that are compressible and fast drying.

Contrary to what you may read in other motorcycle camping sources, you probably will not have room to pack a pair of sneakers or walking shoes. When riding two-up, two pair of sneakers or walking shoes requires a considerable amount of packing space. You will be lucky to find room to pack your shower shoes—much less two more pairs of walking shoes. Therefore, you must be content to use your shower shoes for casual camp wear. For several years, we used flip-flops, but recently we started using Crocs, which are very comfortable and dry quickly. When traveling, we stuff each one with a pair of socks.

Pack as few personal items as possible. Determine what items you must have and what items could be left at home. For example, I must have a toothbrush, toothpaste, floss, hairbrush, and razor. I like a regular-sized toothbrush but cut two inches off the handle to make it smaller to pack. I use a travel-sized toothpaste tube, floss, and hairbrush. I use my bath soap to lather up for shaving. I place my medicine in small travel-sized containers. The total amount of space required for all these items is very small. Robin requires a few more items, but the total space required for her personal items is also relatively small.

Pack clothes and personal items in containers that have other uses. Most backpackers and motorcycle campers prefer to pack all of their clothes and gear in stuff sacks before packing it in their backpacks. In fact, backpackers are so fond of using stuff sacks that most books and articles on camping and backpacking spend a considerable amount of space describing procedures for buying, making, and using these sacks. Furthermore, camping supply stores offer a large selection of stuff sacks and compression sacks in a wide range of sizes. These stuff sacks are considered desirable because they are very lightweight, they further compress your clothes into the smallest possible space, and they require virtually no additional packing space.

For several years, we also packed all our clothes and personal items in six or seven stuff sacks, but we gradually realized that the stuff sacks were sometimes inconvenient and that they have no other uses after setting up camp. We once tried using them as pillows but found them to be uncomfortable. Furthermore, we discovered that when each person has two or three stuff sacks filled with clothing and personal items we had difficulty finding specific items and sometimes had to empty two or three sacks before we found the particular item we wanted.

After several trips, we decided to try a different strategy. In particular, we decided to pack our clothes and personal items in containers that have other uses in camp. For example, we pack a complete set of clothes (underwear, T-shirt, socks, and shorts) in soft flannel pillow covers and use the pillows to sleep on. We purchased these pillow covers with foam filling, but discarded the filling and use our clothing instead. When we need to wear the clothes inside the pillow cover, we can replace them with clothes worn on previous days. We pack the rest of my clothes and personal items into a small soft-side cooler. When we arrive at our campsite, I can lift the cooler by its strap and carry my clothing and personal items to the tent in one trip. If we decide to leave the clothes in the cooler overnight, I can find particular items easier in the cooler with a zip top rather than in one of several stuff sacks. If we are staying in a base camp for several days, we remove the clothes from the cooler and use the cooler to store perishable food. Robin packs the rest of her clothes and personal items in her ultra-light daypack. When we set up camp, she can use the day pack to carry small items on our hikes.

I pack most of my clothes and personal items in this soft-side cooler.

Pack related items together. When packing for a trip, try to keep related items together so that you can easily pack your bike and later find what you need when you need it. For example, pack all your tent parts together, with the exception of your stakes. When you are ready to set up your tent, all the parts are handy. Combine all your tools (including your ax and crow bar and tent stakes) in a tool bag and pack it in a saddlebag. Pack your clothing and personal items (towel, lights, medicine, personal hygiene kit, radio, etc.) together. Pack some of your clothes into your pillow and the rest, with your personal items, into a soft-side cooler or stuff sack. Then you can pack your pillows, cooler, and stuff sacks together in the tour pack or into a T-Bag. When you are ready to take your clothes and personal items into the tent, everything will be together. Pack all your kitchen gear together in a saddlebag. Once you develop a packing system, both you and your companion will be able to pack and unpack easily and you will be able to find anything you need without having to look in several different places.

Pack rain gear where it is accessible. When packing your bike, pack your rain gear where you can find it quickly when it begins to rain. You want to be able to find your pants, gaiters, gloves, and jackets without having to unpack saddlebags or move other items. Many motorcycle riders pack their rain gear at the top of one saddlebag. We sometimes pack ours in a saddlebag, but most of the time we pack it in our daypack, which has been tied on top of the tent and sleeping gear.

Pack your tent where it is accessible. When you arrive at your campsite, you want to be able to unpack and set up your tent before having to unpack any other gear. We pack our tent on the luggage rack, but if you are not riding an Electra Glide with a tour pack and luggage rack, you may have to pack your tent elsewhere. If you pack a duffle bag on the back seat, you could pack your tent at the top of the duffle bag or tie it on top of the duffle bag. If you are riding two-up, you could pack your tent at the top of your T-Bag.

Pack sleeping bags in a water-resistant or waterproof stuff sack. If you have down sleeping bags, you must diligently protect them from rain and all other sources of moisture. If you have synthetic bags, you do not have to be as concerned about moisture, but you still need to protect your bags from getting soaked. When riding a touring bike, use a large water-resistant nylon compression sack or a rubber-coated dry bag. Stuff both sleeping bags in the bag and then use cinch straps or cord to cinch the bag as tightly as possible to make a long, small-diameter bag that can be easily tied with the tent and sleeping pads onto the luggage rack. When riding a cruiser, you may wish to stuff each sleeping bag into an individual waterproof stuff sack and then pack them either in or on the T-Bag.

Keep wet and dry items separate. During most camping trips, some items are bound to get wet. They may get wet because of rain, sweat, dew, washing, or water activities. Whatever the reason, you need a system for preventing your wet items from soaking your dry items, especially your clothes. The best way to accomplish this task is to pack wet items in plastic bags before packing them in the same saddlebag, tour pack, or T-bag with your dry items. Some motorcycle campers use garbage bags, but we prefer plastic shopping bags, especially those given by upscale department stores. These bags typically measure about eighteen inches by eighteen inches. They are large enough for most wet items, they have handles, they are strong, they require almost no packing space, and they can be used for many different purposes. Pack at least four of these bags—two for each person.

Conclusion

How can you pack all your camping gear and clothes on a motorcycle—especially when riding two-up without a trailer or chase vehicle? The keys to packing for motorcycle camping trips are to purchase gear made for backpackers and to develop a system for packing this gear on your motorcycle.

When developing your packing system, you should consider several safety measures. First determine the total weight of your camping gear and clothing. Know your bike's GVWR, and try to keep your total weight under this value. If you are overweight, like me, try to lose some of the weight. After considering your bike's GVWR, refer to the Motorcycle Safety Foundation's general recommendations for carrying loads. Some of the more important recommendations can be found in your state's motorcycle operator's manual. In addition to these MSF recommendations, I have added several additional tips for packing a motorcycle. Following basic principles of motorcycle packing will help to make your trip safer and more comfortable.

After reading this chapter, read *Proficient Motorcycling: The Ultimate Guide to Riding Well* by David Hough. This book presents a good introduction and explanation of a bike's GVWR and explains a number of safe packing guidelines. Then visit the Motorcycle Safety Foundation Web site for more advice regarding loading your motorcycle.

Motorcycle Packing List

Waist Pack
Sunglasses, cell phone, small micro-tool, butane lighter, lip balm, spare keys, and checkbook
Left Saddlebag
10-by-10-foot tarp and a bike cover
Camping tools (ax, crowbar, gloves, pliers, knife, stakes, and cord)
Hammock and straps
Tablecloth
Passenger's personal items
Left Engine Guard Bag
Fix-A-Flat and water bottle
Right Saddlebag
Kitchen items (insulated cups, eating utensils, cooking utensils, paper towels, aluminum foil, dishcloths, dishtowels, spices, cook set, stove, and 2 fuel canisters)
Small soft-side cooler (with beverages, salad oil, and butter)
First-aid kit and paper towels
Camera
Right Engine Guard Bag
Sunscreen, insect repellent, Woolite, and water bottle
Tour Pack
My clothing, headlights, and personal items in a soft-side cooler
MP3 players and radio
Pillow covers (packed with clothing needed for one day)
Shower supplies (bag, soap, towel, washcloth, and shoes)
Passenger's clothing in an ultra-light day pack (or TV if riding solo)
Luggage Rack
Tent, poles, doormat, and footprint
Sleeping bags in a water resistant compression sack
Sleeping pads
Tarp support poles (2) in a pole bag
Daypack with rain gear, baseball cap, and map

9. Chores and Activities

After a long day on the road, you finally arrive at your campground. As you turn into the park drive, you begin to scan the environment to create a mental image of the overall layout of the park and the campground. You begin to look for the registration station. Some parks have self-registration, especially if you arrive after 5 PM, but most parks have an office with a ranger or clerk who will orient you to the campground, get basic information such as your name and home address, and collect your camping fee.

Sometimes, park rangers or office personnel will assign a specific campsite, but frequently they will let you ride around the campground to select the site you prefer. To make the best selection, you must first become oriented to the park and the campground. Develop a mental map of the roads, the bathhouses, the hills, the valleys, and the available sites that have features you want such as proximity to the bathhouse, privacy, and trees to which you could tie your dining fly and hammock. You must eventually decide upon a particular site or two and return to the office to complete your registration. Once you have completed all the paperwork, you may want to ask about the nearest location where you can buy food, supplies, firewood, and perhaps coffee in the morning.

Deep Creek Campground in the Smoky Mountains has a self-registration station.

This chapter describes many of the typical chores and activities associated with camping. Throughout the chapter, I will present several suggestions to help you and your companion stay dry, warm, and comfortable during your stay.

Setting Up Camp

After completing your registration, you must undertake a series of chores in order to set up your campsite. Hopefully you and your companion can work together efficiently to complete these chores in short period of time. Then you can begin to relax and enjoy all the many pleasures the park has to offer.

As you undertake your chores, you will have to communicate with each other frequently, but avoid shouting across the campsite. When you need to talk with your companion some distance away, stop what you are doing and walk closer so that you can talk in a quiet voice. Sound seems to carry more in a campground. You do not want to disturb your neighbors, and you do not want to create a bad first impression that may create a barrier to later social interaction. Unfortunately many couples have difficulty talking in normal voices and begin yelling at each other as soon as they arrive at their campsite. Do not be one of these couples.

Selecting your campsite. After checking in, you will likely ride through the park to look for the best available site. If your campground is a popular one, you may have only a few sites from which to choose. What features should you look for? Every camper seems to have a different opinion. Backpackers must look for sites that are close to rivers, lakes, or some other body of water because they will need to draw water for drinking and cooking.

Motorcycle campers, on the other hand, do not need to be concerned about proximity to water and can focus upon other factors. If the campground is located near a lake or some other body of water, look for a site that is at least seventy paces (two hundred feet) away from the water's edge. There are several reasons for creating some distance between your camp and the water. For example, you do not want to create an obstacle that could discourage wildlife from coming down to the water for a drink; you do not want to accidentally pollute the water with your waste; and you do not want to risk injury from wildlife such as alligators and snakes that may live near the water's edge. After considering this initial issue, we use four important priorities for selecting our campsite.

The first priority should be to find a site that has good water drainage. We do not want to pitch our tent in a valley or low area that could flood if it rains during our stay. Many years ago, when we were much younger, we did not understand the importance of selecting a site with good drainage. One evening we stopped at a KOA campground near Birmingham, Alabama. The clerk suggested a site in the tenting area, but I saw another unoccupied site with many trees, so we requested the wooded site and the park staff granted our request. A few hours later, after we had gone to bed, a strong thunderstorm moved through the area and dumped several inches of rain. Unfortunately our site was the low point of the entire campground. Very quickly we found our tent submerged in a large pool of water about three inches deep. After spending the night in our car, we took the clerk's advice and moved the next day to the tenting area to dry out our gear. After this experience, our first priority is to find a site that will not flood.

Many campgrounds today have elevated tent pads filled with gravel designed to drain water away from your tent as well as to keep campers from pitching their tents on fragile vegetation near the campsite. If the campground has such tent pads, this first priority is satisfied and you can shift your attention to the next three priorities. If the campground does not have elevated tent pads, look for a site that has a compacted ground area on a slight incline or on a small mound. Either of these two features would allow water drainage. Avoid sites at the bottom of a hill, in a gully, or obviously lower than surrounding terrain. Also avoid flat areas, because ground that appears flat may, in fact, be slightly concave and collect water. When considering a potential site, try to determine how heavy rainwater will drain away. If you fail to select a site with good drainage and it rains, you will likely find yourself sleeping in a swimming pool.

Our second priority is to find a site that has at least two trees positioned such that we can set up our dining fly. We prefer sites with several trees that allow us to set up a tarp over our picnic table and provide shade for our tent. We also want trees so we can set up our hammocks. If available sites have only a few trees, we prefer sites that have trees on the west side so that our tent will be shaded from the hot afternoon sun. Having morning sun can be good, but having afternoon sun can make camp life a little more uncomfortable. Hot afternoon sun can make it difficult to take a nap, read a book, or otherwise relax. Furthermore, direct sunlight will gradually deteriorate the materials used to make your tent and dining fly. If you will be camping overnight only and you plan to hit the road early the next morning, you usually do not have to be concerned about trees because most of the time you will not set up your tarp.

Our third priority is to find a site that is reasonably close to the bathroom. For many women, proximity to the bathroom seems to be their first priority. I must confess that as I get older and now must get up almost every night, it has become a much higher priority for me. The best sites are across the road from the bathroom rather than right next to it. This way you avoid having other campers walking through your site to get to the bathroom. If you select a site immediately next to a bathroom, many children and inconsiderate adults will walk through your site (even in the middle of the night) rather than walk on the designated trail. This constant traffic through your site can be very annoying. You can politely tell each person where the path is, but discouraging traffic through your site can be a constant problem. The best way to avoid such traffic is to select a site across the road.

Once our first three priorities have been satisfied, we consider spaciousness as our fourth priority. Some campers might use the term "privacy" for this priority. We do not necessarily need bushes or undergrowth to prevent other campers from seeing us. We just want a sufficient amount of room so that we can move about in our campsite without having to interact with our neighbors. Similarly we do not want our neighbors so close that they have to walk in our site when attending to their routine camping chores. In other words, we do not like feeling confined to a small tent and table area, as is frequently the case in many RV parks and crowded open-field campgrounds.

Another desirable feature is isolation. Occasionally you can find sites that allow considerable privacy, but such sites are rare in many established campgrounds. The best bet for finding a site with both spaciousness and isolation is a primitive or walk-in site. Otherwise most campgrounds, including private, state, and national ones, are designed to accommodate as many camping units as possible, and their sites are usually relatively close to each other.

Another factor you may wish to consider is distance from trash dumpsters. Ideally you want a site close enough to the dumpsters that you can walk there in a few minutes, but you should avoid sites that are immediately adjacent to them. If you select a site that is too close to the dumpsters, you may have to smell garbage during your stay, hear constant noise from other campers slamming the doors and talking loudly, and have animals attracted to the food smells walking in or near your site.

Planning your campsite layout. After selecting your campsite, walk around to determine how best to set up your camp. Try to determine the best place to set up your dining fly and the best place to set up your tent. In some campgrounds, the tent pad, table, and fire ring are pre-positioned and you will have little choice. But in many campgrounds, you will have some freedom to arrange your campsite as you would like. Also look for trees that could be used to set up your hammocks.

If you are camping in bear country, you should locate your cooking/eating area about forty-five feet (fifteen paces) away from your tent/sleeping area. Otherwise you can set up your cooking/eating area about fifteen feet (five paces) away from your tent/sleeping area. The reasons for separating these two areas is to avoid problems with raccoons and other animals that may visit your food preparation area in the night and to prevent accidental damage to your tent fabric from sparks that may float away from your campfire. You do not want to recreate the tent fire scene shown in the movie *Wild Hogs*!

In cool weather, we like to set up our tent on one side of our picnic table with the campfire ring on the opposite side. In other words, we like to position our table between our tent and the fire ring. This arrangement provides ample distance between our tent and campfire but allows us to sit on the table benches under the rain fly before entering or after exiting the tent. We can use the benches to take off or put on our shoes and socks or to sit and relax near the tent door. If it is raining, we have a sheltered place to take off or put on our rain gear. At the opposite end of the table, we can sit on the benches and enjoy our campfire. We also cook and prepare our meals on the end closest to the fire ring.

The tent and fire ring are on opposite sides of the dining area. This was my winter campsite at Monte Sano State Park, Huntsville, Alabama.

As you survey your site, be sure to look for large rocks that would be uncomfortable to sleep on or that could damage your tent floor, large tree roots that could trip you in the middle of the night, dead tree limbs that could fall on your tent, poison ivy, broken glass, ant beds, yellow jacket or hornet nests, and other possible problems.

Setting up your tent. Hopefully you have selected an elevated but relatively level spot with good drainage in the event of rain. In addition, you should have selected a spot that is several feet away from your campfire and cooking areas. The next step is to remove any sharp rocks, pine cones, and twigs lying in the spot where you want to pitch your tent. To help find these objects, lay your ground cloth on the ground and feel around it. Some campers actually lie down on the ground cloth. When you feel a large object, reach under the ground cloth and remove it. You could trace the outline of your ground cloth with your crowbar or a stick and then remove it to find sharp objects. If a rock is

224

embedded in the ground, use your crowbar to remove it and to dig dirt to fill in the depression.

Once the ground is smooth and free from large objects, you are ready to set up your tent. Modern tents are usually easy to set up. In general, the steps are as follows: lay out your ground cloth, place your tent body on top of the ground cloth, assemble your poles, push poles through tent sleeves (if any), insert pole tips into their designated seats, hook tent clips to the pole assembly, reposition the tent if necessary, pull the floor tight, stake the corners, cover the tent body with the rain fly, stake rain fly guy lines, and put out your welcome mat.

Setting up your sleeping quarters. Once your tent is set up, unroll your sleeping pads and (assuming they are self-inflating Therm-a-Rest pads) open the valves and lay them on the tent floor so they will begin to automatically inflate. When our sleeping pads have inflated, we usually blow an extra puff of air in them to provide an extra measure of comfort and then close the valve. Now you are ready to unpack your sleeping bags and place them with your pillows on your sleeping mat. Next bring your clothes, shower supplies, personal-grooming kits, personal music players, books, and headlights into the tent. We typically place these items just inside the door so that we can easily access them later without having to crawl inside the tent. If the tent has two doors, we each place our gear near a different door. If the tent only has one door, we each place our gear in the corner near the door on our side of the tent. Most importantly, we want to be able to find our headlights, personal-grooming kits, and shower supplies after dark without having to enter the tent and rummage around.

Setting up your food-preparation area. Once you have decided where to position your table, you must clean it so that it is sanitary for preparing and eating your meals. Use a cloth rag to brush away old food crumbs, twigs, leaves, and other debris. If the table is sticky, use water and a paper towel to clean the area. After the tabletop is dry, cover it with a plastic tablecloth. To prevent the tablecloth from blowing away, tie it onto the table with one or two pre-cut cords (see chapter 4 for further details). Check the fire ring and remove any trash left by previous occupants. Before sitting down at the table, look under and around it for bees, spiders, debris, or other things that could cause injury. Finally, draw some water, set up your stove, and unpack the rest of your kitchen gear.

Setting up your dining fly. If you plan to stay in your site for several days—or if rain is predicted during the afternoon or evening—you will likely want to set up a dining fly. Setting up a tarp or rain fly takes a little time but provides a lot of comfort from sun, evening dewfall, and rain. Most of the time, you can first tie your fly to trees wherever they are positioned in your site and then move your table under it. In a few sites you may find a heavy, stationary table. In this case you must use whatever trees happen to be close to your table to set up your dining fly.

The best tarp size is at least eight feet by ten feet. You can purchase such a tarp in almost any hardware, building supply, or discount department store for less than ten dollars. If you want a larger and more packable tarp, buy a lightweight ten-foot-by-ten-foot nylon tarp from a camping supply store. It will cost a little more, but it requires a little less packing space.

Tarps can be set up several different ways. If we have our two eight-foot collapsible poles, we like to tie two corners of the tarp to trees and two corners to the poles. Depending upon the positions of trees in the site, you can set up the tarp in different ways. If two trees are positioned on the same side of the table, you can tie each corner of the tarp about five to six feet high on a tree, stretch the tarp across the table, and secure the other two corners with poles. The tarp on the pole edge will be about eight feet high, and the tarp will slope down toward the tree side. Or if two trees are positioned on opposite sides of the table, we tie one corner of the tarp about eight feet high on one tree and the diagonal opposite corner of the tarp about six feet high on the other tree. Then we use the poles to support the off corners. If only one tree is available, we tie one corner about eight feet high on a tree and the diagonal opposite corner to the end of the table or to a ground stake.

Whenever attaching a tarp corner to a pole, you should first insert the pole tip into the tarp grommet; then slip the loops of two guy cords (or ropes) over the pole tips and then stake the cord ends to the ground. Stakes should be set out about four feet from the pole and in direct line with each edge of the tarp. In effect, the two stakes and the pole will form an equilateral triangle that makes a very stable setup. At the free (ground) end of the cord, you must make a loop to hold the stake. To make this loop, you could use a reversed half hitch, a taut-line hitch, or a Prusik knot. Each of these knots will hold the guy line tight but can be easily slipped tighter or looser when necessary. We prefer the Prusik knot because it seems to be the most secure. Each of them will be described in more detail in the next section of this chapter.

If you do not have any poles and your campsite has lots of trees and little wind, you can simply run a piece of cord from each corner of the tarp to a different tree. To assure water runoff away from your tent and campfire, lower one corner of the tarp or make a center ridge by tying a cord high on a tree near the center of the tarp, running it under the tarp to a second tree on the opposite side of the tarp, and tying it high on that tree.

If you only have a few trees in your campsite (or if there is a prevailing wind) you can make a lean-to with your tarp. Lean-tos can be made several different ways. One popular way is to run a length of cord between two trees about seven or eight feet off the ground. Tie this cord as tightly as possible. Then use several one-foot sections of cord to tie each grommet along one edge of your tarp to your cord line. Tying the tarp to the cord line will help prevent grommets from pulling out, especially on windy days. Once all grommets on one edge are tied to the cord line, pull out the bottom edge of the tarp in the direction of the wind—usually to the southwest. Use three or four five-foot lengths of cord to pull out your bottom edge. Using these five-foot cords rather than staking the bottom edge of your tarp to the ground will give you more room to move about under your rain fly. If you are in a hurry and there is little wind, you could simplify your lean-to by just tying two corners of the tarp to trees and staking the other two to the ground. Regardless of the method you use, a lean-to will make it easier to cook and will improve your overall comfort level by blocking both sun and wind.

If your site has only one tree, you can still rig a dining fly. Tie a twenty-five-foot length of cord as high on the tree as possible, pull it tight in the direction of the wind, and stake the opposite end to the ground. Then lay your tarp over the line such that one corner can be tied high on the line and the diagonal opposite corner can be tied low on the line. Use one-foot lengths of cord to tie these corners. Then use two five-foot lengths of cord to pull out the two off corners and stake them to the ground.

Tying knots. Being able to use cord and being able to tie appropriate knots can make your camping trips much more enjoyable. In camp, you need to set up your tarp, your tent, and a clothesline. Each task requires the use of cord and knots. If you are able to tie good knots that can be easily untied when breaking camp, your camping life will run smoothly.

As discussed in chapter 4, cut your cord into five- and ten-foot sections and tie a simple overhand loop at one end of each cord section before departing from your home. Once these loops have been tied, you will never untie them. Depending upon the particular task at hand, these loops can be used in a variety of useful ways.

In the campsite you will be confronted by different tasks that will require different lengths of cord and different knots. For example, a common task is to join two or more cords to make a longer line. If you need to make a twenty-foot line to run from one tree to another (for a dining fly or a clothesline), join two ten-foot sections of cord. The best knot to join two sections of cord is a sheet bend knot. Simply run the free end of one cord through the pre-tied loop of the second cord and then run the free end around the second cord and back under itself. This knot will not slip when the line is tightened. But regardless of the amount of tension placed on this knot, it can be easily untied when you are ready to break camp.

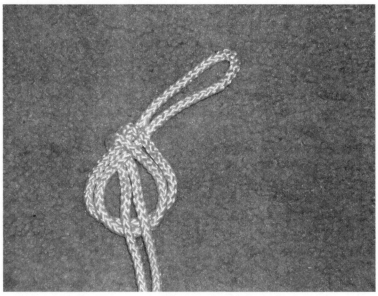

A simple overhand loop

A sheet bend knot

A second common task in a campsite is to run a tight line between two trees or from one tree to the ground. To accomplish this task, first wrap the loop end of a cord around the biggest tree and then run the free end through the loop. In other words, make a lasso around the tree. While the lasso is loose, adjust it as high as appropriate for the situation and then pull the cord tight. Next run the line to the second tree or to a ground stake and tie it tight. Several different knots can be used to anchor the line to the second point. I prefer to run the line around a small tree two times (round turn) and tie a slipped bowknot. If the line needs to be tightened later, I simply pull the end of the bowknot to untie it, retighten the line, and retie it to the tree. Other campers use a clove hitch or a double half hitch. These hitch knots are frequently used because they can be easily untied when you need to re-tighten the line.

A Prusik knot

A bowline knot

A third common camping task is to tie a line to a point, such as a ground stake, so that the knot will hold the line tight but also will slip when you want to make the line tighter or looser. For example, tents with a full rain fly have guy points that must be pulled out away from the tent to allow ventilation and to make the vestibule. Sometimes you may want these points pulled out to their maximum, but other times you may wish to have them closer to your tent. The easiest knot to accomplish this task is a double reversed half hitch. A better knot would be a taut-line hitch. Better yet, use a Prusik knot. All of these knots will hold a line tight but can easily be adjusted to make the line tighter or looser.

One last camping situation requiring a special knot is the occasion when you need to make a temporary loop that can be pulled tight without slipping. For example, you may want to hang a hammock between two trees. In this situation you want a loop (to which you can hook your hammock) that will not slip under relatively high pressure but can be easily untied later when the cinch is no longer needed. The best knot for this situation is the bowline knot. To make this knot, first make a loop in the cord, then run the free end of the cord up through the loop, around the cord, and back through the loop.

Several other knots, such as a figure eight, a clove hitch, and square knots, are discussed in many camping books, but we have not found the need to use them in our camping experiences.

Maintaining Camp

After setting up your camp, you must perform several chores to make your camping trip run smoothly. Some chores, such as washing clothes, are only required every two or three days, but many chores must be completed every day during your camp. If you arrive at your campsite in the afternoon and plan to pack up the next morning, you will have a lot of chores to complete before going to bed. Hopefully you arrived early. If you are staying several days in a base camp, you can spread some of these chores out over time so that you do not feel pressured to get everything done in a short time.

Going for food and supplies. Once you have completely unpacked, one of the next tasks is riding to the nearest store to buy food and supplies. The items you need to buy on any particular day will depend upon your food preference for the night, the weather, and the length of time you plan to stay in your site. Some of the things you might buy include ice, food, charcoal, firewood, aluminum foil, paper plates, paper towels, batteries, a gallon jug of water, and if you are staying a few days in your base camp, a couple of cheap folding chairs.

Some couples will split up—one person stays in the campsite to set up the tent and food-preparation area while the other rides to the store for food and supplies. Several years ago, we met such a couple at Potawatomie State Park in Door County, Wisconsin. After unloading their gear on the picnic table, the man rode to the store while the woman set up the entire campsite, including the tent and sleeping gear.

We prefer to ride to the store together, to see what is available and discuss our food and meal options that particular day. When we are on vacation, we never plan our meals ahead of time. We like to decide at the last moment based upon our mood and what is available. Most of the time, we reach a consensus very quickly. Once we decide what we want to eat, we know the supplies we will need to purchase. After purchasing our food and supplies we pack them on the bike and head back to the campsite.

Finding firewood. Frequently we do not attempt to find firewood because we do not want or need a campfire. Perhaps we want to attend an evening program or perhaps we want to go to bed early so we can get on the road early the next morning. But occasionally we want to have a fire, especially if we are staying in the site for another day or two. We enjoy having a fire in the morning, especially if it is cool. So after getting our food and supplies back to our campsite, I may go back out to find firewood while Robin begins to prepare our meal.

Occasionally you can find wood lying around the campground, but most of the time you will have to buy it. Many campgrounds sell seasoned firewood in the office, and occasionally park staff will deliver it to your campsite. Most of the time, however, you will have to ride back to a store and bring it back yourself. On these occasions, ride alone because you will have to tie the firewood onto the backseat of your bike. It is too bulky and too heavy to carry in your saddlebags or on your luggage rack.

Never transport firewood from another state or distant location to your campsite, even when car camping. Always obtain your firewood from the park or a nearby vendor. Wood from distant locations may be infested with insects or microorganisms that could harm the trees and vegetation in the park. For example, the emerald ash borer has spread from Michigan over at least nine other midwestern states and has killed over twenty million ash trees since 2002. Adult beetles bore holes into ash trees to lay their eggs. Eggs hatch into larvae that feed on the tree for several weeks—eventually killing the tree. When ash trees are cut for firewood, they may contain adult beetles or larvae. Bringing ash or other firewood from another area may introduce an infestation to plants and animals that have never been exposed to it before and do not have the defenses to withstand its harmful effects.

Several types of wood are sold as firewood. As a general rule, soft wood (such as southern pine, cedar, and cottonwood) can be used to start your fire but should be avoided after the fire is burning well. Soft woods produce lots of smoke and will deposit a gum residue on your food or pots. Instead use hardwood such as oak, ash, hickory, poplar, and birch to maintain a hot and relatively smokeless campfire. In particular, many experts believe that oak and ash make the best firewood because their logs are easy to split, produce few sparks, produce little smoke, and have high heat value.

Splitting wood. When you purchase or find firewood, it probably will be cut the right length for a fire, but many pieces may be too large in diameter to be efficiently used as fuel. Ideally firewood should be no larger than the diameter of your wrist. When you buy a load of firewood, many pieces will likely be much larger and you will have to split some pieces with your ax before making your fire.

Some hardwoods are relatively easy to split with your camp ax, while other woods are more difficult to split. Red oak and ash, for example, split easily, while elm and butternut are very difficult to split. Poplar, a wood that is commonly sold as firewood here in the South, requires some effort but can be split with a camp ax. Birch, which is frequently sold for firewood in northern Wisconsin, also requires some effort but can be split if you strike the log with the ax blade parallel (rather than perpendicular) to the bark edge.

When you have a log that splits easily, split it several times to make several small pieces to start your fire. When you find a log that is difficult to split, set it beside the fire as a windscreen and allow it to dry out and heat up so it will later burn efficiently. After sitting next to a hot fire for a while, the large log will begin to flame up. When it does, you can move it onto the fire as needed. These larger logs can be used after your fire has become very hot and has a good bed of coals.

You must be very careful when you split wood. You do not want to sink your ax into your leg or foot. It is a good idea to wear camp gloves and boots rather than flip-flops. It is also good to refrain from drinking alcoholic beverages until you have finished splitting your firewood. To split the wood, place one end of the log on the ground so that it is standing straight up. If it will not stand naturally, use another log to support it. Once the log is in place, spread your legs wide and drive the ax straight down to the ground. If the ax accidentally glances to the side, its momentum will take it to the ground rather than into your leg.

If the piece of wood splits only partially, leave the ax in place and use a second piece of firewood to strike the ax head and drive it through the log. If a log does not begin to split when the ax hits it, place it beside the fire to heat up for later use. If you want to split a small piece of wood that will not stand on its own, hold it in place with another small piece of wood in one hand and hold your ax in the other hand. With a short chop, strike the small piece of wood and it should split. Never hold a piece of wood with one hand when trying to split it with an ax in the other hand.

To avoid injury, hold a small piece of wood with another small piece.

Starting campfires. When you check into your campground, ask about regulations regarding fires. Most campgrounds permit campfires, but some do not. If fires are permitted, build yours in the fire ring and keep it small enough to keep under control. It is a good idea to have water nearby in case it gets too big. You want to keep your fire small so you will be able to extinguish it when you leave your campsite or when you go to bed.

There are two basic methods for safely starting a campfire—the "textbook method" and the "easy method." The "textbook method" is the way Scouts are taught to make fires. First, start with some tinder or highly combustible materials such as dry newspaper, fat pine, or commercial fire starter. Place kindling such as small dry wood sticks that can usually be found on the ground near your campsite (or shavings cut from larger pieces of firewood) on top. Next place larger sticks, about the size of a large pencil, around the bed of kindling. I usually arrange these larger sticks in the form of a tepee, but others like to shape them in the form of a bed or a log cabin. The wood should be arranged such that plenty of air can get to the base of the fire. Once this wood is in place, light the paper at the bottom of the pile, and as the wood begins to burn, add more sticks. Start with smaller pieces of wood, and once a bed of coals develops, gradually work up to larger pieces of wood.

I call the second method the "easy method." It is the method we use. When we go to the store to buy our supplies, we buy a small bag of Match Light charcoal. When we are ready to start our fire, we place about fifteen to twenty briquettes in a small pile, lay several small pieces of firewood on top in the form of a tepee, and then light the charcoal. There is no need to mess with tinder or kindling, and there is no need to worry about getting sufficient air. The wood will begin burning quickly and you have a campfire. If you want to cook on your fire, it will be ready in a few minutes.

Never attempt to start a fire with gasoline. This practice is extremely dangerous. Gasoline is highly combustible and explosive. Using it to start a fire could cause serious injury or death. Similarly, avoid using other flammable materials as these could also cause injury.

Regardless of the method used to start the fire, place the logs that were difficult to split around the fire in the form of a square. Build three sides a little higher to make a windscreen. These larger pieces will not interfere with the fire but will dry out and gradually begin to flame up. After the fire has burned for some time and after the smaller pieces of wood have been used, move the larger logs onto your bed of coals one at a time. Keep your fire small and under control at all times. Bonfires are dangerous and inappropriate in public campgrounds. If you want one, make it on your own property.

Drawing water. After setting up your camp, you will probably need to collect some water to have available in your kitchen or picnic table area. Backpackers can only pack small water bottles and typically must gather water from nearby creeks and ponds several times a day. Each time they get water, they must sterilize it before drinking it or using it to cook their food. Motorcycle campers, on the other hand, have little difficulty finding clean, potable drinking water. Many parks have water faucets in their campsites or very close to them. A few parks have wells and pumps located around the campground. All you have to do is walk over to the faucet or pump and draw your water. Use your small water bottles to hold the water. If you plan to stay in your site for a few days, consider packing or buying a one-gallon water jug. Having a water jug with a handle at your table makes it easy to wash your hands, rinse dinnerware after washing, and measure out specific amounts of water when needed for cooking meals.

Preparing meals. Sometimes you may desire to cook your meal in your campsite. You must consider the cooking gear you packed and the supplies available in the store and then decide what meal you would like to prepare. You should also consider your plans for the following day. If you plan to stay in your base camp for a few days you may wish to buy more food, provided you have a way to protect it from animals. On the other hand, if you plan to pack up early and get on the road, you do not want a lot of food to pack. Whatever your plans, purchase the food and supplies you need and bring them back to the campsite.

You can cook a wide variety of meals in your campsite. Some couples like spaghetti, macaroni, pasta primavera, or some of the other frozen pasta entrées. Most grocery stores have a wide selection of pasta dishes from which to choose. We typically like to have a little meat, some potatoes, and a salad or vegetable. Sometimes we buy a dessert, and sometimes we buy something for breakfast the next morning. See chapter 6 for more details about cooking and eating.

When preparing our meals, we like to work together. I may chop onions, potatoes, green peppers, and any other vegetables while Robin prepares the aluminum foil wraps or some other chore. Other couples may prefer to split the duties so that one prepares the meal and the other cleans up afterward.

Cleaning up after meals. At home, many people like to relax after eating their meals and postpone cleanup for several minutes or several hours. (I know some people who put their dishes in the sink and wait until another day to clean up.) But when you camp, delaying cleanup is a bad practice. Instead clean up your site immediately after finishing your meal. You need to wash all your dishes and pack them away, seal remaining food in bags and pack it away, and dispose of your garbage in provided receptacles. In general, you must get all food and food smells out of your campsite as quickly as possible.

The reason for cleaning up so quickly is that food smells will attract wild animals, such as raccoons, skunks, and opossums, that could strew garbage around the campsite and perhaps damage your camping gear. When you pack away your food and garbage, don't put it in your leather saddlebags, because animals will be able to smell it and could destroy your leather bags to get it. In some campgrounds food smells could even attract bears that could injure you or your companion.

A few years ago I camped with some friends at Moraine View State Park near Bloomington, Illinois. We were traveling together to Wisconsin and had been on the road all day. I was tired. After finishing our evening meal, my friends wanted to stay up a little longer and talk. I wanted to take my shower and go to bed. I assumed they would clean up our site before going to bed. But they were novice campers and did not get all the food and garbage securely packed away. During the night a dozen raccoons must have invaded our site. I slept through the whole affair, but when I woke the next morning, our site was littered worse than a garbage dump. Tiny shreds of paper were strewn far and wide. It took a considerable amount of valuable travel time to get everything cleaned up before we could get on the road.

Dealing with insects. Whenever you spend time outdoors you will likely encounter mosquitoes, ticks, flies, and other biting insects. Mosquitoes can be very annoying at dawn and at dusk. If you attend evening park programs, you will likely encounter some mosquitoes. Ticks are especially plentiful in grass and brush. If you walk by and brush the grass, one or more ticks may get onto your clothes. See chapter 11 for more information about insects. Be ready for such insects by having some type of insect repellent. We use Deep Woods Off with DEET, but many campers prefer other products. Whatever your choice, keep it handy and be ready to apply it when the time is appropriate. We carry a small emergency spray bottle in one saddlebag guard bag. If the insects are especially bad, we will buy a larger bottle when we ride to the store for supplies. Caution! When using Off and possibly other products, do not place the container on your plastic tablecloth. The spray or liquid will quickly eat a hole in the plastic.

Repairing gear and solving problems. On almost every camping trip you will encounter a problem or two. Most of these problems will be relatively minor, but a few may be somewhat more challenging.

They are just a part of camping. When a problem emerges, you will need to spend time evaluating the nature of the problem, collecting information, devising a solution for the problem, implementing the solution, and evaluating the effectiveness of the solution. Most of the time, a pair of pliers, a roll of duct tape, some cord, and a knife can solve your problems.

Bathing. Most campgrounds have bathrooms with showers. Some campgrounds have very nice showers, while others do not. After eating supper and cleaning up your campsite, you may want to attend evening programs if they are available. After that, the next chore is to take a shower before going to bed. Not only does a shower rinse away sweat and dirt accumulated during the day and food smells acquired during your meals, but it also refreshes you, helps you to stay warm during the night, and helps to keep your sleeping bag clean by reducing the amount of dirt and body oil transferred to your sleeping bag liner.

We typically wait until the end of our day to take our showers. It is the last thing we do before going to bed. We each use a plastic shopping bag as a shower bag. In it we pack a pair of shorts and a T-shirt, a small personal hygiene kit, soap, a washcloth, and a backpacker's towel. Since it is usually dark when we are ready for our showers, we strap on our headlights. We put on our shower shoes and walk together to the shower building. If the campground does not have showers, we either use the bathroom sink or heat a little water at our campsite and use our washcloths to wash away as much oil, sweat, and dirt as possible.

Campground showers vary considerably in terms of their overall quality. Some showers are nice, while others are cramped, dirty, have poor temperature control, or have insufficient water pressure. In fact, showers in the same facility may vary. If several showers are available, check each one. You want to get the one that is most comfortable. Hopefully it will have good water pressure, good temperature control, ample space (especially important for us big guys), a private dressing area (especially important for most women), a bench, and several hooks for hanging your shower bag, towel, and dirty clothes. When undressing, put your watch, glasses, and headlight in the shower bag. Keep your shower shoes on.

Try to use as little water as necessary when showering. To conserve water, wet your body and then turn the shower off as you lather up. When you are ready to rinse, turn the shower back on for a few minutes. This procedure will conserve a valuable natural resource that is becoming scarcer every year. If everyone followed this bathing procedure, we would help our children and grandchildren to have the same resources we take for granted.

After our showers, we brush our teeth, take care of other personal needs, and meet back at the campsite to secure everything before retiring for the night.

Preparing for bed. After your shower, hang up your towel so it can dry overnight. The best places to hang it are on the picnic table bench or some other location under your tarp or on your bike under your bike cover. Then take one last look around your campsite to be sure all food and gear has been properly packed. Be sure your campfire is completely extinguished. Also be sure your tarp is securely tied and that one corner has been lowered to drain water away from your tent if it rains overnight. As you enter your tent, leave your shower shoes in the vestibule or just outside the door so you can find them if you have to get up in the middle of the night.

Before going to bed, put on long pants and socks—if it is not too hot to wear them. Long pants and socks will help protect your sleeping bag and will help keep you warm if the temperature drops during the night. Once you are dressed, arrange your clothes and gear so you can easily find them if you need them. I place my glasses, my headlight, and my sleeping cap in the corner of the tent nearest my head. If I need them during the night I know where they are. I usually wear my watch to bed and listen to my MP3 player as I drift off to sleep. When I am ready to remove the MP3 player, I put it in the corner with my other necessities so I can find it the next morning. I put the clothes I plan to wear the next morning together near the door so they are ready when I want to get dressed for the day.

When visiting friends in Wisconsin, we frequently camp at Governor Dodge State Park near Dodgeville.

Washing clothes. If your trip lasts longer than a few days, you must wash clothes. Be sure you have packed a small travel-sized bottle of Woolite. If you have packed clothing made with fast-drying materials, washing is not a problem. If your campground has a laundry (and most do), just put all your clothes into one washer and add a few drops of Woolite. Don't use much or you will have difficulty rinsing out the soap. If your campground does not have laundry facilities, wash your clothes in the bathroom sink with a little Woolite. You may wish to wash a few clothes in the bathroom sink every day rather than waiting until everything is dirty. After washing your clothes, you can put them in a commercial dryer for a few minutes or, if the weather is nice, hang them on your clothesline. Clothing made from polyester and nylon fabrics will dry in a very short time.

Enjoying Leisure Time

Once your chores have been completed, you are free to engage in a wide variety of relaxing and enjoyable leisure activities. This is the fun time. This is the reason so many people enjoy camping.

Walking and hiking. Once your campsite has been set up and your chores have been completed, you might consider taking a stroll around the campground. For most campers, this stroll is a standard routine that is repeated several times a day. Walking is good exercise and opens the door for meeting other interesting people. As you walk, look at other campsites and try to get ideas about how to do things a little better.

Most state and national parks offer a few hiking trails. If you are in good physical condition, you may wish to consider hiking one or two of these local trails. The Smoky Mountains NP and most other national parks offer numerous hiking trails that range in difficulty level from short easy trails to very steep, strenuous trails. Another great park for hiking is Devil's Lake SP near Baraboo, Wisconsin. It has several bluff trails ranging in difficulty levels. But the hike is definitely worth the effort. When you reach the top of the bluff, you will be treated to a spectacular view of Devil's Lake.

Visiting neighbors. If a person is sitting in a site, speak to him or her. Many times a conversation will develop. You might notice something unique in their campsite or ask about local activities or restaurants or ask where they are from. Many times they will ask you similar questions. If they know you are riding a motorcycle, they will ask you about your bike and sometimes will tell you that they used to own or ride a bike in the past. Most people who enjoy camping, like you, are away from their family, friends, and natural surroundings. In other words, they are relatively alone. Consequently they frequently enjoy meeting and talking with strangers. Walking and talking with neighbors will sometimes lead to long-term friendships.

Relaxing. When staying in a base camp for a day or two, one of the main things we like to do is relax. After all, this is our vacation and we do not want to be going at a fast pace the whole time. We like to bring our hammocks, paperback books, and personal music players. We may stroll around the campground a few times a day or perhaps hike to a waterfall and back, but we also like to take midday naps. On a recent trip to the Gulf of Mexico, we spent three days doing nothing more than eating, walking, and sleeping. It was a very relaxing trip. It was surprising how much we slept. Obviously we needed the rest.

Enjoying park activities and programs. Many campgrounds have interesting programs and activities either in the park or nearby. At the Smoky Mountains, for example, dozens of hiking trails and mountain streams for tubing are nearby. Land Between The Lakes National

Recreation Area features a planetarium, a nature center with many reptiles and animals, a living history farm, and a bison range. Other campgrounds have cave tours, horse rentals, snorkeling, exhibits, or many other activities. Most national parks and many state parks have free evening lectures on park history or nature. These lectures are usually well prepared and very educational. When we camp, we try to attend as many of these programs as possible. Usually a list of park activities and programs will be available at the office or posted on an information board somewhere in the park.

Taking pictures. We take lots of pictures on every camping trip. We take pictures of the campground sign at the main entrance, our campsite, our activities, our neighbors and their camping rigs, unique buildings, geographical features, special problems encountered, and so forth. These pictures provide concrete reminders of our adventures, fun times, and the difficulties we have shared together.

Touring and sightseeing. Whenever we stay in a base camp for a few days, we like to ride around the area to see local attractions. After setting up our camp and completing some basic camp chores, we find information and brochures about interesting attractions and good restaurants in the area. Then we go exploring. On a recent trip to Cave-in-Rock State Park in southern Illinois, we rode to the Garden of the Gods Wilderness Area and enjoyed walking a scenic trail through many beautiful rock formations.

Nelson Dewey SP near Cassville, Wisconsin, is situated on a bluff that overlooks the Mississippi River.

Sleeping. You will probably spend more time sleeping than doing any other activity. To be comfortable in various weather conditions, you should have a good tent, a good sleeping bag, and a good sleeping pad. See chapters 2 and 3 for detailed information about these pieces of gear. Many non-campers seem to have unreasonable fears about what could happen while they are sleeping. Some fear that someone or some animal will come to their campsite or tent to harm them. Others fear that snakes or spiders or some other creature will get in their tent. All of these fears are unfounded. The biggest problems campers are likely to have when they are sleeping are 1) difficulty adjusting to a different sleeping routine, which may cause one or two sleepless nights; 2) noise from people, birds, and animals, which may take a day or two to adjust to; and 3) having to get up and walk several yards to a bathroom in the middle of the night. If you have difficulty sleeping the first night or two, consider taking an acetaminophen or ibuprofen tablet before going to bed.

Breaking Camp

Eventually the time comes to pack up your gear and move on. As you pack up, you want to be sure that you do not leave anything in the campsite, that you pack your gear as clean and as dry as possible, and that you pack everything as small as possible so that it will easily fit back on your motorcycle.

Packing your gear. When the time comes to break camp, you and your companion should be ready to work together without shouting and making excessive noise that would disturb your neighbors. Hopefully it will not be raining. One person should attend to affairs inside the tent while the other attends to affairs outside the tent. The person in the tent must stuff sleeping bags into their stuff sacks, roll air mattresses, fold and pack clothes into their respective containers, and place everything just outside the tent door. Once the tent is empty, he or she should clean up any trash and dirt. The person outside the tent must carry items to the bike, pack up the kitchen gear, and take down the tarp.

After the tent is empty, you both should work together to take it down, wipe off dirt and moisture, and either fold or stuff it into its stuff sack. We always count our tent stakes and ropes before packing them to be sure we have not inadvertently left one behind. Then you must fold and pack the tarp and bike cover.

Once everything has been packed in its respective stuff sack or container and these items have been placed on the ground near the bike, we visually inspect everything to be sure we have not forgotten anything. Then, we pack everything on the bike—in its designated place. We start by packing most of our gear in the saddlebags. One person can pack each bag. Then we put our clothes and personal items in the tour pack. Once we are certain all our small items have been packed, we are ready to finish packing by tying our tent, air mattresses, tarp support poles, sleeping bags, and daypack on the luggage rack.

Once we begin to break camp, the whole process takes approximately forty-five minutes unless our gear is wet. If it rained during the night or if there was a heavy dewfall, we use our doormat and other cloth rags to dry our gear as much as possible before packing it. It usually takes an additional fifteen to thirty minutes to wipe away as much water and mud as possible from our tent, rain fly, and other gear.

Cleaning the site. After our tent and gear has been packed, we walk around the campsite and pick up trash. We also check the fire ring to be sure it is clean. We are relatively clean campers and usually do not drop much trash on the ground. But frequently we find trash left by previous campers. We believe that we should leave the campsite cleaner that we found it, so we pick up all trash whether it is ours or not. After all the trash has been picked up, we take it to the nearest receptacle.

Taking the last look. Once everything has been packed on the bike and the site has been cleaned, we usually visit the bathroom and return to our site in a leisurely manner. We want to enjoy one last look at the campground and our site. Sometimes we say goodbye to our neighbors. Eventually we crank the bike, walk around the site one more time to be sure it is clean and that we have not forgotten anything, and then hit the road in search of our next destination.

Cleaning Gear and Repacking

After you have completed your trip and returned home, you must complete a few more chores before you can relax. First, open up your tent, sleeping bag, tarp, bike cover, kitchen gear, tool bag, and any other gear that may have become dirty or wet during your trip. You can hang you tent on a clothesline or set it up in an open room. After you have opened these items, clean them and allow them to dry completely. Be sure to dump all the water out of your water containers and allow them to dry. If your containers are musty, fill them with a Clorox/water solution and let them stand for a couple of days. Once your gear is clean, try to leave it open to dry four days before repacking it.

Second, wash all your clothing, towels, washrags, and dishtowels. Third, restock supplies such as soap, toothpaste, sunscreen, paper towels, first-aid supplies, medicine, and food items that were used during the trip. Finally, repack all your gear and clothing so that they are ready for your next trip.

Conclusion

What chores must be performed to make my camping trip comfortable? And what activities can be enjoyed after completing these chores? Camping trips require a little work but can be very relaxing and a lot of fun. This work will be a lot easier if you have done your homework. You must learn specific skills such as tying good knots, splitting wood, building fires, and setting up tarps. These skills are relatively easy to master, and once you have mastered them, your camping trips will run very smoothly and will be extremely enjoyable.

As you learn basic camping skills, your chores will require less time and effort. And you will have more time to enjoy many different activities such as relaxing, watching birds and wildlife, talking with fellow campers, visiting local attractions, hiking, swimming, or going shopping. The more you camp, the more proficient you will become. Veteran campers quickly come to treasure these camping experiences and activities that cannot be enjoyed at home or work and spend a lot of free time dreaming about the next camping trip.

After reading this chapter, learn as much as possible about camping skills. One good book is *The Backpacker's Handbook* by Chris Townsend. Other good books include *Camping Made Easy* by Michael Rutter, *Camping's Top Secrets* by Cliff Jacobson, *The Complete Idiot's Guide to Camping and Hiking* by Michael Mouland, *Camping and Wilderness Survival* by Paul Tawrell, and *Backpacker Tent and Car Camper's Handbook* by Buck Tilton with Kristen Hostetter.

10. Ethics

Camping out under the stars provides a profound sense of personal freedom. Nothing else compares to being outside, breathing fresh air, hearing the sounds of birds, and smelling the flowers and other vegetation. When you arrive at your campsite, you have escaped the hectic commuter traffic, job pressures, noisy neighbors, family issues, home repairs, and other routine life demands. You are in the midst of nature and have a profound sense of relief and freedom. You are relatively anonymous and thus are free to act more or less as you would like. Everyone is on an equal standing. You may meet other people, but most of the time you will only know them for a day or so before one of you moves on to another destination.

People celebrate this freedom in different ways. Some like to read; some like to talk with neighbors; some like to sit around the campsite and watch others; some like to relax and nap; some like to walk; some like to attend educational programs; some like to sightsee; and some like to shop. There is no prescribed way to enjoy your camping vacation. This sense of personal freedom is further enhanced by the common practice of most park law-enforcement personnel of being friendly and helpful while keeping a low profile.

Mammoth Cave National Park offers great camping, several different cave tours, and evening nature programs. This site is in the Headquarters Campground.

Unfortunately many people who visited parks in the past to enjoy their natural beauty actually engaged in behaviors that were destructive to the park. For example, hundreds of past visitors to Mammoth Cave, Kentucky, wrote their names on the ceiling with the soot of candles or lanterns. Today parts of the cave ceiling are covered with graffiti and names of past visitors. Visitors to other parks collected various souvenirs, such as rocks, stalactites, pieces of driftwood, flowers, and plants such as sea oats. Campers and backpackers frequently cut trees for different purposes (i.e., making fires, shelters, and beds) and trampled fragile vegetation to make paths and campsites. In general, many past park visitors believed they had the freedom to do whatever they wanted in the park, to leave their mark, and to take whatever souvenirs they could find.

Soon after people began visiting state and national parks, conservationists realized that the visitors were slowly and systematically destroying the parks and would eventually ruin them and their natural resources if such practices were allowed to go unchecked. Such repetitive, thoughtless destructive actions would prevent future generations from being able to enjoy our parks in their natural condition.

The American Conservation Movement

Many years before the American Civil War, several citizens became concerned about the relatively rapid pace of the clearing of our American forests and the possible extinction of some indigenous species (especially the bison) that lived there. The great forests and wilderness areas of America had played a big role in defining our national identity. But the growing number of people immigrating here and their quest to settle and civilize previously unsettled lands was gradually destroying our forests and their wildlife. From 1847 to 1872, several citizens, including Henry David Thoreau, gave impassioned speeches, wrote letters, and wrote books calling for a system for the preservation of our forests and wilderness areas. At first the general consensus of our political leaders was that each state should develop a park system (our nation was founded upon the principle of creating strong state governments rather than having a strong national government). To assist them, the federal government actually gave tracts of land to some states with the stipulation that they preserve the land and never sell it. For example, in 1864 the federal government passed a bill giving Yosemite Valley to the state of California (later this park was reclaimed by the federal government). A few years later, New York established the Adirondack Forest Preserve and the Niagara Falls reservation. Thus began the tradition of creating state parks.

In 1872 the federal government adopted a different approach and created Yellowstone, the first national park in the nation—and the world. Additional efforts were made to acquire and preserve other land tracts that had unique scenic beauty, like the Grand Canyon, or that provided refuge for animals, birds, fish, and other wildlife. To facilitate the acquisition and management of this land, the Forest Reserve Act was passed in 1891 and ultimately created the U.S. Forest Service.

Theodore Roosevelt became president in 1901. During his presidency, a considerable amount of attention was focused upon land usage versus conservation. One underlying issue was how to support new technology (such as electric lines, telegraph lines, and irrigation projects) while still preserving our natural resources. One of the laws passed by the U.S. Congress (1906) was the American Antiquities Act, which authorized the president to declare areas in need of protection as national monuments. The first area declared as a national monument was Devil's Tower in Wyoming.

About the same time, John Muir published several books and papers extolling the beauty of scenic wildernesses and advocating the creation of national parks for the long-term preservation of these lands. Muir died in 1914, one year before Congress passed a bill establishing the Rocky Mountain National Park and two years before Congress established the National Park System. Over the next several years, it became apparent that many natural resources needed protection from wide-scale destruction for profit. In particular, timber harvesting, mining, hunting, fishing, and souvenir gathering needed to be regulated.

Once several state and national parks were established, visitors began coming by the thousands and later by the millions every year. Conservationists realized that they had to refocus their attention on protecting the land and wildlife from the people who came there to enjoy the parks. Visitors engaged in all kinds of destructive actions. They cut trees to make campsites, they wrote their names on rocks and cave ceilings, they carved their names into tables, buildings, fence posts, or whatever wooden surfaces were available, and they removed historical and archeological artifacts as personal souvenirs. Such inconsiderate acts by one visitor would have a relatively small impact, but the cumulative damage caused by millions of visitors every year would certainly destroy the natural beauty that our government agencies were trying to preserve. So rules and regulation had to be developed and enforced.

Congress passed the Wilderness Act (PL 88-577) in 1964. This act created a "national wilderness preservation system for the permanent good of the whole people, and for other purposes." It defined wilderness areas as undeveloped tracts of land with no permanent roads and little signs of human habitation. Some of these wilderness areas are managed by the U.S. Forest Service; other areas are managed by the National Park Service; and others are managed by other government agencies. The act also affirmed the importance of preserving our natural resources and introduced restrictions on certain activities in the area, such as mining, logging, and the use of motorized transportation. The overall intent of this law was to preserve the wilderness in its original state, to preserve its natural resources, to keep wildlife and its habitat in as primitive conditions as possible, and to reduce the destruction associated with various commercial and recreational activities. In 2008 there were 702 wilderness areas; they can be found in all but six states.

Congress enacted the Federal Land Policy and Management Act (PL 94-579) in 1976. It directed the secretary of the interior to establish comprehensive rules and regulations designed to preserve and protect public lands owned by the National Forest Service and the

Bureau of Land Management. The intent of the act was to preserve the land areas in their natural condition, provide food and habitat for fish and wildlife, and provide outdoor recreation. The law specifically directed the secretary to preserve and protect the scientific, scenic, historical, ecological, environmental, air, atmospheric, water resource, and archeological value of the land.

Over the past twenty to twenty-five years, camping has become one of the most popular recreational activities in America. Every weekend during the spring, summer, and fall millions of people flock to our state and national parks. According to a report by Property and Environmental Research Center entitled *Parks in Transition* (www.perc.org), visitors to state parks across the United States increased from 193 million in 1980 to 750 million in 1997. According to another report by the National Park Service (www.nature.nps.gov/stats), visitors to national parks increased from 220.5 million in 1980 to 277.6 million in 2006. Many parks become extremely overcrowded during the camping season. For example, the Great Smoky Mountains National Park had more than nine million visitors in 2006. Anyone who visited this park during the summer-fall camping season probably encountered overcrowded campgrounds, frequent traffic jams, and difficulty finding parking places near popular attractions. In the same year, the Grand Canyon had approximately four million visitors and Yellowstone had approximately three million visitors. Each year seems to bring more and more park visitors. Many park campgrounds require advance reservations, and they still fill to capacity during the camping season. As a result, it is difficult to secure campsites on weekends. The overcrowding has become so severe that experts are now recommending that campers, hikers, and backpackers avoid popular campgrounds and consider visiting other less-well-known areas.

Leave No Trace Principles

During the 1960s and 1970s, many conservation-minded citizens as well as park personnel began to realize that lists of rules and regulations were not enough to stop the cumulative destruction caused by millions of park users. People were coming year after year, setting up campsites, gathering wood, hiking through forests, throwing their waste on the ground, making fires, and collecting souvenirs. Something had to be done to stop their gradual destruction of our precious natural resources.

Several conferences were held, and participants at these conferences concluded that regulations alone were not enough to get park and land users to change their destructive behaviors. Experts agreed that land users needed to be educated regarding the past destruction of public land and the importance of preserving it for future generations. The intent of these educational programs would be to get park users to voluntarily change their overall behavior patterns in public parks and wilderness areas. Furthermore, these programs asked park users to become *advocates* for park preservation and be willing to educate other park users regarding proper ethical behaviors in the wilderness. As a result, several educational pamphlets and books were published to present the new ethics regarding appropriate behaviors in a public wilderness or park environment.

These educational and advocacy efforts were uncoordinated until the National Outdoor Leadership School, joined by several national land management agencies, developed the Leave No Trace (LNT) educational curriculum for wild-land visitors. Thus began the focus on outdoor ethics. Today LNT promotes seven ethical principles for outdoor users:

- Plan ahead and prepare.
- Travel and camp on durable surfaces.
- Dispose of waste properly.
- Leave what you find.
- Minimize campfire impacts.
- Respect wildlife.
- Be considerate of other visitors.

These principles seem to be aimed more at back-country hikers and campers, but they can be slightly modified and expanded to apply to motorcycle camping.

Park Rules and Regulations

Today every campground has a list of rules and regulations. When you arrive at a park, look for a copy of them. In many parks a copy is given to you when you register for your campsite. In a few parks, they are posted on a bulletin board. They are designed to preserve and protect the park's natural resources from the thoughtless, destructive actions of its visitors.

Most of these rules and regulations are common to all campgrounds, but a few may be specific to one particular campground. These regulations are generally intended to prevent problems that have frequently occurred in the past. Regardless of your camping experience, take the time to review these rules and regulations and try to abide by them. If you are a veteran camper, you probably are familiar with most of these rules and regulations and understand the rationale behind them. If you are a novice camper, you may not understand the underlying rationale for some of the rules, but be assured that each rule is designed to prevent a common problem that could cause problems between park users or destroy the natural beauty of the park. Regardless of your personal beliefs and past camping experience, study the rules and regulations carefully and commit yourself to abiding by them.

Major rules are posted at the entrance of Tims Ford State Park, Tennessee.

In addition to this written list of rules and regulations, a few unwritten rules are common in most campgrounds. For example, be quiet and respectful toward other campers, do not drive nails into trees, walk on established trails and pathways rather than through other campers' sites, keep your campsite clean and neat, and so on.

Ethical Principles for Motorcycle Camping

If you take the time to think about it, you should be able to figure out the proper ways to behave in any public park simply by using your common sense. First, be considerate and respectful toward other people, and second, help preserve the park's natural beauty and animal habitat. These two ethical principles should guide your behavior whenever you are camping, or even if you are just visiting a state or national park. If everyone followed these two ethical principles, there would be almost no problems in our parks.

Sometimes it is difficult to translate these abstract principles into practice, so I have developed a list of twelve specific ethical principles for lightweight motorcycle camping. If every camper followed these ethical principles, all park visitors would enjoy their visits, animals would be able to live in their natural habitat undisturbed, and future visitors would be able to enjoy the parks' natural beauty as much as you have. These ethical principles are based upon the LNT ethical principles, common campground regulations, and basic principles of common courtesy. Hopefully you will be willing to embrace each of the following ethical principles and encourage other campers to do the same.

Arrive early. Plan your day so that you are able to arrive at the campground before 4:00 or 5:00 PM. You need plenty of time to register, set up camp, go for food and supplies, prepare your meal, clean up your campsite, and take a shower before 10:00 PM, when most campgrounds request that you begin observing quiet hours. If you arrive late you will feel pressed for time and may make more noise trying to complete your tasks before bedtime. Furthermore, you may not be able to complete your chores before 10:00 PM and you may disturb your neighbors after they have gone to bed. If you can't get to a campsite early, consider staying at a motel for the night.

Set up your campsite immediately and use the tent pad. After registering for your campsite, return to the site and set up your tent before going to the store for supplies. Most campgrounds include this principle as one of their rules, because an unoccupied site may appear to another person as an open site. If a second person were to assume the site was open and set up a tent on your site, both you and the other camper would think you had a claim to the site, and this dispute may lead to an argument that could disturb other campers. Probably both of you would be reluctant to move, and park personnel would have to make a difficult decision. Setting up your tent clearly demonstrates that the site is occupied and avoids a large number of campsite disputes.

When you begin to set up your campsite, position your tent on the designated tent pad. If there is no designated pad, place your tent somewhere within the defined campsite limits on a durable surface such as hard-packed dirt or gravel. Do not place it back in the woods away from the designated site. Keeping your tent on a durable surface within the designated site helps prevent additional damage to the vegetation of the park. Placing your tent under the trees or in the nearby meadow will likely damage fragile vegetation that serves as food and habitat for various wildlife species. If many campers set up their tents on the grass and in the woods, considerable damage could occur over a few months or a few years. Depending upon the extent of the collective damage, it could take years to overcome it.

If the parking area for the campsite is a gravel bed, you can usually place your tent on the parking pad if no other acceptable location is available. If the parking area is paved, ask before setting up your tent on the pavement. Some parks, such as Gulf State Park in Gulf Shores, Alabama, have rules prohibiting setting tents on paved parking areas, presumably because they do not want tent stakes driven into the pavement.

Be considerate of others. In any campground, there will be other people who, like you, want to enjoy the park, its solitude, and its natural resources. Like you, they want to enjoy the quiet and peacefulness that can only be found in a natural environment. When you arrive at your campsite, speak to your new neighbors. If they show a willingness to talk, take a few minutes to visit. Ask about their hometowns or their camping rigs. Most people are more than willing to talk with you and will likely ask you similar questions. Many times this brief conversation establishes a foundation for future social interactions and offers of assistance. If you have established a connection with your neighbors, they may invite you to visit with them after you complete your chores, may offer you food or drink, and may be willing to assist you should you need any help setting up a tarp, moving a picnic table, or with some other task.

Another act of consideration is to avoid walking through other campers' campsites. When you need to go to the bathhouse, the water pump, or some other place in the park, walk on established roads and pathways. Do not be tempted to take shortcuts through other campers' sites. This is one of my pet peeves and a peeve of many other campers. Campsite occupants have rented the entire campsite, and as such they consider it their temporary motel room, home, and property. Do not disrespect your neighbor's home.

Another act of consideration is to obey posted speed limits. The reason for obeying these limits is to demonstrate courtesy to other park users and to avoid the possibility of causing injury to another person or damage to someone's property. Park visitors typically feel safe in a park and are much less vigilant. They are relaxed and frequently amble around without looking for other cars or motorcycles. Children and pets sometimes impulsively run into the road. Many campers like to walk and ride their bicycles in the roads. Sometimes they like to stop and visit with their neighbors. Sometimes they may be driving a car, see something of interest (like a deer or some other wildlife), park their car, and walk into the road to get a better look. They may be oblivious to motorized traffic. In general, campgrounds are especially congested places. As drivers we should recognize these potential problems and drive slowly. We must be prepared to stop quickly for pedestrians, children, pets, and bicycle riders. To be able to stop quickly, drive no faster than fifteen miles per hour in the campground and obey other park speed limits. Always give the right of way to pedestrians, bicyclists, and children.

Sign at Edgar Evins State Park, Tennessee

Yet another act of consideration is to help keep bathrooms clean. When many people share a public bathroom, they can mess it up in a hurry. Although park employees typically clean bathrooms once a day, the bathrooms may not stay clean for long, and they will get nasty during the day unless everyone helps to keep them clean. Be sure to dispose of all your paper and garbage. If another camper has left paper or trash in the bathroom, put it in the trash receptacle. When you use the sink area, wipe up water and soap before leaving. Flush the toilet and be sure it is ready for the next person. If the toilet is stopped up, notify park personnel. Be sure to leave the shower as clean as possible for the next person.

Avoid making excessive noise. Virtually all campgrounds request that you keep noise to a minimum and observe quiet hours from 10:00 PM to 8:00 AM. This rule seems to make common sense. Everyone in the campground, including you, wants to enjoy the peace and quiet associated with being outdoors. If they wanted to hear a lot of noise, they would stay in a motel in the middle of the city. Unfortunately many campers seem to forget this basic rule and make lots of noise that disturbs their neighbors.

The most common example of excessive noise occurs when inconsiderate people turn up the volume of their radios or boom boxes. Many people like to listen to their music at high volume levels, but a campground is not the place to do this. The noise from radios and boom boxes can be heard all over the campground and will annoy many other campers. Sometimes the noise is so loud that others cannot listen to their own music, read their books, or carry on normal conversations. Although the person playing the loud music may not realize it, other people may not like their type of music and do not want to be forced to listen to it.

Do not be one of these campers. If you want to listen to music, bring a personal music player (i.e., a small cassette radio, CD player, or MP3 player) and a set of ear buds. You can enjoy your music at the volume you like without disturbing your neighbors. If you and your companion want to listen to the same music, buy a splitter and a second set of ear buds.

Another common example of campground noise is couples who are unable talk with each other at normal volume levels or use their "inside voices." When they arrive at the campsite, they immediately begin shouting at each other as they begin to pitch their tent and set up their campsite. After the site has been set up, they continue shouting at each other as they make simple requests and demands. The question, "Where is my towel?" and the answer to this question may be shouted at such volume levels that it can be heard several campsites away.

Some campers like to drink alcoholic beverages, stay up late, sit around the campfire, and talk until the wee hours of the morning. Unfortunately when everyone else goes to bed, what may seem like normal conversation will sound very loud to neighbors who are trying to sleep. Most of the time, other campers try to ignore the noise, but sometimes a neighbor may request the couple to be quiet. If you are asked to reduce your noise level, do not get defensive, do not get angry, and do not continue to talk. Just be apologetic and go to bed. Continuing to talk after someone has asked you to be quiet is disrespectful and unethical. If you are unable to whisper, go to bed and save the conversation until another day. If you want to stay up all night and talk, go to a motel room or a deserted area in the park. Besides, if you are going to get on the road early the next day, you should get to bed around 10:00 PM so you will have a good night's rest.

One last source of noise is "loud pipes." Many motorcycle riders like having loud pipes. If you are one of them, get to your site as quickly as possible and turn off your bike. Avoid starting your bike or riding it in the campground during quiet hours (i.e., between 10:00 PM and 8:00 AM). Better yet, consider changing to quieter pipes.

Limit your alcohol consumption. Unfortunately a lot of campground problems are associated with alcohol consumption. Frequently, nice, well-behaved people come to campgrounds to have a party. They begin drinking and may invite a few friends. After a few more drinks, they change into loud drunks who want to stay up all night talking incessantly and arguing. They do not know when to go to bed and are obnoxious to everyone else in the campground. Their loud speech, music, and behaviors frequently keep other campers awake all night.

If intoxicated people are asked to be quiet or to go to bed, they often get louder and may want to fight. Furthermore, they engage in a number of other behaviors, such as urinating in public and using profanity, that are offensive to other people. When neighbors or park rangers confront them, they can become belligerent. We have experienced obnoxious drunks on many past camping trips. It is a shame that some people are unable to maintain their decency after consuming alcoholic beverages.

As a result of frequent alcohol-related problems, many campgrounds now have rules designed to control this obnoxious behavior. For example, many have rules that limit the number of people who can occupy a campsite, rules that limit the number of vehicles on a campsite, and rules that either restrict alcohol consumption to the campsite or completely forbid its use in the park.

In past years, parks with rules forbidding alcohol possession were lenient in their enforcement of the rule, but now some of them have become very strict regarding possession of alcoholic beverages. I enjoy drinking a beer or two while camping, but after suffering through many sleepless nights caused by drunken neighbors, I understand the rationale for these rules. Park managers want their campgrounds to be nice places where parents can bring their children without exposing them to profanity, arguments, fights, public urination, and other behaviors associated with excessive alcohol consumption. Restriction of alcohol consumption will help keep campgrounds peaceful and pleasant family environments.

Keep fires small and under control at all times. Many campers like to have campfires, but campfires that get out of control can cause forest fires. In addition, frequent campfires can have a negative environmental impact due to repeated gathering of wood and repeated scorching of the ground. By removing dead wood from the forest, we remove the food and habitat of many wildlife species. That, in turn, removes the food of other animals that feed on that wildlife. As a result, most campgrounds have a set of rules related to campfires. If you plan to have a campfire, become familiar with the rules. First be sure campfires are permitted. Most campgrounds allow campfires, but some do not. The ethical thing to do is to make sure that fires are permitted before starting one.

If campfires are permitted, the park will usually have a fire ring in each campsite. Confine your fire to the fire ring provided. Do not move the ring to another location or start a fire in another location in the campsite. The reason for confining your fire to the existing ring is that fires have a negative impact on the spot of land where they are built. In addition to discoloring the ground, the heat will kill insects and the microscopic plant life that could serve as food for other animals. If every camper built a fire in a different place, collectively they would quickly cause a considerable amount of damage to the ground, insects, and plant life in the park. By using the existing ring, you avoid damaging additional ground or plants. If you want to go another step toward protecting the environment, avoid building campfires as much as possible. Instead cook with a backpacker's stove or use charcoal if a grill is provided.

If you decide to have a campfire, buy your firewood either from the campground vendor or a local store rather than scavenging it from the ground, and bring it back to your site. Purchased firewood is usually cut to an appropriate length and will be seasoned so it will burn efficiently as fuel. You may be able to find some deadwood lying about the campground, but most of the time it will not be enough to support your fire. Previous campers have probably collected most of the available wood. Do not wander through the park looking for large logs. It will likely be a lot of trouble getting this wood back to your campsite, it may be against regulations in some parks, and it would likely remove natural food sources and habitat for park wildlife.

Under no circumstances should you ever cut living or "green" trees or bushes. In addition to it being difficult to burn, cutting living plants unnecessarily damages the environment and animal habitat.

If you choose to have a campfire, keep it small and under control. Have water nearby in case the fire gets too large. You should be able to extinguish the fire completely should a problem develop. Another basic principle is never to leave your fire unattended. If you must leave your campsite, extinguish your fire completely. At the end of the day when you are ready to go to sleep, extinguish it completely. To extinguish your fire, douse it with water, stir the ashes with your crowbar or with a long stick, and douse it again. Repeat this sequence until the fire is completely out. Some outdoor ethicists recommend scattering your ashes before leaving your site.

Keep your campsite clean. There are at least three reasons for keeping your site clean. First, it will prevent the wind from blowing your trash into another camper's site. Second, it will prevent animals from shredding your trash and depositing it all over the campground. And third, it will help to keep wild animals from becoming accustomed to eating human food and becoming a nuisance to other campers. Keep a trash bag handy and put your trash in it as soon as possible. When you must leave your campsite and when you are ready to go to bed, take your garbage and recyclables to the dumpsters and dispose of them properly.

Some campgrounds still have the old-style garbage cans with lids, but many have changed over to large dumpsters and recycle bins to facilitate collection and to prevent animals from getting access to the garbage. Keep your glass, plastic, and aluminum cans separate and place them in the recycle containers. Never throw garbage, glass, aluminum, and plastic products into the fire. They will not burn completely, they may give off unpleasant fumes, and they will be an unsightly mess that the next campsite occupant will have to clean up.

If you smoke cigarettes, put your butts in the garbage. Do not throw them on the ground or in the fire. They are unsightly and take years to decompose. Occasionally children camping in the site after you may pick up your butts and put them in their mouths.

Soapy water is another type of waste that should be disposed properly. Never pour your "gray" water into creeks, rivers, or other bodies of water. Many campgrounds forbid disposing of gray water on the ground. Regardless of whether or not there is a specific rule regarding gray water, try to dispose of your dish and bathwater in an appropriate dumping place. If no gray water dumping station is available, pour the water into a flush toilet.

When the time comes to leave your campsite, pack your bike completely and then police your site. In other words, systematically walk around your site and pick up all trash, whether it is yours or a previous camper's. When you police your site, you may occasionally find some of your own gear (a rope or tent stake) that you have accidentally overlooked. More importantly, you will be leaving your site ready for the next occupant.

This sign is posted at the exit of 29 Dreams Resort near Birmingham, Alabama.

Minimize your environmental impact. When you camp in a park, leave everything as you found it. Do not be tempted to carve your name or initials in a tree, write your name on a wall, rearrange landscaping rocks or timbers, or take souvenirs such as rocks or pieces of wood. A well-known directive for park preservation is, "Take only pictures, leave only footprints, and bring home only memories." If possible, go another step further and try to have a "negative environmental impact." In other words, clean up trash and waste left by other campers. If possible, repair things that were damaged by previous campers.

Respect wildlife. In many parks you are likely to see several different animals and reptiles. These animals and reptiles may include squirrels, raccoons, skunks, bears, foxes, coyotes, bobcats, birds, toads, lizards, and snakes. They lived in the park before your visit and will live there after you leave. A common park rule is "Do not molest the animals." You should not approach them, tease them, throw rocks at them, or attempt to injure or kill them. Instead respect their right to exist in the park and leave them alone.

If an animal presents a problem, inform a park ranger. For example, if you see a bat on the ground or a raccoon walking aimlessly in the middle of the day or some other animal behaving strangely, do not approach it or touch it. Leave it alone. Stay away and inform a park ranger.

As mentioned previously, you should not feed animals or give them access to your food. When humans feed animals or leave food in unoccupied campsites, animals become dependent on human food and lose their ability to find food in their natural environment when the human food is no longer available. Furthermore, if you feed wild animals, they will lose their fear of humans and become beggars. Besides being a nuisance to future campers, they will be more aggressive in approaching humans and taking their food. A common belief is "A fed animal is a dead animal." As they lose their ability to find food on their own, larger animals like bears may have to be killed because they can become dangerous if they lose their fear of humans and attempt to take their food. Do not be the cause of an animal's death.

Do not trample or cut vegetation. When walking or hiking through the park, stay on designated paths. Do not take shortcuts through the woods or brush, because you may end up trampling vegetation. If everybody walked on vegetation, plants would be unable to grow and provide the cover needed by some species of animals.

Another important principle is not to cut live trees, shrubs or other plants (like sea oats). There is no reason to cut live wood for a fire, because it will not burn efficiently and will give off a lot of smoke. Do not drive nails in trees; if you find nails driven by previous campers, remove them with your crowbar. Do not throw knives or hatchets into trees. In addition to being dangerous for other people, such actions unnecessarily damage the habitat of many animals.

Avoid trenching. Many years ago, campers routinely dug trenches around their tents to keep water out and to keep their clothing and gear dry.

Children and other novice campers were routinely taught to pack a small shovel and always dig their trench before engaging in recreational activities. Today our thinking has completely reversed itself. We now believe that trenching is not necessary and may be potentially harmful to the park and its animal inhabitants. We believe it is not necessary because most tents now have bathtub floors and large rain flies that make it virtually impossible for water to seep into the tent and because most campgrounds now provide elevated tent pads made with porous materials that facilitate rapid movement of water away from your tent area. Unnecessary trenching by many campers can increase soil erosion and can damage soil and plants that serve as food and habitat for small organisms in the food chain. Occasionally you may encounter a situation that seems to require some trenching. For example, a few years ago while camping at a private campground near the Smokies, we had a summer thunderstorm that produced a considerable amount of rain in a relatively short time. We were camped beside a mountain river. As a result of the storm, we suddenly had another small river running under our rain fly and through our table area. To divert the river through our table area, I had to dig a small trench further to the side and use the dirt to fill in the low area near our table. Most of the time, however, you can stay dry and never have to dig a trench.

Leave firearms at home. Firearms, including pistols, have been prohibited in most state and national parks for many years (these regulations may change in 2010). Although some bikers seem to think pistols are essential, they really are not, and they are prohibited in most public campgrounds.

Environmental Concerns

About ten to fifteen years ago, a new ethical issue began to emerge among campers and other outdoor enthusiasts. This issue, sometimes called eco-concerns, focuses upon the environmental impact of our lifestyle. In regard to motorcycle camping, these eco-concerns focus upon procedures used to grow and manufacture materials that are used to make camping gear and clothing. Ironically, the technology that has produced high-quality camping gear also has produced several potentially harmful environmental effects. Considerable evidence suggests that many agricultural and manufacturing procedures pose potential threats to our environment and personal health.

Specific problems. To understand the reasons for eco-concerns, it is necessary to first understand how camping gear is made. In particular, we should understand how materials used to make gear are typically grown and/or manufactured. In this regard, two different general concerns have emerged.

The first general concern relates to the overall amount of fossil fuel required to manufacture, transport, warehouse, and sell each particular product used for camping. Environmentalists have pointed out that the standard manufacturing processes rely heavily upon the use of non-replenishable fossil fuel energy. Factories typically burn oil or coal to heat their buildings, to power their lights, and to run their machinery. After products have been produced, trucks burn gas or diesel fuel to transport goods to wholesalers and to retail outlets. Wholesale and retail outlets must burn fuel to heat and light their buildings. Overall, a considerable amount of fuel is burned to manufacture, transport, and store any particular product sold to consumers. When fossil fuels are burned, they release tons of carbon dioxide into our atmosphere, which presumably accelerates the process of global warming and the consequent extinction of plant and animal species. Many environmentalists are concerned that global warming resulting from burning fossil fuels has already had caused the death and near extinction of several plant and animal species. More importantly, these environmentalists believe that global warming will have a catastrophic effect upon our planet in a relatively short time unless we quickly change our energy consumption patterns. See the September 2007 issue of *Backpacker* magazine for many more details about this issue.

The term *carbon footprint* is now being used to quantify the amount of energy that is expended each year by a person or product. The concept can also be applied to quantify the amount of energy that is expended to produce a particular camping gear product. The Web has several sites that can be used to estimate carbon footprints. The calculation methods and statistics vary from one site to another, but all the sites agree that most Americans are expending two to three times the amount of energy and carbon than is environmentally desirable. These sites urge Americans to become more environmentally conscious and to reduce their carbon footprint. Many sites also urge Americans to voluntarily pay *carbon offsets* (fees) to select organizations that support environmentally friendly projects such as planting trees and using solar or wind energy to generate electricity.

A second concern focuses upon specific chemicals used to manufacture camping gear. Many chemicals used to make camping gear can be harmful to our environment and health in different ways. For example, people working in fields and factories may be exposed to harmful and sometimes deadly levels of chemicals. Furthermore, because these chemicals become embedded in their clothing, these workers may take the chemicals home after work and expose their spouses, children, and other family members. After the manufacturing process has been completed, consumers, users, and anyone else who comes into direct contact with some products during their lifetime can be exposed to potentially harmful levels of the chemicals. Waste from the manufacturing process is typically released into the air or rivers where it can be inhaled, absorbed through the skin, or ingested either directly from the water supply or indirectly by eating fish, fowl, or animals that were exposed to the chemicals. Finally, many products thrown into landfills do not degrade and may release small amounts of the chemicals into the soil for many years. Examples of specific materials and the potentially toxic chemicals used to make them are summarized in the following paragraphs.

Cotton is used to make lots of clothing for the general population and for campers. Traditional methods used to grow healthy cotton plants involve the application of a considerable amount of potentially harmful chemicals such as fertilizers, pesticides, and herbicides. Pesticides, in particular, have been the focus of much concern. Pesticides are liberally applied to prevent boll weevil and other insect infestations. Unfortunately field workers in many countries are exposed to extremely high doses of these pesticides by physical contact and by inhalation. And when they go home at night wearing clothing covered with pesticides, they expose their children and other family members to high doses. According to the World Health Organization, approximately three million cases of pesticide poisoning and twenty thousand deaths have been reported each year (mostly in third-world countries). Herbicides are another concern. They are applied early in the growing cycle to control weeds and then again at the end of the growing cycle to kill the leaves of the plants to facilitate picking. Unfortunately these herbicides can be inhaled by anyone working in the fields or living nearby and can be ingested due to runoff into our water supply. After cotton has been converted into cloth, chromium and heavy metals such as copper and zinc are used to make dyes that are used to color the fabric. These metals can be especially hazardous to textile workers but pose an environmental problem because they are frequently released into the air or dumped into nearby rivers where they can be ingested by other people and animals through foods and drinking water. Prolonged exposure can cause skin ulcerations, breathing problems, and possibly cancer.

Wool is usually made from the fur of sheep. Typical methods used to raise sheep and make wool raise several concerns. First of all, some environmentalists are concerned about methane gas (a powerful greenhouse gas that presumably causes global warming) that is produced from the digestive process in sheep (as well as cows) and belched into the air. Sheep are frequently dipped in pesticide baths to keep insects from causing infections; they are also fed antibiotics to prevent infections; and they are fed with food that has been mixed with formaldehyde to increase wool production. After the wool has been harvested, chlorine (which is also used to make household cleaners and to sanitize water) is applied to the fabric to reduce shrinkage. Excessive exposure to chlorine can cause pneumonia, emphysema, hypoxia, pulmonary edema, asphyxia, cardiac arrest, and death. Later in the manufacturing process, heavy metals are used to make dyes to color the fabric.

Polyester is made from petroleum—a non-renewable resource. When we eventually deplete all the world's supply of petroleum, future generations will have no more. Burning petroleum to make polyester produces carbon dioxide—a powerful greenhouse gas that depletes the earth's ozone layer and is assumed to produce global warming. Furthermore, silver is sometimes used during the manufacturing process to help some types of polyester (e.g., polyprophelene) reduce odor retention.

Nylon is made from coal—another non-renewable resource that contributes to global warming by depleting the earth's ozone layer.

Leather is used to make boots and various articles of riding apparel. Cows are also a major producer of methane gas, and leather products are tanned with chromium.

Plastic products frequently are made with polyvinyl chloride (PVC or vinyl). PVC is a pliable material that is used to make several materials for camping gear. It may be identified with the number 3 inside the universal recycle symbol or the letter "v" under it. After it has been manufactured, it contains traces of several toxic chemicals such as mercury, dioxins, and phthalates (e.g., DEHP) that can leech out and possibly poison anyone who comes into contact with the product by inhalation, skin absorption, or ingestion. Excessive exposure to these chemicals can cause lung cancer, lymphomas, leukemia, brain cancer, and liver cirrhosis.

Hard plastic is used to make some drinking bottles and cups. To harden the plastic, many manufacturers use bisphenol-A (BPA). When these bottles are heated (e.g., in a dishwasher, hot drinks, direct sunlight), BPA could leech out of the plastic into liquids that are placed inside the bottle and perhaps cause health problems to anyone who drinks the liquid. BPA is a synthetic variation of estrogen and may cause reproductive and other problems. It may be found in bottles that have either the number 3 or the number 7 inside the universal recycle symbol.

Eco-friendly (green) choices. To overcome the potentially catastrophic environmental and health problems resulting from our wasteful lifestyle, environmentalists urge us to adopt a new approach to life—we must learn to reduce, repair, and recycle products rather than waste and pollute. In this country, environmentalists have asked consumers to estimate and modify their *carbon footprint.* Europeans have been urged to examine their *ecological rucksack.* In other words, we must learn how to reduce our fuel usage by adjusting our home thermostats, by taking shorter and fewer trips, by walking, by riding bicycles, and by driving more fuel-efficient vehicles (e.g., motorcycles) rather than larger fuel-consuming vehicles. We all must learn to repair and recycle our consumer goods, including camping gear, to get the maximum life out of products rather than throwing them into landfills.

Campers must also learn to camp comfortably with less equipment and try to purchase eco-friendly (or green) camping gear whenever possible. Some examples of green camping gear are described in the following paragraphs.

Many companies (e.g., Patagonia and Marmot) now make clothing with eco-friendly materials such as organic cotton, hemp, cocona (from coconut shells), bamboo, and Tencel. All of these new materials use fewer chemicals than older materials. Some companies (in particular Patagonia) now make polyester clothing (e.g., Capilene) from recycled polyester. Other companies are making shoes and boots with recycled rubber and use other eco-friendly processes. For example Patagonia makes Ecostep soles from 30 percent recycled scrap rubber and latex harvested from Hevea trees.

Other companies are making camping gear from recycled materials. For example, Mountainsmith makes the Phoenix backpacks from recycled materials. Sierra Designs makes the Verde sleeping bag from recycled Climashield insulation and Cocona. Big Agnes makes the

Skinny Fish sleeping bag from 100 percent recycled Climashield HL green insulation.

Yet other companies have begun to make camping gear with materials that are made with few, if any, toxic materials. For example, Sierra Designs makes the Electron RC 2 tent from PVC-free tape, toxin-free poles, and no dyes. SIGG, Kleen Kanteen, and New Wave Enviro now make reusable water bottles from aluminum, stainless steel, or BPA-free plastic to avoid the potential problems associated with plastic water bottles made with BPA.

When the time comes to replace your camping gear, investigate eco-friendly gear as a possible option.

Conclusion

How should one behave on a camping trip? Are you free to do anything you want? Motorcycle camping provides an incomparable sense of freedom and pleasure of being in the midst of nature. You are free to relax and unwind in many different ways. But it should not be viewed as an opportunity to destroy our precious natural resources or to prevent other people from enjoying these resources.

Whenever you visit a park, be sure to exercise common sense so that you do not offend other campers or damage the natural resources of the park. Read and obey park rules and regulations, try to be a good neighbor, and help preserve our natural resources so that our children and grandchildren will be able to enjoy them. When in doubt, follow the twelve ethical principles presented in this chapter. At home, try to become more knowledgeable about environmental issues and how our personal decisions may contribute to global problems.

After reading this chapter, read more about outdoor and camping ethics. You can visit the Leave No Trace Web site (www.lnt.org), read *Backwoods Ethics* by Laura and Guy Waterman, read *The Backpacker's Field Manual* by Rick Curtis, and learn more about environmental issues. For more information about environmental concerns, you can visit any of the following sites: www.climatecrisis.net, www.greenyour. com, www.ecollo.com, www.wecansolveit.org, www.climateprotect. org, www.besafenet.com/pvc, and www.closetheloop.com.

11. Problems

Motorcycle camping usually is an immensely enjoyable recreational activity. Campers are away from their jobs and family pressures; they are surrounded by trees, grass, wildflowers, and nature; they are able to breathe plenty of fresh air; occasionally they can smell smoke drifting up from nearby campfires and foods being cooked by neighbors; they are able to enjoy brisk morning temperatures; they can hear birds singing and occasionally see animals walking near their sites; and they have a sense of personal freedom that exceeds anything they experience in their normal daily lives. Camping life is good!

Unfortunately problems can sometimes occur. Like life in general, problems are a part of camping. The better you understand potential problems, the better you will be able to deal with them. Backpackers and mountain climbers, who travel and camp in remote wilderness areas, are acutely aware of potential problems. These campers enjoy camping several miles away from other people, telephones, transportation, and emergency assistance. If they experience severe weather, animal attacks, choking, chest pains, allergic reactions, food poisoning, broken bones, severe lacerations, or other problems, the problem can quickly turn into a life-or-death emergency. Because they are many miles from civilization, they will be unable to get medical assistance for several hours or even for several days. Therefore, backpackers and other people who camp in remote wilderness areas must learn basic medical procedures and survival techniques before venturing into the back country. To help them prepare, most books and magazines written about backpacking and ultra-light camping include chapters and articles describing various life-threatening scenarios and presenting strategies for surviving them. These books and magazines typically assume "worst case scenarios" and present their recommendations as "survival techniques."

Bluff-side trails provide spectacular views but can be dangerous. Robin paused by the balanced rock at Devil's Lake State Park near Baraboo, Wisconsin.

Fortunately motorcycle campers who stay in established state or national park front-country campgrounds do not need to learn survival techniques. These lightweight campers typically camp in campgrounds where other campers can call for help, where cars and trucks can provide emergency transportation, where cell phones are plentiful and anyone can call 911, and where park personnel are readily available to provide emergency assistance. If a problem develops, motorcycle campers can usually get on their motorcycle and quickly ride to another location where assistance is available. If they did experience a potentially life-threatening problem, they will not have to know survival techniques, other than perhaps CPR. If an injured person needed to be transported to a hospital, paved roads are nearby. Emergency personnel will be able to get to the injured person quickly, will be able to administer treatment within a few minutes, and will be able to evacuate the person quickly. Therefore, books on motorcycle camping, such as this one, do not need to discuss survival techniques. Instead this book will focus upon problems that could occur in established campgrounds, ways to prevent these problems, and ways to treat these problems should they occur.

Almost every trip we have taken has confronted us with a new problem or two that has required us to spend a little time thinking about how to prevent that problem in the future or how to resolve or treat it if it occurs again. On one trip, for example, Robin broke her ankle. After gathering our wits and assessing the situation, we rode to the nearest emergency room to get it set. Facing and resolving such problems with your companion will create a bond that will last for years. After surviving the problem, you will be able to look at pictures of your trips many years later and laugh about the problems you faced together.

A few simple precautions will prevent many problems. For example, be sure your gear is in good shape before you leave home. If you have a stuck zipper on your sleeping bag or tent, fix it or replace it before departing on your trip. When you register for your campsite, inquire about potential problems in the park. Signs frequently will alert you to these problems. If, for example, your campground is located in a bear habitat, posted signs will alert you to this fact and rangers will advise you regarding your personal safety. Read and obey the signs, listen to the rangers' advice, ask questions, and follow their recommendations. If you do, you will probably never have a problem. Finally, drink alcoholic beverages in moderation. Alcohol impairs judgment, perception, and coordination. Many serious injuries such as burns, lacerations, and broken bones occur as a result of intoxication.

Overall Risks

I have been car and motorcycle camping for about forty-five years. Each year I take about ten trips and spend about thirty to forty nights in campsites. Some years I have spent as many as eighty or more nights in campsites. I have never been seriously injured in my campsite during any of these trips—thanks be to God. Robin has accompanied me on many of these trips and was injured only one time—she stepped in a hole at night and broke her ankle. Furthermore, in all these trips I have never been aware of other campers being seriously injured or killed. It seems obvious to me that the risks of injury while camping are very low.

Statistical data on camping-related injuries and fatalities are difficult to find. Several national parks and states publish search and rescue (SAR) statistics, and some publish hospitalization statistics. Examples of such studies include a ten-year retrospective study of 1,912 SAR missions in Yosemite National Park by Hung and Townes (2007 and a five-year retrospective study of 516 recreational injuries and nineteen deaths in Mount Rainier and Olympic National Parks by Stephens, Diekema, and Klein (2005). One study by Flores, Haileyesus, and Greenspan (2008) examined factors related to approximately 500,000 admissions to sixty-three hospitals scattered across the United States. In particular, this latter study attempted to determine specific factors related to 212,708 injuries sustained while engaging in outdoor recreational activities.

When reviewing these and other studies one should remember that statistics are typically based upon all park visitors and not specifically upon campers. Most serious injuries and fatalities usually occur when campers or day users hike, climb, or wander away from the campground and engage in other dangerous activities. Males are more likely to be injured and killed while engaging in outdoor recreational activities than females, and young males (under thirty-five years of age) are more likely to be injured and killed than males over the age of thirty-five. Furthermore, many injuries and fatalities are associated with the use of alcohol or other drugs. These injuries could have been prevented had the victim obeyed park rules and used a little "common sense."

Flores and his colleagues (2008) used data taken from a sample of hospitals to estimate the rate of outdoor recreational injuries as 72 per 100,000 visitors. Data from this study were also used to estimate injury rates related to several different outdoor recreational activities. The rate of injury related to camping was estimated to be less than 1 percent of the population, and many of these injuries were burns and lacerations sustained by young children. The rates of injury related to other activities were as follows: snowboarding, 18 percent; sledding, 8 percent; hiking, 4.6 percent; personal watercraft, 2.6 percent; fishing, 2.4 percent; and swimming, 1.5 percent. Another study by the National Park Service (www.nationalparktraveler.com) reported 872 injuries and 136 fatalities during 2007 in all the national parks combined.

All of the studies cited above, plus many more, agree that falling is the primary cause of outdoor recreational injuries and fatalities. Stephens and his colleagues (2005) found that falls accounted for 37 percent of the 535 injuries in Mount Rainier and Olympic National Parks between 1997 and 2001. Hung and Townes (2007) reported that falling was the most common cause of fatalities in Yosemite National Park between 1990 and 1999. And the October 2008 issue of *Backpacker* magazine reported that falls caused 4,616 mountaineering disasters between 1951 and 2006. (The second-highest factor caused only 971 disasters.) If you go to the Web and search for "hiker falls" you will find news stories for over a dozen deaths and many more serious injuries in state and national parks during 2008. When hikers fall, they are likely to sustain head injuries, internal injuries, broken bones, and lacerations. Furthermore, they frequently fall down into places where rescue and evacuation is difficult to accomplish and thus medical treatment may be delayed for several hours—exacerbating the effects of the injury. On the basis of several separate studies, it seems reasonable to conclude that falling from high cliffs, bluffs, or ridges causes over a third of all serious injuries and fatalities in state and national parks.

After falling, the next most frequent causes of outdoor recreational injuries and deaths are drowning, heart attacks, hypothermia (usually caused by getting lost in caves or in the forest at night), and heat stroke. Other occasional causes of injuries and death in wilderness areas are lightning, avalanches, bee stings, mosquito-borne viruses, and assaults by other people (The National Park Service reported twelve murders in 2007.) At the bottom of the list of risks are snakes, spiders, mountain lions, bears, and alligators. Information about these dangers and their "Backpacker Terror Indexes" are presented in the October 2008 issue of *Backpacker* magazine.

Intoxicated Neighbors

In our camping experience, the most common and most serious problem has been intoxicated neighbors. Frequently groups of people decide to use the campground for an all-night drinking party. We have endured many of these drunken parties over our camping lifetime. In addition to disturbing our sleep and our peaceful camping experience, these intoxicated people frequently cause problems for other people. Others in the campground are forced to listen to their profanity, arguments, and loud music all night long. The rest of us never know what one of the drunks will do that could damage our property or cause injury. Intoxicated people are frequently destructive to other people's property—intentionally or not—and cause many serious injuries and deaths. If another camper asks them to settle down or to reduce their noise level, they frequently become even more obnoxious and belligerent and may try to provoke a fight.

Perhaps our worst experience with intoxicated neighbors occurred several years ago in a private campground near the Ocoee River. We were chaperoning a group of college students who were planning to raft down the river the next day. I am proud to say that our group was well behaved. However, next to us was a group of employees from a nearby factory who decided to have an all-night party. They were loud and used frequent profanity; they broke bottles by throwing them in the fire ring and against trees; they urinated in the open; they crashed a car into a tree; and they yelled and argued all night long. Early in the evening, we informed the park management about this developing situation, but nothing was done to stop the party. Empty bottles, cans, and trash were strewn all around the campground the next day. Fortunately none of our party participated or was injured.

It is not always easy to predict who will become intoxicated neighbors. The campers in the site next to you may seem perfectly normal during the day. But they may change into loud, belligerent drunks at night. On one trip a few years ago, I selected a campsite in a remote area of a campground to be away from other campers. After I had set up my site, three families with lots of teenagers moved into the site next to me. Although they had the whole campground from which to select their site, they chose the site next to me, and they stayed up all night partying. Needless to say, I had a long night.

The best way to prevent the problem of intoxicated neighbors is to stay only in campgrounds with good nighttime security. If campgrounds have hosts or rangers on duty or provide emergency phone numbers, disturbances can be reported and will hopefully be stopped before they get out of hand. Deep Creek Campground in the Smoky National Park, for example, did a good job a few years ago of keeping a potential party under control. One weekend trip we selected a good site near the creek and began to relax. Later that afternoon, we noticed that a large group arrived, pulling a commercial generator and portable stadium lights on a trailer. And they selected a site near ours. We were horrified and assumed we were in for a long night. But as soon as the lights came on that night, rangers visited their site and convinced them to turn off their lights and go to bed. The night was quiet. You also don't need to worry about loud drunken parties in Wisconsin state parks. These parks generally have good nighttime security and do a great job of controlling noise.

If you camp in a park with minimal nighttime security and a disturbance develops—and officials do not come to stop it—you have few options. You could pack up and leave, but packing is hard to do after you have settled in for the night. If a host or ranger is on duty, report the disturbance and request their intervention. Sometimes you might be tempted to politely ask a member of the group to reduce their volume, but frequently polite requests do not help and may actually make the problem worse. Drunks seem to resent other people asking them to be quiet.

The next morning you certainly should complain to park officials and request a refund of your camping fee. Odds are you will not get a refund at that time, but make your request in writing. Even if you do not get a refund, the written complaint and refund request will likely get the attention of park officials. Also write a letter to the park director and/or to the director of the state parks department giving details of the incident, including the date and description of the disturbance and the lack of official intervention. Then repeat your request for a refund. You may not get your money back, but your documentation may save future campers from having to endure a similar experience.

Injuries

When you are outdoors working with fires, knives, and axes in unfamiliar places, you may occasionally have an accident that causes an injury. Some people are more careless than others, but no matter how careful you try to be, you will likely experience an injury or two if you camp very often.

Burns. The injuries I have experienced most often have been minor burns. I sometimes get careless around the campfire and when cooking. I get in a hurry and try to move a log in the fire or move a hot grill or pick up a hot pot with my bare hands. I am especially likely to get burned if I have consumed a beer or two. Burns can also come from excessive exposure to sun and wind as you are traveling.

The best way to avoid campfire burns is to wear camp gloves when working around the fire or with hot pots. The best way to avoid cooking burns is to use pliers or dish towels when handling hot pots. And the best way to prevent sun and wind burn is to wear sunscreen, even on cloudy, cool days.

If you get a minor burn, wash the burn with soap and water and then apply an aloe cream or gel. We keep a travel-sized bottle of aloe gel in our first-aid kit. If the burn produces blisters, you should seek professional medical attention.

Severe burns can occur from careless use of gasoline or other flammable materials and from using fire in a tent. Never use gasoline to start a fire. It can be extremely dangerous. If a person actually catches on fire, extinguish the flames by wrapping the person in a blanket or towel and rolling him or her on the ground. Have the person lie down and treat him or her for shock. Do not try to remove clothing, and immediately call for emergency medical assistance.

Broken bones. Campgrounds generally have rocks, tree roots, logs, holes, and uneven ground surfaces that you would not find in your home or motel room. These obstacles could cause a fall resulting in a broken bone. As mentioned earlier, Robin broke her ankle on a camping trip. One night she was walking out to the road to get something and she stepped in a small hole. When we realized the bone might be broken, we did not try to apply a splint. Instead we just tried to keep her foot as still as possible as we rode to the nearest hospital. Backpackers who camp many miles away from cars, roads, and assistance may have to apply splints to broken bones and fashion some type of crutch before they can walk out of the wilderness. Sometimes they may have to be carried out. They may have to wait a considerable amount of time before they have access to medical care. On the other hand, lightweight campers staying in state or national parks have immediate access to transportation. If a serious break occurs, emergency medical treatment can be summoned within a few minutes.

Lacerations. Another common injury is a serious cut. Lacerations can occur when people are not careful working with axes and knives. They can also occur in many other situations when a person unexpectedly encounters a sharp object. If a serious laceration occurs, first try to stop the bleeding. Ideally you should cover the wound with a sterile piece of gauze from your first-aid kit and apply pressure. If the gauze pad gets soaked with blood, apply a second pad on top of the first. Do not remove the first pad. If you do not have a sterile pad, use a clean white cloth; if you do not have that, use any cloth or towel you have to stop the bleeding. If considerable bleeding has occurred, the victim should be treated for shock. Have him or her lie down with the feet slightly elevated and cover the victim with a blanket or sleeping bag. Call 911 or ask someone to help transport them to the nearest medical facility.

Other soft-tissue injuries. According to the study by Flores and his colleagues (2008), strains and sprains accounted for a significant number (34 percent) of hospitalizations related to outdoor recreational activities. Other factors include dislocations, contusions, abrasions, and traumatic brain injury.

Cold Weather

When you first start camping, you may frequently find yourself unprepared for cool nights. You are likely to be unprepared because in your everyday life you spend most of your time in your car, home, and other buildings where your body is easily able to maintain its core temperature and where you do not need extra warm clothing for extended outdoor living. As a result, you become accustomed to dressing in a minimum amount of clothes. On the other hand, when you camp you will be outside for many hours. Much of the time, your body will be relatively inactive. After prolonged periods of inactivity in relatively cool temperatures (in the low fifties) without adequate clothing, your body core temperature will begin to drop, especially if you are wet from rain or sweat. As a result you may begin to shiver uncontrollably, and you could develop hypothermia. If you develop hypothermia, you will likely become a little confused and make poor decisions, which could increase your risk for a serious accident.

The best way to prepare for cold weather is to pack the right type of clothes. You must wear moisture-wicking underwear, thermal underwear, and plenty of garments designed to be worn as layers. Also bring a sleeping bag that is rated at least ten degrees lower than the expected low temperature. Cotton garments and leather pants and jackets should be left at home, because they are poor choices for keeping your body core temperature within the normal range. More information about sleeping and clothing is provided in chapters 3 and 5.

If you begin to shiver, go to a warm building. Hot-air hand dryers in bathrooms are useful for warming you up. If possible, take a long warm shower. If your clothes get wet, try to put on dry clothes and dry your wet clothes as soon as possible. If you are unable to maintain your body core temperature, go to a motel and wait for warmer weather.

Thunderstorms

Thunderstorms are relatively common in many parts of the country, especially during the spring-summer-fall camping season. If you camp much at all, you will likely experience thunderstorms on a fairly frequent basis. Most of the time, they create only minor problems such as soaking your tent and perhaps some other gear that requires a little time to dry out.

However, thunderstorms always have the potential for causing serious injury or death. You should always recognize this potential and take precautionary actions. One of the major threats from a thunderstorm is lightning. It kills about eighty people every year in the United States and injures many more. Another threat from a thunderstorm is high wind that can cause large trees or limbs to fall onto your tent. Heavy rains from thunderstorms can cause flash floods. Sometimes thunderstorms spawn large hail and tornadoes that could injure you and damage your gear.

The morning after a thunderstorm requires time and effort to get dried out. This was our campsite at the Smokemont campground, Great Smoky Mountains National Park.

The best prevention for thunderstorm-related problems is to monitor local weather forecasts. If strong thunderstorms are predicted during the day, you may wish to pack your gear and seek shelter. Any building is better than staying in the open. The best buildings are brick or stone buildings with few glass doors and windows. A basement is an ideal place to go, but few buildings in the South have basements. Hospitals, medical clinics, libraries, banks, government buildings, and college buildings are usually good choices. If thunderstorms are forecast during the night, you may want to consider spending the night in a motel.

If you get caught in your campsite by a thunderstorm, move to a shelter such as a bathroom, the park office, a recreation building, or a covered picnic shelter. You definitely want a roof that will keep you dry and protect you from falling limbs, flying debris, and hail. If possible, choose a building with solid walls and only a few windows that can protect you from wind and possible tornadoes.

Plants

Several plants can produce a strong allergic reaction if you come into contact with them. They include poison ivy, poison oak, poison sumac, and wild parsnip, among others. A few people apparently do not have this allergic reaction, but many people have a moderate reaction characterized by itch and skin rash. Some people may have a strong reaction and experience difficulty breathing after contact. The way to prevent accidental contact is to learn how to recognize these plants so you can avoid contact with them.

Poison ivy and poison oak have a distinctive three-leaf cluster. Either plant may grow as a vine on a tree or as sprouts from the ground. Poison ivy leaves can be small, as shown in the picture, or very large. Poison oak leaves usually are lobed and always grow in three-leaf clusters. Frequently the stems of poison ivy and oak are pink or red. Most campgrounds have poison ivy near campsites, but three that I remember as having a considerable amount are Parksville Lake in the Cherokee National Forest, Edgar Evins State Park near Cookeville, Tennessee, and Blue Mound State Park near Madison, Wisconsin.

Poison ivy may grow on the ground or on a tree as a vine.

The leaves of poison oak are lobed.

Poison sumac is a bush or small tree that typically grows in wet areas such as swamps, marshes, and other moist soil areas. Its leaves grow in pairs along a reddish stem with a final leaf at the end of the stem. The leaves are oblong in shape, have smooth edges, and have a point at the tip. They turn to beautiful shades of red and orange in the fall.

Wild parsnip is a weed that has recently invaded midwestern prairies. It looks like a yellow wildflower, but repeated skin contact can produce a severe allergic burn reaction. Wild parsnip has become very common near campsites in Wisconsin and Minnesota. It is especially plentiful in Governor Dodge State Park near Dodgeville, Wisconsin.

When you first arrive at your campsite and begin to plan your setup, look for these plants. If they are present, use this information to plan the location of your tent and picnic table. Try to set up your camp to avoid accidental contact with these plants. When you tie ropes to trees, look for these plants on the ground and on the trunk of the tree. When walking in the woods or brush near your campsite, wear boots rather than shower shoes.

If you accidentally contact one of these plants, remove any clothing that may have contacted the plant and wash the affected area with soap and water and then apply an antipruritic cream or lotion such as Calamine lotion. If you have an allergic reaction, you may wish to consider taking a Benadryl tablet from your first-aid kit.

Several other plants are poisonous to eat. Since motorcycle riders have ready access to grocery stores, there is little reason to eat wild plants and berries. Especially do not be tempted to eat wild mushrooms. The best advice is to refrain from eating any wild plants unless you have extensive training in edible foods and you are able positively to identify edible and non-edible species.

Insects

Whenever you camp you may come into contact with several different types of insects, including mosquitoes, bees and other stinging insects, chiggers, ants, and caterpillars.

Mosquitoes. Mosquitoes are commonly found in many parts of the country. If you camp, you are likely to encounter mosquitoes. They are more likely to be out during the early morning hours and the evening hours; they breed in standing water and thus are likely to be more numerous if you camp near swamps, marshes, backwaters, and other places where water stands still. Here in the South and in other parts of the country, they present only a minor annoyance, but in some parts of the country, such as the northern midwestern states (Minnesota, North Dakota, South Dakota, and Wisconsin) they can make your camping trip miserable if you are unprepared for them. Our worst problem with mosquitoes was on a June 2008 trip to Peninsula State Park in Door County, Wisconsin. Mosquitoes were abundant when we woke up in the morning and before we went to bed at night. They were especially annoying on the shore of Nicolet Bay.

In addition to the immediate discomfort caused by their bites, mosquitoes can carry several serious diseases including malaria, yellow fever, West Nile virus, and several different types of encephalitis. Therefore, when you camp, be prepared for mosquitoes.

The best way to prevent mosquito bites is to apply mosquito repellent. Most experts recommend a product with DEET, such as Deep Woods Off, because it lasts longer than other products and repels more mosquitoes. We have used this product for several years and have found it to work very well. Reviews of various products usually rate Deep Woods Off very highly in terms of its ability to reduce mosquito bites for long periods. Whether we are camping or not, we always carry a can in case we run into a swarm of mosquitoes or other insects. A few campers prefer to use products that are more environmentally friendly, such as Skin So Soft lotion or citronella candles. If you plan to camp in a known mosquito-infested area, you may wish to consider packing mosquito repellent clothing and a head net.

If you get bitten by mosquitoes, wash the bites with soap and water and dab a small amount of an ammonia-based product such as Itch Eraser on each bite. We pack a small tube of Itch Eraser in our first-aid kit and use it often.

Biting flies. Several parts of the country have biting flies. We first encountered such flies at the Florida Gulf beaches during the month of September. They attacked our legs and made it impossible to enjoy being on the beach. We have also encountered deer flies and horse flies during past summer camping trips to southwestern Wisconsin. They like your legs and back and can bite through your clothing. Black flies reportedly are plentiful during the month of June in the northern boundary waters between Canada and the United States. They especially seem to like your legs and the mucous membranes of your face (eyes, nose, and mouth). If you encounter problems with biting flies, remember that you have a motorcycle nearby and can easily ride to another location.

Bees and other stinging insects. Campers should also be aware of stinging insects such as bees, wasps, hornets, and yellow jackets. More people reportedly are hospitalized because of allergic reactions to insect stings than because of any other type of animal attack. Stinging insects can present problems all summer, but they seem to be most aggressive on hot days during the end of summer. In general, look where you are walking and where you put your hands. Yellow jackets make their nests in the ground. If a person steps on their nest, the yellow jackets are likely to attack in a mass, inflicting several stings. During their attack, they will get inside clothing to sting the victim. Be careful to stay on well-worn paths when you are walking in the woods. Hornets build very large nests in trees and usually swarm around them. If you see a nest, do not disturb it. Instead move away as quickly as possible. Bees, especially the Africanized bees, have become more aggressive. Try to avoid them all.

If you are stung by any of these insects, first wash the skin around the sting. You may want to take a Benadryl tablet and to apply Itch Eraser. If it was a honeybee, try scraping the stung area with a credit card to remove the stinger. If you have meat tenderizer, dab some on the sting with a cotton swab or cloth. If you receive several stings or if you have difficulty breathing, you should seek immediate medical attention.

Chiggers. Chiggers or red bugs can also causes problems for campers. I have camped for over forty years and never had a problem with chiggers until a recent trip to Gulf State Park in Gulf Shores, Alabama. After registering for our site, we began to set up our camp in a grassy field. To drive in my tent pegs, I put first one knee on the ground and then the other. As it turned out, the weather was warm and I was wearing a pair of shorts. I did not feel the bites at the time, but a little later I noticed dozens of red spots on each knee. At first I thought they were mosquito bites where I had missed spraying repellent, but later I realized they were chigger bites. They itched a little so I dabbed each one with Itch Eraser. After a brief stinging sensation, the bites did not bother me anymore, but they were visible for about a week after the trip.

Ants. Ants, especially the fire ants found throughout the South, can cause problems for campers. When you first begin to plan your camp layout, look for ant mounds. If mounds are present, set up your tent and dining area as far away from them as possible. You do not want to accidentally step in one after dark. If you did, you would likely receive numerous bites before you could get the ants off your body. If previous campers left food on the ground or poured a sweetened beverage on the ground, it may attract ants. While it is light, look for spilled food or drink on the ground, especially around the table. If you find any, remove as much as possible and rinse the ground with water. If you are bitten by ants, apply Itch Eraser.

Stinging caterpillars. Finally, I have to mention stinging caterpillars. Although these insects are rarely discussed as potential problems for campers, we learned firsthand that they can cause a stinging skin irritation. We learned this lesson after our trip to the Deep Creek Campground in the Smoky Mountains National Park. We arrived at the campground early one morning and got what seemed to be a choice site under some trees near the creek. As we began to unpack and set up our site, we noticed several white fuzzy caterpillars. They were on the picnic table; they were on the landscaping timbers that defined the tent pad; they got on the tent as we were setting it up; and later we found a few inside our tent. We generally tried to avoid contact with them, but we did not realize that they could cause us considerable discomfort.

During the first night, I had the sensation that small needles were sticking my legs inside my sleeping bag. At first I thought it was a stiff nylon thread or a twig and I moved about several times to adjust my sleeping position and rubbed my legs to reduce the sensation. But it continued. The next day my legs were stinging and Robin complained that her neck was stinging. We had no idea what could have caused our problems, but a few days later, when we were packing up to leave, we found four of these caterpillars in our tent.

A few days later, when our symptoms seemed to worsen, I began to suspect that the caterpillars were the cause of our problems. The first thing I did was to call the park to ask if the caterpillars may have caused our problems, but the person with whom I spoke was unaware of any problems caused by caterpillars. Then I began to search the Web, and sure enough, I found several sites that described skin irritation caused by the fine hairs of caterpillars.

As we learned from the Web site, most caterpillars do not cause skin irritation, but a few stinging (or *urticating*) caterpillars do exist. They do not attack people, but they will release toxin if people accidentally come into contact with them. Some of the well-known stinging varieties are saddleback caterpillars, flannel moth caterpillars, and puss caterpillars. If you contact a stinging caterpillar, you may experience the sensation that needles are sticking you followed by a rash, stinging or burning sensation, numbness, and nausea. The irritation varies in severity from person to person. Untreated, it subsides in about seven days.

If you know you have come in contact with a caterpillar, you can do a few things immediately after exposure to reduce the discomfort associated with the contact. First, change your clothes and wash the contacted area with soap and water. If a stinging sensation or rash develops, stick a piece of duct tape on the skin area and pull it off quickly. Hopefully this procedure will remove many of the stinging hairs. After using tape to remove the hairs, apply a cortisone cream from your first-aid kit.

Arachnids

Ticks. The most common of the arachnids are ticks. They are found in tall grass and weeds almost anywhere in the country. They typically rest on the grass and wait until a warm-blooded animal brushes against the grass. When an animal or person touches the grass, the tick jumps or climbs onto the host animal. Once on the host, the tick will walk around for a while until it attaches to the skin and begins to suck the blood.

Ticks present a major health concern because they can carry several different diseases including Rocky Mountain Spotted Fever and Lyme disease. Lyme disease may be transmitted by small deer ticks in all parts of the country, but according to the Center for Disease Control almost all of the reported cases are concentrated in upper midwestern and northeastern states. Most of the cases were caused by tick exposure in the person's own yard rather than in a campground.

To prevent problems caused by ticks, stay on paved or hard-packed pathways and avoid walking in tall grass as much as possible. If you must walk in tall grass, wear long pants and tuck the legs into your socks and also use an insect repellent such as Deep Woods Off. Each evening take a shower and inspect your body. Be alert to ticks that may be crawling on your body. You should especially examine your hair, the back of your knees, your armpits, your groin area, your lower legs, and your waist.

Several methods have been recommended for removing an embedded tick. The method that seems to be most accepted is to grasp the tick as near to your skin as possible with a pair of tweezers and slowly pull until the tick releases. Do not jerk the tick out and do not pull the tick with your fingers. If some parts of the tick remain in the skin, remove them with the tweezers. Once you have removed it, kill the tick by cutting it with a knife or stepping on it with your boot and wash the wound with soap and water.

Spiders. When you camp, you are likely to see many different spiders. Most of these spiders are harmless. In particular, the daddy longlegs (a common spider found in most campgrounds) is harmless and in fact is a good spider to have around camp because it kills other types of spiders. If a daddy longlegs gets on or in your tent, just grab one of its legs and throw it away from your tent.

Two spiders deserve a little more attention. One is the black widow. It is a glossy black spider with a red spot (frequently described as an hourglass) on its back. They have potent neurotoxin venom, but their bite usually is not fatal to most healthy adults. They are very easy to spot during daylight hours. They like moisture and seem to have an affinity for pit toilets, woodpiles, and for objects that have been lying on the ground for a few days. I have seen many in my yard but have never seen one on a camping trip. But be alert to their presence. Whenever visiting an outhouse, lift the seat, look, and run a stick around the base before sitting down. When picking up wood or other objects lying on the ground, use gloves and move the object first so you can look under it before picking it up.

The second poisonous spider to know is the brown recluse. It is a tan-brown spider with a dark violin or fiddle mark on the back of its head and upper body. It is primarily found in the southern states ranging from Texas to Georgia and from the Gulf Coast up to central Iowa, Illinois, and Indiana. It likes dark, dry places such as attics and storage sheds, but it may also be found underneath logs, rock piles, and stacks of lumber. Typically they do not attack humans but may bite when touched or crushed. To avoid being bitten, look before picking up wood and stones from the ground and wear gloves. If you are bitten, the bite is unlikely to be fatal and may, in fact, cause very little discomfort, but it can cause a serious reaction in some people.

If you suspect that you have been bitten by either a black widow or a brown recluse spider, seek medical attention. If pain or swelling occurs, apply ice packs.

Scorpions. Scorpions generally are nocturnal and avoid human contact. They can be found in many parts of the country. Most are not dangerous to healthy adults. I was stung on my back by a small one several years ago when we were camping at Henderson Beach State Park near Destin, Florida. The sting was about as noticeable as an ant bite. I had walked back into the brush to take a picture of our campsite. Robin playfully said to me, "Something's gonna get you." As I walked back to the site, I noticed something stinging my back and asked her to see what it was. She lifted my shirt, screamed, and ran away. I had no idea what it was. Fortunately this scorpion, like most, was relatively harmless.

However, one very dangerous type, the Arizona Bark Scorpion, lives in the desert southwest, especially in Arizona. Most of the time, its sting is not fatal to healthy adults, but it can kill people who are allergic to it or who have been weakened by other medical problems.

To avoid scorpion stings, shake out your sleeping bag before entering it at night and shake out boots and clothing before putting them on.

Reptiles

The three major types of reptiles are snakes, lizards, and alligators. Although all three could cause problems for campers, they rarely do so.

Snakes. People seem to be most fearful of snakes, but this fear is generally unfounded. We have never seen a snake, venomous or non-venomous, in an established campground. I have seen many in my backyard and on hiking trails but never in a campground. Snakes generally try to avoid human contact and will move away from areas frequently used by humans. If a snake ventures into a campground, a camper will likely report it and a park ranger will probably remove it to a remote area of the park. Furthermore, most snakes in the wild are harmless and, in fact, are beneficial to man because they control mice and other snakes. According to several sources (e.g., *American Family Physician*, April 1, 2002) only five to ten deaths a year in the United States are caused by venomous snakebites. Many bites result when people try to capture snakes for recreational or religious activities.

There are four types of venomous snakes in the United States. Generally they live in southern states and are most active in the evening on dry, hot, late summer days. The most common venomous snake is the copperhead. It is more likely to live near humans and is known to hang around houses in the flowerbeds here in the South. Of the four snakes, it would be the one campers would most likely encounter near a campground. Its bite is painful but not deadly for most healthy adults. Bite victims should be taken to a hospital for observation, but most of the time antivenin and other aggressive medical treatments will not be necessary.

A second venomous snake is the cottonmouth water moccasin. This snake lives near water and has been known to attack people who invade its territory. To avoid this snake, camp two hundred feet (seventy paces) or more away from rivers, lakes, ponds, ditches, and other bodies of water, and be very cautious when walking near water.

A third venomous snake—the rattlesnake—is perhaps the best known. There are several different species, and one or more of them can be found over a large area of the United States. The diamondback rattlesnake is considered the most dangerous of all the venomous snakes in the United States.

Another venomous snake is the coral snake. It is different from the first three in that it is not a pit viper and thus its head is much smaller than the heads of the other venomous snakes. It apparently prefers to live in remote, heavily forested areas and in rotting wood. Thus it is very unlikely to be found in an established campground. It is a colorful snake with red, yellow, and black bands. Other snakes, such as king snakes, have red and black bands, but the coral snake is the only one that has yellow bands adjacent to red bands. To help remember this specific combination, many people memorize the saying "Red touch yellow, kill a fellow."

The primary ways you might encounter a snake is to walk in relatively isolated areas or to pick up logs or flat pieces of wood, metal, or plastic lying on the ground. Be watchful for snakes when in the woods, but do not go out looking for them. When walking about the campground after dark, use your headlight to see where you are putting your feet. Most of the time, you should be okay. On the other hand, be cautious around lakes, slow-moving rivers, and other bodies of water in the South. Water moccasins can be more aggressive.

The best way to prevent snakebites is to keep your distance from the reptiles. Use a stick to move objects on the ground. Look where you put your hands and where you step, especially in tall grass or near water, fallen logs, and rocks. If you see a snake, give it room. Do not try to kill it or capture it. Apparently several people are bitten each year while trying to kill or capture snakes.

In the highly unlikely event that a person is bitten by a venomous snake, get a good description of the snake (head shape, color, body markings, length, and diameter), wash the bite with soap and water, immobilize the bitten area, keep it lower than the heart, and get medical attention. Most experts believe that cutting the skin and applying tourniquets may actually cause more harm to the victim and consider these methods to be ineffective. Using a suction device found in some snakebite kits may be helpful but usually is unnecessary. The primary thing to do is to get the person to a medical facility as quickly as possible.

Lizards. Campers are likely to see a variety of lizards, but they are generally harmless. Only one venomous lizard lives in the United States. This lizard—the Gila Monster—is found in Arizona and adjacent parts of California, Nevada, Utah, and New Mexico. These lizards are much larger than most others. Generally they live underground and thus should pose relatively little threat to most campers. Use the same precautions as for snakes and scorpions. If a person is bitten, take him or her to a medical facility.

Alligators. One last reptile to mention is the alligator. These reptiles generally do not pose a threat for campers, but they are common in Florida and several southern states. Alligators rarely attack humans, but I know of a man who was attacked while swimming in the small lake at Open Pond campground in the Conecuh National Forest in south Alabama. The alligator grabbed his arm and tried to pull him out to deep water. The man fought against the alligator's pull and lost his arm in the struggle. Avoid alligators by camping several feet away from water, and exercise caution when swimming or walking near water.

Other Animals

Various other animals living in or near campgrounds can also cause problems. One major concern with animals, although unlikely, is rabies. If you see a bat, raccoon, coyote, fox, skunk, or some other animal that appears injured or is wandering aimlessly or is behaving in an unusual manner, stay clear and notify park officials. Generally speaking, if you do not attempt to touch or capture animals and you do not feed them, you should never have a problem.

Raccoons. By far the peskiest animals for campers are raccoons. They typically sleep in trees during the day and descend into campgrounds shortly after dark. If they are present, they will visit your campsite during the night looking for food or garbage. They have opposable thumbs that allow them to open many different types of coolers and lockable boxes. They seem to be especially fond of eggs and corn but will eat almost any food they find. When they come to your campsite, they will pick up your spoons, plates, and other objects lying on the table or on the ground. They will try to open any containers. If they find paper or plastic with food smells, they will shred it into a thousand pieces and strew them all about your site.

Raccoons were very pesky at the Moraine View State Recreation Area near Bloomington, Illinois.

We have experienced many minor raccoon problems during our camping trips, but by far the worst was at the Myakka River State Park near Sarasota, Florida. The first evening, as we were eating our supper, we were visited by at least six raccoons. They were extremely forward in begging food and slowly crept to within two or three feet of us. At first I yelled at them, but my yelling did not seem to scare them. Then I threw sticks at them, but again they were not frightened. In a moment of desperation, I threw a glass of water on one and he quickly retreated. Then I began to throw water on others, and finally they all left our campsite. Previous campers had obviously fed these raccoons and by doing so had encouraged the raccoons to harass us (and probably many more campers who stayed at this park after us). Another park where we encountered many raccoons was Moraine View State Recreational Area near Bloomington, Illinois.

Raccoons look very cute and seem docile, but do not be deceived. They can be vicious when provoked. They can easily kill or cripple feral barn cats that are relatively tough fighters. To prevent raccoon problems, never feed them and never leave food or garbage in your campsite. Do not try to touch or handle them or any other wild animal.

Skunks. Skunks also come out after dark and could present a possible problem for campers. They will commonly roam through a campground during the night looking for food. If they feel threatened, they may spray your gear with an offensive odor that will be very difficult to remove. This is another reason for keeping your site clean and keeping your food packed away. If you see a skunk at night, remain calm and walk slowly away from it. If your gear is sprayed try using baking soda, soap, vinegar, tomato juice, and/or beer to remove the smell.

Porcupines. Porcupines are nocturnal animals that live in northern states east of the Mississippi River (e.g., Wisconsin, Michigan, and New York) and in all states west of the Mississippi River. We have no experience dealing with them, but other campers have experienced a few problems with them. The most common problem is a pet dog that gets too close to the porcupine and gets quilled. Occasionally campers sleeping in hammocks report being quilled when a porcupine wandered under their hammock during the night. These quills have barbs similar to fish hooks and must be removed to prevent further injury. Removal is painful but necessary.

Bears. Many books and magazine articles on camping seem to go overboard when discussing bears. They go into lengthy discussions regarding preventing and fighting off bear attacks. Although my experience with bears is admittedly limited, I think much of the discussion is over-dramatization.

Two basic types of bears live in the lower forty-eight states. They are the black bear, which can be found in many states, especially North Carolina, and the brown (or grizzly) bear, which is primarily found in the northern Rocky Mountain states. Both types are much more plentiful in Canada and in Alaska. Generally speaking, both types of bears are shy and usually try to avoid contact with humans.

In a bear habitat, the campground will probably have a steel locker to store your food, toothpaste, sunscreen, and other fragrant items.

Robin and I have camped dozens of times in the Smoky Mountain National Park (Tennessee and North Carolina) and in the Cherokee National Forest (North Carolina); we have never seen a bear in an established campground. We have seen them on hiking trails and in Cades Cove but never in the campgrounds. Based upon my personal experience, I believe that the risk of having a problem with a bear is very small.

However, a recent article in *Backpacker* magazine reported that bears in some western parks (especially Yosemite National Park) have become very adept at stealing food from campers in their campsites. And when bears learn to steal food from humans, they could easily injure someone. To keep these bears under control, park rangers tranquillized several that were lingering too close to campgrounds and tagged them with radio wave transmitters. After the bears were released, the rangers could monitor their movements in the dark. If a bear gets too close to a campground, the rangers locate it and harass it with loud noise until it leaves the area.

For the most part, bear attacks on humans are very rare, but a few are reported every year. Considering the thousands of hikers, campers, and visitors who come with reach of bear habitats every year, one could conclude that a bear attack is one of a camper's least worries.

However, it is prudent to recognize the possible risk of bear attacks and to exercise caution when camping in a bear habitat. Seven basic rules follow: 1) never feed bears; 2) keep your food in metal lockers and put your garbage in metal garbage receptacles so that bears cannot get it when you leave your campsite or go to sleep; 3) never bring food, toothpaste, sunscreen, or other fragrant items into your tent; 4) remove clothing worn when cooking food before entering your tent; 5) do not approach or follow bears or their cubs; 6) make noise when hiking so you do not accidentally surprise a bear that may be feeding or resting near your trail; and 7) never chase bears into the woods. Some people carry a can of bear-repellent spray, but most people do not feel the need to purchase this item. If you have any questions about the risks in a particular park, ask a ranger.

When you arrive at a campground in a bear habitat, you will see signs warning you that you are in a bear habitat and that you must follow food storage regulations. When you register for your campsite, the ranger will suggest ways to safeguard your food. The primary rule is to keep your site clean and secure all food when you leave your site and when you go to bed. Place all your garbage in garbage receptacles. If you had a car, you could store your food in the trunk, but if you are riding a motorcycle, you must store your food, along with other fragrant products, in the metal food storage locker. Do not store food in leather saddlebags. Several animals in addition to bears could destroy your bags to get your food.

Conclusion

What problems could be encountered on a motorcycle camping trip? Motorcycle camping is usually an enjoyable experience with a relatively low risk for injury or death. But like in life in general, problems sometimes develop. Some of the more common problems are falls, insect stings, and drowning. To avoid these problems, you must know what types of problems to expect, avoid excessive alcohol and drug use, practice common sense, have a first-aid kit handy, and know how to respond should a problem occur.

After reading this chapter, learn more about potential problems in parks and campgrounds by reading other books and Web sites. Look for information that describes possible problems, their prevention, and their treatment. Examples of such books include *Lightweight Backpacking and Camping* by Ryan Jordan and *Camping and Wilderness Survival* by Paul Tawrell. Also visit Web sites related to each specific problem (e.g., poison ivy, brown recluse spiders, or copperhead snakes) to learn more about prevention and treatment.

12. Closing Comments

The financial benefits associated with motorcycle camping should be evident from your very first trip. Since you do not have to pay for expensive motel rooms, you should notice that you have more money to enjoy other activities on your trip or to take more trips. But after completing a few successful trips, you will probably begin to notice many more benefits associated with camping. For me, one of the greatest pleasures in life is to snuggle up in my sleeping bag in my tent on a cool night, especially when it is raining. Once you become proficient with routine camping chores, you will be able to relax and enjoy many pleasures that camping can offer. You will probably begin to notice many pleasures that you may have never experienced before in your daily life.

Intangible Benefits

Perhaps the greatest intangible benefit of camping is just being able to stay outside for long periods of time. Like the pleasure associated with riding motorcycles and the pleasure dogs seem to experience when sticking their heads out of car windows, being outdoors provides pleasures that are difficult to explain. You seem to breathe more deeply when camping, and your body seems rejuvenated by the extra oxygen being transported through it. The air at a state or national park always seems fresher than the air at your home or work. It seems especially fresh if you are camping in the mountains or near lakes, rivers, or the shore. Furthermore, being outdoors allows you to enjoy soft breezes that gently blow against your skin and plenty of sunlight that helps lift your spirits and reduce the stress of everyday life.

On a trip to Wisconsin, I camped overnight at the Kickapoo State Park near Danville, Illinois.

Camping also seems to liberate your mind from the problems of your normal daily life. When camping, you must focus your attention upon many new tasks, such as finding the best campsite, setting up your tent and dining area, finding firewood, splitting the wood, deciding what to eat and where to find it, and preparing for rain. As you focus your attention on these tasks, you will quickly forget all your other worries and problems. Living in a campsite for several days (away from your family, neighbors, coworkers, and other daily reminders of problems) seems to make your pressing problems seem less significant. Sometimes when you are able to forget a pressing life problem for a while, you may experience a flash of insight when you least expect it that will help you solve the problem.

Camping can teach you how to be more independent and self-sufficient. You learn how to tie better knots, how to start fires quickly, how to cook outdoors, how to solve a variety of problems, and how to live without the conveniences that many others depend upon. You become proficient at setting up and breaking your camp, and this skill allows you to pack up your home whenever you wish and move it to whatever location you want. You learn how to prepare great-tasting meals with only a campfire or a small stove and a few small pots. You learn that you do not need large stoves, refrigerators, multiple pots and pans, and microwave ovens to live comfortably. You learn to clean up after a meal without using a dishwasher and trash compactor. You learn how to stay dry, warm, and comfortable in a wide range of weather conditions without needing heating or air-conditioning. You learn that you are able to travel on a limited budget without expensive housing costs, meals, moving expenses, airline tickets, taxi fees, and tips. You learn that all you really need are a few small pieces of camping gear, a few batteries, some warm clothes, and a campfire. In other words, you learn to live independently—like our pioneer forefathers did. And this knowledge can be empowering. It provides a tremendous amount of self-confidence.

Camping can teach you many things about history, biology, and other subjects, too. For example, it can teach you more about plants, animals, and ecosystems in the parks. You can also learn about the environment, ecology, and geology. Many parks are located in places that have historical, biological, cultural, or archeological importance and most offer educational programs designed to teach park visitors about the park's heritage. For example, before the devastating hurricanes Ivan and Dennis, park rangers at the Fort Pickens Park in the Gulf Islands National Seashore near Pensacola, Florida, used to teach many free programs. One such program was an orientation to small marine animals that live in the grass beds just offshore in the Pensacola Bay. At the beginning of the class, rangers supplied snorkels and masks and then taught participants the basics of snorkeling. Then they led us to the grass beds in the bay and taught us how to catch and identify various marine animals living there. I learned at least two important lessons from this short program. I learned more about the environmental and habitat needs of small creatures living in the backwaters of the ocean, plus I learned a new water recreational skill.

Another park that offers interesting educational programs is Mammoth Cave National Park in Kentucky. Every day during the camping season, park rangers lead several cave tours and teach a variety of evening programs on the social history, ecology, geology, plants, and snakes of the park. Guntersville State Park, near Guntersville, Alabama, offers programs on eagles and other indigenous birds. In general, many parks offer programs and activities on a variety of educational topics including American history, art, pioneer life, and environmental issues. And many state and national parks also offer nature centers where you can learn more about the animals and plants that live inside the park.

If you happen to select a park that does not offer such programs, you can always bring a bird, tree, plant, or flower field-identification guide and teach yourself how to recognize different species.

Another pleasure associated with camping is the opportunity to relax more than you are able to do most at other times in your life. You will be miles away from your routine daily demands, and you have few responsibilities or planned activities. You do not have to rush to keep scheduled appointments. You can go to bed as early as you would like, you can sleep as long as you like, and most importantly you can take a nap any time you want. You can read a book, listen to music, play your musical instrument, or do whatever helps you relax. We especially enjoy reading and napping in our hammocks in the afternoon. And we find that we sleep many more hours on a camping trip than we do in our daily life at home.

Blue Mound State Park is located on the top of Blue Mound near Madison, Wisconsin.

Camping offers the perfect combination of social interaction and solitude, regardless of your particular needs. When you feel like talking with others, you can usually find plenty of campers and park employees who are more than willing to talk with you. Many of them, like you, are miles away from their family, neighbors, and coworkers. They are relieved of their everyday pressures and responsibilities and have lots of free time. Many believe that no matter what type of tent or camper a person has, all campers belong to a common brotherhood because they all must learn how to deal with similar problems. Consequently other campers are usually willing to talk with their neighbors and offer assistance if needed. To initiate social interaction, all you have to do is to walk around the campground and speak to anyone you see. If they seem willing to talk, ask where they are from or where a good restaurant is located or what recreational activities are available nearby. A conversation will usually start, and sometimes a long-term friendship will develop.

On the other hand, when you want solitude, just read your book or take a nap in your hammock. Other campers may speak to you, but they will usually recognize your need for privacy. Most veteran campers are very good at respecting their neighbors' need for solitude and usually follow an important unwritten rule of camping—do not disturb those who want to be left alone.

Camping offers a wide range of pleasurable smells you usually cannot experience in your daily life. On every camping trip, you will notice distinctive aromas. Some of the smells are common to many campgrounds. For example, the smell of smoke wafting from a campfire, the smell of coffee brewing, or the smell of bacon cooking in the morning will likely be noticed in most campgrounds. Rain seems to have a relaxing smell for many people. If you are camping in a campground near the coast, you will enjoy the smell of the salt sea air. If you camp in a pine forest or in the mountains, you will notice a rich aroma that seems to provide both pleasure and relaxation. At certain times of the year, you may notice jasmine, magnolia, honeysuckle, privet, and other flowering plants blooming near your campsite. The more you camp, the more you will notice the many aromas drifting through your campsite.

Camping also offers a wide range of pleasurable sounds you usually cannot hear in daily life. For me, one of the most relaxing sounds is a gentle rain hitting on my tent or dining fly. During the day, you hear the voices of other people (both adults and children) echoing through the rocks and trees. At night you may hear a variety of birds and animal calls. Perhaps you will learn to tell the difference between a barred owl and a screech owl, or the difference between a whippoorwill and a Chuck-will's-widow. If you have the opportunity to hear a Chuck-will's-widow, hopefully it will not spend several hours calling out near your tent when you are trying to sleep—as one did near our tent at Gulf State Park in Gulf Shores, Alabama, a few years ago. Some campers enjoy these bird songs so much that they purchase CDs and other educational materials that will help them learn how to identify each bird species by its song.

Camping offers the opportunity to see and enjoy many aspects of nature that you would likely never experience in your routine daily life. For example, if you camp at Mammoth Cave campground, you will likely see deer walking through the campground and perhaps through your campsite early in the morning. If you camp at Cave-in-Rock State Park, Illinois, you may see coveys of turkeys walking through the campground. If you camp at Cades Cove in the Smokey Mountains National Park, you may see mother bears with their cubs near the campground. If you camp at any of the Wisconsin state parks along the Mississippi River you may see bald eagles and a variety of migratory birds. And if you camp in a wooded site at Peninsula State Park near Fish Creek, Wisconsin, you may see (and hear) pileated woodpeckers perched on trees near your tent.

Campfires provide a tremendous amount of comfort and pleasure. In most campgrounds, you can build a campfire any time you wish. At night a fire warms your body and clothes and helps reduce the chill that can occur when you first enter your empty sleeping bag. In the morning, a fire helps reduce the shock of climbing out of your warm bed and stepping into the chilly morning air. In the morning, a fire can also be psychologically comforting, because once it has been started, you know that your coffee or hot chocolate will soon be ready. Most importantly, a fire can comfort your soul. The flames of a fire can be hypnotizing. You can spend hours any time of day just staring at the flickering flames, and as you stare at the flames, your worries seem to vanish.

When you spend the whole day outdoors, you will likely notice sunrises and sunsets. In particular, sunsets in Peninsula State Park near Fish Creek, Wisconsin, are spectacular! Be sure to have your camera ready.

Meals can provide a lot of pleasure to campers. Food cooked in your campsite seems to taste much better than food cooked at home or bought in restaurants. Perhaps the food tastes better because you use special recipes that you only use when camping; perhaps it tastes better because the smoke from your campfire provides a special flavor; perhaps it tastes better because the fresh air activates your taste buds; or perhaps it tastes better because your appetite has been stimulated by spending several hours outdoors engaging in vigorous camping chores and activities.

In general, camping provides many pleasures beyond its financial benefits. The more you camp, the more pleasures you will notice. Each veteran camper describes his or her list of pleasures differently, but they all agree that camping provides many benefits in addition to just saving money. If you decide to join the ranks of lightweight campers, you also will probably grow to love camping as an enjoyable recreational activity in itself, and someday you might choose to stay in a campground rather than a motel even if money is not an issue.

Highway Safety

Before concluding, I want to shift gears and make one last point. To assure that you will have a pleasant camping experience, you must drive safely on the highways. Whenever traveling, especially when riding a motorcycle, you must be especially vigilant. You must look out for distracted drivers (who may be trying to dial their cell phones or do something else while driving), impaired drivers (who may be intoxicated from alcohol, marijuana, prescription pills, or other drugs), and aggressive drivers (who think they are driving on a race track rather than on a public highway and who show no regard for the lives of other people). Any of these drivers could cause a crash that will ruin your trip.

But more importantly, you must watch out for your own unsafe driving habits. According to the National Highway Traffic Safety Administration, motorcycle riders themselves pose the greatest risk to their own personal safety. Year after year, nearly half of all motorcycle fatalities have been single-vehicle accidents. Furthermore, we know from anecdotal accounts and newspaper reports that many more motorcycle riders cause multiple vehicle crashes. Thousands of motorcyclists have died or been seriously injured in crashes that were caused by their own careless riding mistakes rather than by other drivers. They are killed or seriously injured because they ride too fast, they become impaired by alcohol, marijuana, or some other drug, or they do not follow fundamental driving rules described in all state drivers' manuals. Approximately 75 percent of all motorcycle fatalities and serious injuries are probably caused by motorcycle riders' own mistakes rather than by other drivers.

This billboard near Sturgeon Bay, Wisconsin, urges drivers to drive defensively.

Therefore, to assure safe and enjoyable camping trips, you must resolve to examine your own riding habits, identify your unsafe habits, and try to adopt safer practices. A list of twenty-five defensive riding practices is offered at the end of this chapter. How many of these practices do you follow? How many do you disregard?

If you want to learn more about motorcycle safety, first refresh your memory of basic highway safety principles by re-reading the motorcycle operator manual published by your state. Most state manuals are prepared in conjunction with NHTSA and the Motorcycle Safety Foundation. Other good references are *Motorcycle Roadcraft: The Police Rider's Handbook to Better Motorcycling* by The Police Foundation of London, England; *Proficient Motorcycling: The Ultimate Guide to Riding Well* by David Hough; *Street Strategies: A Survival Guide for Motorcyclists* by David Hough; and *Motorcycling Excellence: Skills, Knowledge, and Strategies for Riding Right* by the Motorcycle Safety Foundation. Each of these books provides additional details related to basic principles of motorcycle safety. Also browse NHTSA's Web site (www.nhtsa.dot. gov) for recent analyses and information about motorcycle safety.

Conclusion

Camping offers you both an economical way to travel and a major source of pleasure and satisfaction. Through camping, you will meet many interesting people, you can learn many useful skills to help you become more self-reliant, and you can learn a considerable amount of information about geology, ecology, and history. You can learn to identify different birds, wildflowers, and trees living in various regions of the United States. You can learn how to be more self-sufficient and to appreciate the difficult challenges our pioneer ancestors must have faced. Through camping you will probably begin to appreciate our wilderness areas and how unrestricted land development and pollution will gradually destroy them and the animals that live there. Moreover you will see how man, animals, and plants are dependent upon each other. Through your experiences you will hopefully come to understand the importance of becoming a steward of the gifts given to us by God.

If you have never camped before, consider trying it. For your first trip or two, plan short weekend trips to nearby parks and be sure the weather will be warm and dry. You can buy the gear you and your companion will need for about a hundred dollars. If you try it, you will probably enjoy your experience and will begin to think about buying better gear and taking longer and more distant camping trips.

Once you give camping a try, you will soon come to enjoy all the smells, sights, sounds, and other sensory pleasures derived from being outdoors. Sleeping in a warm sleeping bag on a cool night or sitting at a picnic table under your dining fly, eating a meal you just cooked, and being miles away from your normal routine and daily pressures provide peak experiences. Savor them as often as possible.

Defensive Riding Practices

- Keep your bike properly serviced.
- Wear a helmet and other protective safety gear (eyewear, boots, gloves, long pants, and long sleeves).
- Remember that the extra weight of your passenger and camping gear will make your motorcycle more difficult to control, especially when stopping, accelerating, and leaning. The extra weight will make U-turns or other sharp turns more dangerous.
- Do not ride after drinking alcohol, smoking marijuana, or taking other mind-altering drugs (including certain prescription drugs like Xanax, Valium, or narcotic pain medicines).
- Learn to recognize common hazards (like gaggles and gators) and constantly scan for them.
- Limit your riding time each day to no more than eight hours or 450 miles.
- Take breaks about every hour, or more often when tired.
- Keep your speed under the posted limit.
- Reduce your speed to forty miles per hour or less, and tap your brakes when approaching congested intersections, driveways, or other potentially dangerous areas.
- Reduce your speed and tap your brakes when other drivers get too close to your vehicle.
- Reduce your speed when passing stopped or slow-moving vehicles.
- Reduce your speed in darkness, in rain, in fog, and when road shoulders are not wide enough to see animals that may be lurking nearby.
- Reduce your speed when riding in neighborhoods where children or pets could run into the road.
- Reduce your speed and downshift before entering curves.
- Ride in the driving lane (the far-right lane) as much as possible, because it usually offers an escape route to the right and better control over the space in front, to the left, and behind your vehicle.
- Maintain at least a four-second-space cushion behind the vehicle in front of you.

- Look beyond the vehicle directly in front of you. If you cannot see beyond the vehicle, increase your space cushion.
- Check your mirrors and turn your head before changing lanes.
- Be patient when riding behind slow vehicles and wait until you can execute the safe passing procedure described in all state driver's manuals.
- Come to a complete stop and place at least one foot on the ground at stop signs and red lights.
- Look twice each way before entering the roadway.
- Accelerate smoothly and signal lane changes, turns, and stops before executing them. Avoid making sudden movements.
- When riding in a straight line on dry pavement, apply your front brake with your rear brake to make emergency stops.
- When leaning into a curve or when riding on wet roads, dirt, or gravel, avoid using your front brake.
- Take a motorcycle safety class to learn more about motorcycle safety.

Bibliography

Coyner, Dale. *The Essential Guide to Motorcycle Travel: Tips, technology, advanced techniques.* Center Conway, N.H.: Whitehorse Press, 2007.

Curtis, Rick. *The Backpacker's Field Manual: A comprehensive guide to mastering backcountry skills.* New York: Three Rivers Press, 2005.

Fellows, Kay. *Upper Mississippi Valley by Motorcycle.* Rockledge, Fla.: The Motorcycle Publishing Company, 2006.

Flores, Adrian, Tadesse Haileyesus, and Arlene Greenspan. "National estimates of outdoor recreational injuries treated in emergency departments, United States, 2004–2005." *Wilderness and Environmental Medicine* 19 (2008): 91–98.

Frazier, Gregory. *Motorcycle Touring: Everything you need to know.* St. Paul, Minn.: Motorbooks, 2005.

Gray, Melissa and Tilton, Buck. *Cooking the One Burner Way, 2nd ed.* Guilford, Conn.: The Globe Pequot Press, 2000.

Herod, Lori. *Foil Cookery, 3rd ed.* Arcata, Cal.: Paradise Cay Publications, 2007.

Hough, David. *Proficient Motorcycling: The Ultimate Guide to Riding Well.* Irvine, Calif.: Bow Tie Press, 2000.

Hough, David. *Street Strategies: A Survival Guide for Motorcyclists.* Irvine, Calif.: Bow Tie Press, 2001.

Hung, Eric and David Townes. "Search and rescue in Yosemite National Park: A 10-year review." *Wilderness and Environmental Medicine* 18 (2007): 111–116.

Jacobson, Cliff. *Basic Essentials of Cooking in the Outdoors, 2ⁿᵈ ed.* Guilford, Conn.: The Globe Pequot Press, 1999.

Jacobson, Cliff. *Camping's Top Secrets, 3ʳᵈ ed.* Guilford, Conn.: The Globe Pequot Press, 2006.

Jordan, Ryan, ed. *Lightweight Backpacking and Camping: A field guide to wilderness hiking equipment, technique, and style.* Bozeman, MT.: Beartooth Mountain Press, 2005.

Molloy, Johnny. *The Best in Tent Camping—Southern Appalachian and Smokey Mountains, 4ᵗʰ ed.* Birmingham, Ala.: Menasha Ridge Press, 2007.

Molloy, Johnny. *The Best in Tent Camping—Tennessee.* Birmingham, Ala.: Menasha Ridge Press, 2005.

Molloy, Johnny. *The Best in Tent Camping—Wisconsin, 2ⁿᵈ ed.* Birmingham, Ala.: Menasha Ridge Press, 2007.

The Motorcycle Safety Foundation. *Motorcycling Excellence: Skills, knowledge, and strategies for riding right, 2ⁿᵈ ed.* Center Conway, N.H.: Whitehorse Press, 2005.

Mouland, Michael. *The Complete Idiot's Guide to Camping and Hiking, 2nd ed.* New York: Penguin, 2000.

The Police Foundation of London, England. *Motorcycle Roadcraft: The Police Rider's Handbook to Better Motorcycling.* London, England, 1996.

Rutter, Michael. *Camping Made Easy: A manual for beginners with tips for the experienced, 2ⁿᵈ ed.* Guilford, Conn.: The Globe Pequot Press, 2001.

Stephens, Bradford, Douglas Diekema, and Eileen Klein. "Recreational injuries in Washington state national parks." *Wilderness and Environmental Medicine* 16 (2005): 192–197.

Tawrell, Paul. *Camping and Wilderness Survival, 2ⁿᵈ ed.* Lebanon, N.H.: Tawrel, 2006.

Tilton, Buck with Hostetter, Kristen. *Backpacker Tent and Car Camper's Handbook: Advice for families and first timers.* Emmaus, Pa.: The Mountaineers Press, 2006.

Tobey, Peter, Ed. *Two Wheel Travel: Motorcycle Camping and Touring.* New Canaan, Conn.: Tobey Publishing Co., 1972.

Townsend, Chris. *The Backpacker's Handbook.* New York: McGraw Hill, 2005.

Waterman, Laura and Waterman, Guy. *Backwoods Ethics,* 2nd *ed.* Woodstock, Vt.: The Countryman Press, 1993.

Woofter, Bob. *Motorcycle Camping Made Easy.* North Conway, N.H.: Whitehorse Press, 2002.

Youngblood, Ed, Ed. *Heroes of Harley-Davidson.* St. Paul, Minn.: Motorbooks International, 2003.

About the Author

Frazier Douglass was born in Birmingham, Alabama, and inherited an analytical approach to solving life's problems from his father (who was a chemical engineer) and his grandfather (who was a mechanical engineer). After graduating from high school, he attended Auburn University and earned a bachelor's degree and a master's degree in psychology. He spent nine months in military training learning how to be an operating-room technician and then moved to Wisconsin where he began teaching psychology at the University of Wisconsin-Richland.

After teaching for five years, he began doctoral study at the University of Wisconsin-Milwaukee. He earned his PhD in clinical psychology in 1978 and moved back to Alabama where he began working with drug-dependent and mentally ill patients in a community mental health center. After ten years, he changed careers and began teaching psychology at Athens State University (a small university in north Alabama). He has continued to teach at Athens State for the past twenty years.

He began camping with his father when he was about eight years old and has camped in many campgrounds across the central United States. During the late 1990s, he served as the campground host at Brigham County Park near Madison, Wisconsin, for three summers. During the past ten years, he has taken many motorcycle camping trips and has visited campgrounds in Alabama, Florida, Tennessee, Kentucky, Georgia, Illinois, and Wisconsin. He especially enjoys testing new camping gear and experimenting with unique ways to solve common camping problems.

He also has been riding motorcycles for most of his life. He bought his first motor scooter (a Cushman Highlander) at the age of twelve to manage a large newspaper route in Birmingham. After crashing that scooter into a bus, he has bought and ridden several other motorcycles. He has owned Yamaha, Honda, and Harley-Davidson motorcycles. Currently he owns a 1988 FXR Low Rider and a 1996 Harley-Davidson Ultra Classic Electra Glide Shriner Edition. He usually rides the Electra Glide on his camping trips.

He took his first motorcycle camping trip in 1998. Although this trip turned out to be a cold and miserable experience, he was determined to learn how to camp comfortably on his motorcycle trips. For the past eleven years, he has slowly acquired the knowledge and skills needed to camp in a wide range of weather conditions—whether riding solo or two-up. Today he maintains a Web site devoted to motorcycle camping (www.motorcyclecampingtips.com), writes camping gear reviews for www.trailspace.com, and writes motorcycle camping articles for the Wisconsin-Illinois Biker Information Guide.

Index

P

packing xvii, xxi, 6, 7, 17, 21, 23, 35,
36, 38, 39, 43, 53, 55, 56, 69,
71, 72, 76, 77, 78, 80, 84, 85,
95, 96, 98, 100, 101, 102, 103,
104, 106, 107, 108, 109, 110,
111, 112, 113, 114, 118, 121,
122, 124, 127, 129, 130, 143,
147, 149, 150, 153, 154, 155,
156, 157, 158, 162, 163, 164,
170, 173, 174, 175, 176, 179,
180, 181, 183, 184, 185, 187,
188, 189, 190, 191, 192, 193,
194, 197, 199, 200, 202, 204,
206, 207, 208, 210, 211, 212,
213, 214, 215, 216, 226, 236,
244, 274, 282, 284
pans xxiii, 147, 148, 149, 151, 156,
157, 161, 167, 170, 172, 199,
297
pants 83, 84, 98, 99, 100, 101, 110,
117, 120, 123, 125, 128, 131,
132, 134, 135, 136, 137, 140,
141, 143, 146, 212, 215, 277,
285, 304
paper towels 95, 103, 112, 113, 120,
149, 200, 217, 231, 245
Patagonia 99, 100, 101, 130, 131, 140,
141, 142, 143, 178, 267
personal-grooming kit 103
Petzel 115
pillow 65, 82, 84, 87, 120, 143, 144,
178, 200, 201, 213, 214
Plastic bags 120
plates 147, 153, 154, 157, 162, 170,
172, 200, 231, 289
pliers 53, 109, 110, 111, 120, 161,
163, 200, 217, 238, 275
poison ivy 224, 279, 294
poison oak 279, 280
poison sumac 279
polyester 23, 81, 83, 99, 100, 125,
126, 130, 131, 133, 134, 136,
139, 140, 141, 142, 143, 144,

240, 266, 267
pots xxiii, 27, 87, 98, 110, 111, 147,
148, 149, 151, 159, 160, 161,
162, 190, 199, 207, 233, 275,
297
Princeton Tec 115
ProLite Gear 29

R

Raccoons 55, 168, 289, 290
rain fly. *See* tarp
rain gear xvii, 98, 99, 100, 101, 116,
119, 127, 133, 137, 178, 179,
191, 200, 201, 203, 215, 217,
224
rain pants 101, 135
REI 8, 9, 29, 34, 35, 36, 39, 40, 44,
46, 47, 49, 50, 51, 52, 54, 56,
58, 59, 63, 69, 73, 81, 87, 88,
89, 91, 97, 99, 100, 101, 130,
131, 138, 139, 140, 141, 143,
145, 153, 154, 178, 201
relaxing xvi, 8, 16, 55, 174, 176, 185,
240, 241, 245, 299
rope. *See* cord

S

safety xii, 55, 186, 197, 209, 216, 271,
301, 302, 304, 305
Scorpions 286
shirts 122, 123, 125, 128, 129, 130,
131, 132, 134, 135, 136, 137,
139, 140, 141, 142, 146
shoes xix, 44, 53, 97, 103, 104, 120,
138, 183, 184, 185, 195, 201,
213, 217, 223, 238, 239, 267,
280
shorts 78, 130, 131, 132, 134, 135,
136, 137, 139, 140, 141, 142,
146, 213, 238, 283
shower bag 97, 103, 104, 120, 238
shower shoes 97, 103, 104, 120, 184,
185, 201, 213, 238, 239, 280
shower supplies 98, 119, 143, 198,

Breinigsville, PA USA
23 June 2010
240420BV00002B/77/P